Sabai | สบาย : The state of being when you're at ease. Comfortable. Relaxed.

Pailin Chongchitnant knows that a busy schedule can make learning new recipes seem intimidating—whether you're familiar with the cuisine or not. In her second book, Pai will empower you to make Thai food part of your everyday routine, with a compilation of authentic and straightforward recipes, like Beef Laab or Green Curry Chicken with Winter Melon, that are quick to make and delicious to eat. From prepping, to cooking, to eating, the dishes in this book can be done *sabai sabai*, as the saying goes.

Pai takes you through every recipe with her signature level of detail and warm, encouraging style. And she's thought of plenty of shortcuts, tips, and tricks to get dinner on the table, no matter how hectic the day has been. There are even QR codes linking to her YouTube videos to support you every step of the way.

Whatever you're in the mood for, you'll find inspiration in Pai's easy, yet flavorful, creations:

- **SNACKABLE APPETIZERS** like Fish Sauce Wings or Flaky Roti with Yellow Curry Dip;
- **SNAPPY MAINS** like Weeknight Chicken Khao Soi or Minimalist Pad Thai;
- **SIMPLE YET SATISFYING DESSERTS** like a Banana Coconut Sundae or Black Beans & Sticky Rice.

With a full section on Thai pantry staples and common ingredient substitutions, *Sabai* has everything you need to make your favorite dishes at home. You'll also love the section on how to compose the perfectly balanced Thai meal, with specific recipe pairings and ideas to make sure you've got the sweet, salty, sour, and spicy elements covered. Step into the kitchen, relax, and let your taste buds—and Pai—be your guide.

SABAI
สบาย

100 Simple Thai Recipes for Any Day of the Week

PAILIN CHONGCHITNANT
ไพลิน จงจิตรนันท์

appetite
by RANDOM HOUSE

Appetite by Random House® and colophon are registered trademarks of Penguin Random House LLC.

Library and Archives of Canada Cataloguing in Publication is available upon request.

ISBN: 9780525611714
eBook ISBN: 9780525611721

Cover and book design by Talia Abramson
Photography by Janis Nicolay
Floral pattern on endpapers and throughout:
Lovely Mandala/Shutterstock
Printed and bound in China

Published in Canada by Appetite by Random House®,
a division of Penguin Random House LLC.
www.penguinrandomhouse.ca

10 9 8 7 6 5 4 3 2

appetite
by RANDOM HOUSE

Penguin
Random
House

To Kaan: Never forget your roots.

CONTENTS

Introduction

The Two Things I Want

After more than 12 years of teaching people all over the world how to cook Thai food, I've had a lot of time to think about what it is that I ultimately want people to take away at the end of my lessons. And I've come to the conclusion that there are two things.

First, I want people to experience the Thai flavors that I grew up with. While Thai food at most restaurants outside Thailand is enjoyable, ask any Thai person living abroad and they will all agree that it can be a challenge to find one that really tastes like home.

Second, and perhaps more important, I want people to feel that they *can* cook real Thai food, and that they can do it regularly, on any given night of the week. I've been amazed by the number of emails I've received over the years in which the writer uses the word "intimidated" to describe how they felt about cooking Thai food before watching my videos. I want to assure you that it's not any harder than any other cuisine, and it's not more complicated. There *is* a bit of a learning curve if you're new to these ingredients and techniques, but it will all fall into place with a bit of practice.

Cooking Thai Food Is Not Hard

For many of us, cooking food from an unfamiliar cuisine usually starts out as a project. You take the time to read the recipe, watch a YouTube video or two, make a trip to a specialty grocer or even a few . . . it's a real investment! And it's truly upsetting if, after all that, the recipe fails. And even if it doesn't, the whole process can still feel like a lot of work.

This first experience too often leaves people with the wrong impression that this new cuisine is too difficult or time-intensive, and so it gets relegated to the land of "weekend projects" forever. Few people realize, though, that it has nothing to do with the cuisine itself.

Cooking any new cuisine for the first time is going to be a bit of work because there's a lot to deal with that you don't normally have to when cooking your "comfort cuisine." You have to get to know the ingredients, source them, and then actually read the recipe word for word because you don't know how to wing it. It's a bit like learning how to ride a bike, and it can seem like you'll never get your feet off the ground.

But I can assure you it's not the fault of the cuisine itself, because when I was living in Thailand, I tried to learn Western cooking, and wow . . . what's oregano? What's a potato masher? Canned tomatoes—people *can* tomatoes? Imagine doing that when you couldn't google any of it. It left me thinking, "Man, this *farang* food is hard!" It happens to everyone.

But once you try a few dishes, get to know some of the ingredients, and understand some new techniques, it will click. Then next thing you know, you'll have enough ingredients in your pantry to pull off many Thai dishes on a whim, and you'll have the confidence to do it too.

Some Thai Dishes Are Complicated, but These Recipes Are Not

When most people think of Thai food, they're usually thinking of dishes served in restaurants or by street vendors in Thailand. But those dishes represent only a fraction of Thai cuisine, ones cooked by professionals. Dishes cooked in the home are much more manageable and simpler. Thai people need quick weeknight dinners too, you know!

That is what this book is for. My goal for this book was to put together a compilation of authentic recipes that are straightforward and quick to make, or what I call "weeknight friendly," while giving you just enough of the "Thai Cuisine 101" info to support you without overwhelming you. For a deeper dive into the foundational principles and cultural context of Thai cuisine, my first book, *Hot Thai Kitchen*, is a great resource.

Recipes You Can Cook Sabai-Sabai

I have never believed in enticing but unachievable promises like "15-minute meals," because we all know those 15 minutes don't include unpacking your grocery bags, washing your vegetables, or doing dishes because you need that pan again, and you have to make sure you chop quickly and do absolutely no cleaning as you go.

I picked the recipes in this book based on whether I can use the word *sabai* to describe the process of making them. *Sabai* is the Thai word that describes the state of being at ease or comfortable. Relaxed. Not rushed. Easy-peasy. From prepping to cooking to eating, everything is *sabai-sabai*, as we like to say. Essentially, these are dishes that are simple, with no tedious, time-consuming steps—definitely no skewering or individually wrapping anything (okay, the salad rolls on page 40 require wrapping, but it's quick and totally worth it). Finally, these recipes are hard to screw up. Nothing here requires you to be particularly skilled or precise, so you can actually cook *sabai-sabai*. Some recipes, such as for braises and stews, may require relatively long hands-off time, and some benefit from an overnight marinade. These are perfect for making on your day off when you've got the time, which makes the day-of an absolute breeze.

In other words, all of these are dishes you can pull off on a weeknight, with opportunity for advance prep if you're into that. Ultimately, I'd love for Thai food, with the help of this book, to be part of your regular meal repertoire. I hope you love reading and cooking from this book as much as I have loved writing it.

How to Use This Book

I have given you more than just recipes in this book: I've also provided useful information that will help you immensely when navigating recipes if Thai cuisine is unfamiliar to you. With these extra tidbits, you'll feel much more equipped to make cooking Thai food a part of your regular repertoire.

SIDEBARS: For most recipes, I've provided additional information in a sidebar that gives cultural context to the dish, suggests a modification, or explains an unusual step. As regular viewers of my YouTube show know, I believe it's important not only to have the how-to but also to understand the dishes you're cooking in a deeper way. You'll be a much better cook in the long term.

INGREDIENTS DICTIONARY: If you are new to Thai cuisine and are unfamiliar with our ingredients, I've provided a Thai ingredient dictionary of a sort (pp. 6–15). I've kept it brief so that you can quickly get just what you need, but if you want a more detailed study, watch the videos on the "Thai Ingredients 101" playlist on my YouTube channel.

EQUIPMENT DICTIONARY: You can certainly cook Thai food with the pots and pans you've got at home, but there are a few items that will help make it much easier. Consult the equipment section (pp. 18–19) for an overview, and you can also check out my website, where I post a comprehensive list of all the equipment I use on the show.

HOW TO COMPOSE A THAI MEAL: Thai home cooking is always served family style, with every meal consisting of multiple dishes that complement each other. While you certainly can make just one dish for a meal, if you want to do it Thai style, I've provided guidance for composing a proper Thai meal (pp. 20–21), to maximize your enjoyment.

RECIPES TO MAKE IN BULK: As with any cuisine, Thai cooking has staple sauces, condiments, and other base ingredients that are used across multiple recipes. You can certainly buy these items, such as curry pastes, but for those who are DIY-minded, I've provided recipes for them (pp. 249–269), so you can make them in bulk and/or in advance.

TIPS FOR EFFICIENT COOKING: Having simple recipes is helpful, but actually being efficient in the kitchen takes cooking to the next level. This doesn't mean you have to chop faster, though that always helps, but it does mean you need to do a bit of planning before you execute. "No wasted movement, no idle moment" is what I'm always striving for when I cook, so I share some pro tips on how you can make everything in the kitchen go a little smoother and a little faster (pp. 22–23).

COOKING TIME: In the recipes, this is the time that it should take you to execute the instructions; it doesn't include prep time. But even the lengthiest ingredient list should take no more than 20–30 minutes to prepare.

A NOTE REGARDING THE ROMANIZATION OF THAI WORDS: I have provided Thai recipe and ingredient names written out phonetically in English letters throughout the book. I have tried to make this as phonetically close to the Thai pronunciation as possible, but for most words it is impossible to make it 100% accurate because there are many sounds in the Thai language that don't exist in English.

In some cases, I've decided to use the most commonly recognizable spelling rather than one that is phonetically closer, for example *pad thai*, which is actually pronounced *pud-tai*. For a few words, the most accurate spelling happens to resemble a . . . shall we say "not nice". . . word in English, so I have chosen a different spelling there.

This is why some dishes here may be spelled differently from how your local restaurant or another cookbook spells them; people choose whatever spelling they think works best. *Pad kra pao, pad gaprao,* and *pad kapow* are all different spellings I have seen referring to the same dish.

I have to note that there *is* an official guide to romanizing Thai words, but this is a complex set of rules that is not very helpful in conveying how words actually sound and is often overly complicated, so I have chosen not to follow it. This is why you see silent h's added to words like *khao soi* and *pad thai* for seemingly no reason, and why Thailand's main airport is called "Suvarnabhumi" but is actually pronounced *su-wun-na-poom*!

The Basic Thai Pantry

The only real hurdle to making Thai cooking a weeknight breeze is gathering the basic pantry ingredients. Thankfully, many of our ingredients last a long time in the pantry, fridge, or freezer, so once you've made your first trip to the grocery store, you'll be well equipped for the next little while.

The Salty

In Western cuisines, granulated salt is added to essentially every dish. In Thai cuisine, however, salt on its own is rarely used in savory cooking because we like to use a variety of sauces that give not only saltiness but also flavor.

FERMENTED SHRIMP PASTE | *GAPI* | กะปิ This salty, purplish-gray paste made from fermented small shrimp (or sometimes krill) is the epitome of funky and is used all over Southeast Asia. It's one of those things that tastes better than it smells. It has lovers and haters. I am a proud lover of shrimp paste! You may have eaten shrimp paste without knowing it, because most Thai curry pastes contain it in small amounts. You can buy Thai shrimp paste in a plastic tub, or the Malaysian type in a plastic-wrapped brick called *belacan*. Where shrimp paste is used in small amounts, such as in curry pastes, you can omit it and add extra fish sauce instead.

Note: Do not confuse this with a product called shrimp paste that looks like an oily orange paste and comes in a glass jar. That shrimp paste is *mun goong* and it is made from shrimp tomalley cooked with herbs and seasonings. It's delicious added to fried rice and stir-fries, but it is not fermented and cannot be used as a substitute for *gapi*.

FERMENTED SOYBEAN PASTE | *TAO JIEW* | เต้าเจี้ยว This delightful chunky sauce is what I call the Thai miso, but with a pourable consistency and the whole soybeans still visible. It's very salty, with an edge of acidity, and its aroma is different from that of Japanese miso. Many a time I have added too much *tao jiew* to a dish—it's actually a lot saltier than it looks (somehow the whole soybeans make it look like you can add a lot of it!)—so this is one ingredient I wouldn't eyeball. It's not used often, but when it is used, it is important to the character of that dish. Healthy Boy is the most popular brand of *tao jiew* outside Thailand. You can substitute Japanese miso or Korean doenjang in roughly equal amounts, but be prepared to taste and adjust.

FISH SAUCE | *NAM PLA* | น้ำปลา A must-have in any Thai home. Made from fermented anchovies and salt, this pungent amber liquid adds a sharp saltiness and a punch of umami that is an iconic characteristic of many Thai dishes, but especially our salads. When buying fish sauce, look for brands that contain as few ingredients as possible, preferably only anchovies, salt, and sugar. Squid, Megachef, and Tiparos are classic, good-quality Thai brands that are inexpensive, easy to find, and perfect for everyday cooking. A good, widely available Vietnamese brand is Three Crabs; it's a little milder and less salty than Thai ones, so this is a good choice if you prefer things less salty. Red Boat is a premium brand that contains no sugar, and it is pricier, but you can really taste the difference. Do not cheap out on fish sauce; the difference is huge.

If you're vegetarian, you can substitute soy sauce in roughly equal amounts. Larger Asian markets do sell vegan fish sauce, but some of them can be rather awful. However, I have sampled a pleasant-tasting one labeled "premium pineapple-made vegetarian fish sauce" from Vietnam. There are many recipes on the internet for vegan fish sauce, but no combination of non-fish ingredients is going to make it taste fishy—so adjust your expectations.

OYSTER SAUCE | *NAM MUN HOI* | น้ำมันหอย This is the queen of stir-fry sauces. It's so delicious in itself, you could drizzle it over some blanched veggies and call it a day. Imagine a combination of the briny flavors of oysters, the umami of soy sauce, and a subtle sweetness—that's the flavor of oyster sauce. A common Thai brand is Maekrua, but the widely available Lee Kum Kee is also great for Thai cooking. Oyster sauce quality varies significantly, with the better ones containing more "oyster extract," which is the oyster poaching liquid. Lee Kum Kee has a few grades, but these two are the most common: the basic Panda brand, which is fine for everyday use, and the premium "lady on a boat" version, which I recommend for recipes that use oyster sauce as a main ingredient. Price and protein content are also a good general indicator of how many oysters were used to make the sauce—the more expensive and the more protein, the greater the quantity of oysters.

SALT | *GLEUA* | เกลือ Salt on its own is not used very often in Thai cooking except for in desserts. When we do add it, most people use iodized table salt, and sometimes sea salt. Since this book will find its way into homes all around the world, I've decided to call for table salt in my recipes because it is the one salt everyone has access to (we don't have kosher salt in Thailand, for example). This is important to note, because salt measures differently depending on the size of the grains—larger, more irregular-shaped grains will not pack as tightly into a teaspoon as the fine grains of table salt. You can, of course, use any salt that you like, just keep in mind that you may need to adjust the amount slightly. Conversion charts for different types of salt can be easily found online.

SOY SAUCE | *SEE EW KAO* | ซีอิ๊วขาว You probably have Japanese or Chinese soy sauce in your kitchen already, but Thai soy sauce is unique. Compared with those more common soy sauces, ours is a little lighter in both color and body, and has a distinctly different aroma and flavor. The literal translation of *see ew kao* is "white soy sauce," which actually refers not to its color but to the fact that it is the thinnest and lightest among our soy sauces (it's still a dark brown color). Healthy Boy is a classic brand available at many Asian markets, but if you can't find it, Japanese soy sauce will work as a substitute. Note: Healthy Boy makes various kinds of soy sauce, and to make sure you're getting *see ew kao*, look for a bottle labeled "thin soy sauce" (yellow label) or "mushroom soy sauce" (brown label); these are two varieties of *see ew kao* (see top photo on p. 15). The mushroom version is one I prefer, though either will work in the recipes just fine. Do not use a non-Thai mushroom soy sauce as a substitute.

SOY SAUCE, BLACK | *SEE EW DUM* | ซีอิ๊วดำ
Translating literally as "black soy sauce," *see ew dum* is a nice-to-have ingredient but not essential because it's usually not integral to the dish. Think soy sauce mixed with molasses—it's thick, mildly salty, a little sweet, and very dark. It's used mainly to add a dark brown color and a touch of richer flavor. Whenever you see a Thai dish with a very dark color, like some dark soup broths or stir-fries, it's probably *see ew dum* in action.

Black soy sauce brands vary significantly in terms of how dark they are, so in my recipes I always give a range, and you should always start with the smaller amount. Healthy Boy brand, for example, is very dark, and it's easy to add too much if you're not careful. Dragonfly brand, the one I grew up with, is lighter and more forgiving, so it is

my preference if I can find it. You can instead use Chinese dark soy sauce, which will give you the dark color, but it tends to be saltier, so if using more than ½ teaspoon (5 ml) or so, you might want to cut back on other salty stuff you're adding.

THAI SEASONING SAUCE (GOLDEN MOUNTAIN SAUCE) | *SAUCE PROONG ROHT* | ซอสปรุงรส
You might be asking yourself, "Aren't they *all* seasoning sauces?" Yes, but there is a specific type of sauce that we literally call "seasoning sauce." I suppose it's because they didn't know what else to call it and didn't want it confused with soy sauce . . . though it kind of *is* soy sauce! *Sauce proong roht* is basically soy sauce with a different character, and it is a bit richer and darker than *see ew kao*.

Although it's not an essential ingredient to stock, you can find Golden Mountain brand seasoning sauce at many Asian markets. Both Maggi Seasoning and Bragg Liquid Aminos taste similar, and either will work as a substitute. In my recipes, *sauce proong roht* is usually used in combination with soy sauce to create a more complex flavor, but if you don't have it or the other options, substituting more soy sauce is fine.

A Note on Storage:

Salty things keep well by nature because salt is a preservative, and in Thailand, most people keep these sauces at room temperature because we go through them fast. But even though they won't spoil, the flavors can change for the worse over time. So, for occasional users, I recommend keeping these items in the fridge. Oyster sauce should always be kept in the fridge, as it isn't as salty as the others and can get moldy over time.

The Sour

In most cases, the sour flavor of Thai dishes comes from only two things: lime juice and/or tamarind. Limes are used when we want a bright, fresh-tasting acidity, such as in salads, while tamarind has a richer, sweeter flavor and is usually used in hot cooked dishes.

Thai Ingredient Playlist

Palm Sugar | *Nam Taan Peep*

LIMES | *MANAO* | มะนาว Limes are pretty straightforward. I'll just mention here that lime juice tastes best when it's not cooked, so if adding to cooked dishes, add it at the end. Freshly squeezed lime juice has the best flavor, though I have found that crystalized lime powder (True Lime brand) is a great substitute in a pinch. Do not use bottled, shelf-stable lime juice, especially in Thai salads where it is a main dressing ingredient, as it can be slightly bitter and doesn't have as much of the lovely citrus flavor. Choose limes that have smooth, shiny skins, which indicate a juicy lime.

TAMARIND PASTE | *NAM MAKAAM PIAK* | น้ำมะขามเปียก Tamarind is a fruit with dark brown sticky flesh encased in a hard, brittle pod. The pulp can range from very sweet to very sour. For cooking, we mix sour tamarind pulp with water until it is a pourable liquid that can be easily incorporated into the dish.

You can buy prepared Thai tamarind paste in plastic tubs or glass jars, usually labeled "tamarind concentrate" or "tamarind paste" and found in the sauces section of your Asian grocery store. As a side note, the name "tamarind concentrate" is a misnomer because this product is not actually a concentrate. Quite the opposite!

I used to use prepared tamarind paste for its convenience, but I have noticed that it's often too diluted and lacks flavor, so I have switched to making my own from store-bought pulp, and the result is a million times better. The pulp is squished together into a block and sold wrapped in plastic. To make your own, see Homemade Tamarind Paste (p. 266).

Do not get Indian tamarind concentrate, as that is a very different product. While Thai and Vietnamese ready-to-use tamarind pastes are diluted pulp with a thick but easily pourable consistency, Indian tamarind *is* a true concentrate. It is extremely thick, sticky, and much more sour than what we use in Thailand.

If you can find fresh tamarind in the pods, great, but don't use them for cooking. These are sweet tamarind for eating fresh, so go ahead and enjoy them as sweet, sticky, yummy snacks!

Once tamarind paste is opened, refrigerate if you'll finish it within a few months, or freeze in an ice cube tray, then transfer to a freezer bag.

The Sweet

In Thai cuisine we mainly use two types of sugar: granulated sugar and palm sugar. On rare occasions, brown sugar is used.

GRANULATED SUGAR | *NAM TAAN SAI* | น้ำตาลทราย You know all about good old granulated white sugar, but I want to mention that even though it isn't the traditional sugar, it is now very commonly used in Thai cuisine for both sweet and savory applications. In dishes where the amount of added sugar is small, we usually go for granulated sugar for convenience, and because adding the more expensive palm sugar wouldn't make any difference in flavor. It's also the sugar of choice when a neutral sweetness is desired, such as in some desserts.

PALM SUGAR | *NAM TAAN PEEP* | น้ำตาลปี๊ป Palm sugar is the traditional Thai sweetener, used before the more convenient granulated sugar became available. It is made by reducing and caramelizing the nectar from the flowers of either the coconut palm or the toddy palm, which produce very similar sugars. It has a gorgeous butterscotch flavor that is delicious on its own, so much so that I often eat it straight up while I'm cooking! Fresh, unreduced palm nectar is sold as a magnificent, refreshing drink that I always seek out when I'm in Thailand.

Palm sugar is usually sold in tan-colored pucks or in tubs as a spoonable paste. Essentially all palm sugar sold outside Thailand (and even most of what is sold in Thailand) is mixed with granulated sugar to some degree, because of the cost and availability of palm nectar. So the key is to find one that has the least amount of granulated sugar, and the only real way to tell is to taste it. The less flavor it has, the more granulated sugar is mixed in. Never trust the label; even if it says "100% pure palm sugar," if it's exported and costs you only a few dollars, it's most certainly not pure.

If using a solid puck, you can shave it with a large knife, then finely chop the shavings. You can also pound the puck with a big stone mortar and pestle so it breaks into smaller pieces. I like to chop or pound a bunch at a time, then store in an airtight container so I don't have to chop the palm sugar every time I need it. Like brown sugar, palm sugar

Note: In my recipes, I call for palm sugar to be finely chopped so that it can be packed and measured in measuring spoons or cups, but if you are measuring by weight, there's no need to chop it finely unless it needs to be dissolved in cold liquid—for example, in salad dressings. I find weighing is the easier way to work with palm sugar and is why I've provided the weight measure in the recipes.

dries out and becomes rock hard over time, so if you're not going to use it up quickly, chop it while still fresh.

If using the tub kind, you can spoon it out, but if it has hardened, heat it up in the microwave briefly to soften, and then spoon it out while still warm.

Is palm sugar the same as coconut sugar? Yes and no. Coconut sugar is a type of palm sugar, but the modern granulated varieties that are sold in health food stores in the West do not taste the same as traditionally made Thai coconut sugar, especially the one that is dark brown in color. Different processing really does make a difference here, so for Thai cooking, it's best to stick with the Thai brands.

Herbs & Spices

Here are some of our core herbs and spices, some of which you may not be familiar with. There are obviously more on the list, but these are the most important and most commonly used ones.

BASIL, HOLY | *GAPRAO* | กะเพรา A little more peppery than the sweet scent of Thai basil, holy basil goes well with dishes that are intensely spicy. If not available, Italian basil is a fine substitute.

BASIL, THAI | *HORAPA* | โหระพา Fragrant and floral, Thai basil adds so much complexity to stir-fries and curries. If not available, you can use Italian basil instead.

CHILIES, DRIED | *PRIK HANG* | พริกแห้ง In the same way that raisins taste nothing like grapes, chilies develop an entirely different character once dried. We use two major types of dried chilies: small (spicy) and large (mild). Don't get too hung up on which specific varieties you need, because fortunately most dried chilies have a similar-enough flavor that they can be substituted for one another in Thai recipes, but you *do* want to be aware of the heat levels, which vary greatly.

Spicy, small dried chilies are used to add heat to curry pastes, and we also roast and grind them up into chili flakes, which can be added to just about anything. The generic no-name dried chilies you can usually find at Chinese grocery stores, as well as Mexican chiles de árbol, are great for this purpose, and they are not too hot. If you find small dried chilies from Thailand, just know that these are *very* spicy. You can remove the seeds and pith of any dried chilies to reduce the spiciness.

Large, mild chilies are most often used in curry pastes because we want to maximize the bright red color and chili flavor without making the curry too spicy. The Thai variety, *prik chee fa*, is essentially impossible to source, but dried guajillo or puya peppers are perfect substitutes. You can find them anywhere Latin American groceries are sold. You can also use Korean gochugaru pepper flakes instead. If these are not available, you can experiment with whatever you can find; anything larger than about 4 inches (10 cm) is likely going to be mild enough. If you can only find small ones, remove the seeds and pith from them. The only caveat is to stay away from very large and dark chilies, such as ancho or pasilla peppers, or anything smoked, like chipotle.

CHILIES, FRESH | *PRIK* | พริก To add spiciness in our dishes, we most often use small and super-spicy bird's-eye chilies, or *prik kee noo*. In North America, you can find these sold as "Thai chilies," and they can be found red (ripe) or green (underripe).

We also use larger, milder chilies to add color and chili flavor without heat, and for this we turn to spur chilies, or *prik chee fa*. These are not easy to find, but you can substitute any other mild red pepper you can find; even red bell pepper will do in a pinch.

"No chilies, no fun" is the mantra of many Thais. Spicy food gives us an adrenaline rush that's become part of the excitement of Thai food, and some dishes need at least a little bit of spiciness in order to be complete. Not only that, but chilies also give their own unique flavor to the dish. So even if your heat tolerance is low, don't omit them altogether, because you'll be missing an important component of the dish! Add as much as you can tolerate, and remove the seeds and pith to reduce the spiciness.

CILANTRO | *PAK CHEE* | ผักชี Cilantro is the most frequently used herb in all of Thai cuisine, as you're about to find out as you cook your way through this book. It is our default finishing herb, adding an element of freshness to just about everything. This is especially important in dishes that tend to be heavier, such as fried rice and noodle soups.

When used as a finishing herb, cilantro is almost always used together with green onions, so much so that markets in Thailand will usually sell the two together in the same bunch! But for simplicity at home, it's fine to use one or the other.

Aside from being an all-purpose finishing herb, the cilantro plant has roots that serve as one of the three members of an herb paste we call *saam glur*, meaning "three friends," the other two being garlic and white

Holy basil | *Gaprao*

Dried chilies | *Prik hang*

Thai basil | *Horapa*

Makrut lime leaves | *Bai Magrood*

Galangal | *Kha*

Lemongrass | *Takrai*

pepper. This paste, which one could call the Thai holy trinity or Thai mirepoix, forms the flavor base of many dishes, from marinades to sauces to curries.

When using cilantro as a finishing herb, always use the whole sprig—leaves *and* stems. When making a paste for cooking, use only the stems (or the roots, if you're lucky enough to find them), because the leaves will turn black in this application. Under no circumstance should you pick off the leaves and throw away the stems, as the stems are actually *more* fragrant than the leaves!

If you have an aversion to cilantro, as I know some people do, feel free to substitute chopped green onions, or in the case of salads, mint.

GALANGAL | *KHA* | ข่า Galangal is a firm rhizome whose aroma is very much like that of a lush pine forest. It's cooling, calming, and refreshing. Although it looks like ginger, and many people will say that you can use ginger as a substitute, I insist that you don't. Not if you expect it to have a similar flavor, anyway!

There are two common uses of galangal: pounded into curry pastes, and sliced into rounds for infusing into soups. While not done as often, it can also be finely chopped and added to salads or stir-fries.

Galangal freezes very well. Slice into thin rounds and freeze in a single layer on a tray lined with plastic wrap before storing in a freezer bag. This will prevent the rounds from sticking to the tray and to each other.

Fresh is best, frozen is second-best, and paste is third-best. Dried galangal and powdered galangal retain flavor better than their lemongrass counterparts, so they can be used if necessary.

LEMONGRASS | *TAKRAI* | ตะไคร้ Lemongrass is a sturdy herb that has a citrusy aroma but gives no actual sour taste to food. It's as core to Thai cuisine as garlic is to Italian cuisine. Lemongrass can be bruised and infused into soups, like a cinnamon stick might be, or finely chopped and added to salads, dips, or stir-fries. It's also a key ingredient in many curry pastes.

I use only the bottom half of lemongrass because the flavor gets weaker at the top. I freeze the tops for making stock, but you can also make lemongrass tea. If making soup where the lemongrass is added to infuse and then discarded, there is no harm in also adding the tops—it'll just be more pieces to fish out later.

Fresh lemongrass is widely available these days, but it can also be found frozen, dried, powdered, or in paste form. Fresh is best, frozen is second-best, and paste is third-best. Avoid dried or powdered, as neither has much flavor left in them. If you find fresh, do stock up, as it freezes very well. I cut it into 2- to 3-inch (5 to 8 cm) long pieces before freezing, for ease of use. Use them without thawing.

MAKRUT LIME LEAVES | *BAI MAGROOD* | ใบมะกรูด
Previously called kaffir lime leaves, these thick, sturdy leaves smell like the grassier sister of lime zest. It's all aroma, though, as makrut lime leaves don't impart any of the sour taste you might expect from something with such a citrusy fragrance.

Makrut lime leaves are extremely versatile. They can be roughly torn and infused into soups and broths, or finely julienned and added to just about anything you can imagine. Make sure those juliennes are really fine, though, as these leaves are tough and too-big juliennes can leave you feeling like you've got a piece of hay stuck in your teeth.

We do not generally use the juice of makrut limes, of which there isn't much anyway, though the zest is often used in curry pastes. Look for frozen leaves if you can't find fresh; if not available, look for dried.

Makrut lime leaves freeze like a dream. Simply put them into a freezer bag and press as much air out as possible.

> **Note:** Makrut lime leaves are double leaves, meaning that each leaf is made up of two single leaves attached end to end. When a recipe calls for "5 leaves," I mean five single, average-sized leaves. You can use more if they're small; you can never add too many of these!

PANDAN LEAF | *BAI TOEY* | ใบเตย
This aromatic, long, blade-shaped leaf is the star of Thai desserts because its floral aroma pairs fantastically with coconut. Most commonly, we simmer the leaf in liquid to infuse its fragrance, though it can be blended with water and strained when its natural green color is also desired.

Fresh pandan leaves are harder to find, though frozen ones are perfectly fine to use. In fact, if I buy them fresh, I end up freezing them anyway. Pandan extract, though not ideal, can be used instead, but be sure to add a little at a time as it can be intense and easy to overdo it.

WHITE PEPPER | *PRIK TAI KAO* | พริกไทยขาว
Unlike in North America, when we say "pepper," we mean white pepper, as it is our default. We use black pepper occasionally, but it's not a staple in every home. If you don't have or don't like white pepper, black pepper is a fine substitute.

Cupboard Staples

COCONUT MILK | *GATI* | กะทิ
The most important liquid in the Thai kitchen. Coconut milk is our only source of creaminess, because we do not use dairy in Thai cooking. Even though canned coconut milk is the most widely available, I highly recommend you look for coconut milk in UHT paper cartons. Because of different methods of processing, the stuff in the cartons has a much better flavor, more similar to freshly squeezed coconut milk. Aroy-D and Chaokoh are two good brands that come in UHT cartons.

Another thing to look at is the ingredient list. Choose coconut milk with the fewest ingredients possible, as that indicates more real coconut flavor. And never buy "light" coconut milk, because all the flavor is in the fat. Stay away from powdered coconut milk too.

Also, if you're looking at a carton of "coconut milk" in the beverage section of the grocery store, walk away. That is a milk substitute meant for drinking, not cooking. It has *no* coconut flavor in it. The fat, and therefore flavor, has all been removed.

COOKING OIL | *NAM MUN* | น้ำมัน
You can use any neutral-flavored, high-heat-resistant oil for Thai cooking. I personally use avocado oil because it is a healthier option, but because that's pricy, I use canola when I deep-fry. You may think we use coconut oil a lot in Thai cuisine, but we actually mostly use coconut milk and rarely the oil. If you want to use coconut oil, choose refined coconut oil, which does not have the coconut flavor. Using virgin coconut oil will make everything taste like coconut!

CURRY PASTES | *PRIK GAENG* | พริกแกง
If you want to make your own curry pastes and keep them in the freezer, great! (See pp. 255–257 for the recipes.) But I want to

How Coconut Milk Is Made Documentary

The Ultimate Guide to Coconut Milk

assure you that there is no shame in buying prepared pastes, and that most Thai people do not make their own. I certainly do it less often now that I am a mom! In fact, if you can't get all the ingredients, instead of making substitutions, I'd rather you buy a good paste to make sure that you're getting the right flavors.

There are many brands of curry pastes these days, and curry paste is one of those things that you have to try to know if it's good or not. I can say this: make sure it's made in Thailand, and make sure it doesn't have any seasoning other than salt in it. You want the paste to be as pure as possible, so that you can do all the seasoning when you're cooking. Mae Ploy and Aroy-D are both good brands that are widely available, though there are many other good ones out there too.

When you try a curry paste, consider these four things: (1) Flavor: Does it have good, bold flavor? (2) Spiciness: Is it too spicy for you? Don't use less paste to cut down on spiciness, because you'll also be lacking the other herbs and spices. It's better to buy a brand that is less spicy so you can use the right amount. (3) Saltiness: Is it too salty if you add the amount that the recipe calls for? (4) Shrimp paste: whether the curry paste contains it is just something to note, especially if you're vegetarian. I personally like curry pastes that contain shrimp paste, but I can always add it myself if need be.

Once curry paste is opened, keep any leftovers in the freezer.

DRIED SHRIMP | *GOONG HANG* | กุ้งแห้ง Basically, *goong hang* are shrimp jerky. Little shrimp are salted and dried in the sun, and in that process they develop a robust, savory flavor. You can buy these in the refrigerated section at Asian grocery stores. I stick with medium-sized ones, which are most versatile. Freeze them and they will last indefinitely.

NOODLES, GLASS | *WOONSEN* | วุ้นเส้น These clear, thin noodles are also called bean threads or bean vermicelli because they are made from mung bean starch. My grandma always has glass noodles in the pantry, as everyone loves them, they're quick to cook, and they're extremely versatile. They're delicious in salads, soups, stir-fries, and spring rolls, and they're a staple for hot pots. They are also often used to bulk up meat-based fillings and stuffing.

To cook, soak them in room temperature water for

7 to 10 minutes, until they're pliable, then drain and cut with scissors a couple of times to shorten, if desired. They're now ready to go into boiling water for 2 to 3 minutes, or straight into the wok for stir-fries, with a bit of extra water or stock. If you realize at the last minute that you've forgotten to soak them, a 2-minute soak in the hottest tap water also does the trick, though you want to be careful with this, as they can overcook if left to soak for too long. If using room temperature water, they can linger in the water longer than necessary with no harm done.

NOODLES, RICE | *SEN GUAY TIEW* | เส้นก๋วยเตี๋ยว Dry rice noodles are a great thing to keep in your pantry because they are versatile and last seemingly forever. Choose brands from Thailand if possible, as Vietnamese ones can sometimes have tapioca starch mixed in and will have a slightly different texture. They come in many sizes and shapes, but the thin ones are the most convenient for weeknight cooking because they don't take long to soak and cook.

The Minimum Thai Pantry and Freezer

I realize this pantry section might seem like a long list of ingredients for some, so below is a list of what I consider the *essential* Thai ingredients that will allow you to make many of the dishes in this book. Everything else not on this list would be nice to have and would allow you to make more dishes, but they're not critical.

PANTRY/FRIDGE
- Fish sauce
- Soy sauce
- Oyster sauce
- Coconut milk
- Red curry paste, or another one of your favorites
- Palm sugar or light brown sugar
- Tamarind paste
- Jasmine rice
- Rice noodles and/or glass noodles

FREEZER
- Thai chilies (fresh)
- Lemongrass
- Makrut lime leaves
- Galangal (if available)

Top: Essential ingredients for Thai cooking.
Bottom: Nice-to-have ingredients, but not necessary.

Ingredient Substitution Guide

When someone asks "What can I use instead of . . . ?" my follow-up question is always "For what dish?" Substitutes are rarely universal, and you can't determine the best substitute until you know what role that ingredient plays in that dish. For the same ingredient, I may suggest different substitutes depending on the dish. Or I may tell you to just omit it. Or I may even tell you not to try to make that dish without it.

Having said that, there are some substitutions that generally work, so I have provided a guide here, but please use this guide in combination with your own good cooking judgment and intuition!

INGREDIENT	SUBSTITUTE
Basil, holy	**Italian basil.** Thai basil can also be used, but the flavor of Italian basil is more similar to that of holy basil, so it's my preferred substitute.
Basil, Thai	**Italian basil.**
Dried shrimp	**Generally, you can omit,** or use Japanese bonito flakes instead.
Fermented soybean paste (*tao jiew*)	**Korean doenjang or Japanese miso,** starting with the same amount, then tasting and adjusting as needed. *Tao jiew* is runnier, but it tends to be saltier.
Fermented shrimp paste (*gapi*)	**Korean doenjang or Japanese miso,** but this works only when used in small amounts. The flavors of these pastes are completely different, but it does work in adding some umami saltiness. Often you can just omit shrimp paste if only a small amount is called for.
Fish sauce	**Soy sauce or Thai seasoning sauce,** in equal amounts.
Galangal	**No good substitute.** Look for frozen galangal, which works well in all recipes, or dried galangal, which works in soups.
Lemongrass	**No good substitute.** Look for frozen lemongrass, which sometimes comes prechopped. Dried and powdered lemongrass are not recommended.
Makrut lime leaves	**No good substitute.** Look for frozen, which works well in all recipes. Dried leaves work in soups and curries. Lime zest doesn't have the same aroma, but can be added for a similar citrus effect.
Oyster sauce	**Vegetarian stir-fry sauce,** sometimes labeled as "mushroom vegetarian sauce," in equal amounts. Or substitute slightly less of soy sauce or Thai seasoning sauce.
Palm sugar	**Light brown sugar,** in equal amounts by weight and volume; 1 tablespoon (15 ml) packed finely chopped palm sugar = 1 tablespoon (15 ml) packed brown sugar.
Tamarind paste	**Lime juice,** in roughly equal amounts, though you always want to taste and adjust. In small amounts where it's used just to add a touch of acidity, a dash of Worcestershire sauce works too.
Thai seasoning sauce	**Maggi Seasoning, Bragg Liquid Aminos, or soy sauce,** in equal amounts. If the recipe already calls for soy sauce, you could use two different types of soy sauce.
White pepper	**Black pepper** in equal amounts.

Thai Cooking Equipment

MORTAR & PESTLE, STONE | *KROK HIN* | ครกหิน

Mortar and pestles are our blender, food processor, and spice grinder all in one, and every Thai home has one because we make a lot of herb pastes in Thai cooking. It's more work to use, but they are superior to machines in that they can grind anything, wet or dry, no matter how small the amount, and without ever having to add extra liquid. If you don't have one yet but want one, I recommend getting a granite mortar and pestle that is at least 6 inches (15 cm) in external diameter, which is a good all-purpose size. If you want to make curry pastes in it, get an 8-inch (20 cm) one. For the record, I have 4-inch (10 cm), 6-inch (15 cm), and 8-inch (20 cm) stone mortars, and one clay salad mortar (see below).

MORTAR & PESTLE, SALAD | *KROK SOM TUM* | ครกส้มตำ

Most Thai homes have a larger light-duty mortar made from clay or wood that comes with a wooden pestle. These are made specifically for pounded salads, such as the famous green papaya salad, or *som tum*. They're generally less useful than the granite one, so there's no need to own one of these unless you plan on having Thai pounded salads on the regular.

STEAMER | *SEUNG* | ซึ้ง

When I came to Canada, I was surprised to learn that many people here do not own a steamer, a core piece of cookware in Thai homes. The steamer is the reason whole fish are part of everyday Thai home cooking. Steaming also cooks things very quickly compared with baking, takes less time for preheating, and doesn't leave any greasy mess to clean, like frying does.

You can get a multitiered steamer from any large Asian grocery stores that sell cookware, and I recommend getting one that is 14 inches (35 cm) in diameter, if you have the storage space. Yes, it's big, but you want to be able to fit a dinner plate into the steamer, with plenty of room to get it in and out.

If you don't have the storage space, you can get a steamer rack or trivet for a few dollars and put it at the bottom of a stockpot or a wok, as long as you have a lid for it. It's harder to get things in and out of a stockpot, so make sure you have steamer tongs too.

Bamboo steamers can be great, and you can put those in a wok or on top of a pot of the same diameter. The only downside is that they are often too shallow or small to steam a large dish or a whole fish.

WOK | *GATA* | กะทะ

Arguably the most useful piece of cookware in the kitchen. You can use it to stir-fry, sear, boil, steam, deep-fry . . . you name it, it can be done in a wok. When I was growing up, we had pots for simmering and boiling, and one wok for everything else. We didn't own any flat skillets until we started dabbling in Western cooking.

If you have a gas stove, a carbon steel wok is your best choice. If well seasoned and maintained, it will be stick-resistant. It can also develop the smoky "wok flavor" after repeated use and can withstand very high heat, which is useful for stir-frying. It won't get as nonsticky as Teflon, though, so you still need to make sure the pan is hot and oiled before adding stick-prone foods. Round-bottomed woks are recommended only if you have the kind of stove designed to accommodate and stabilize the rounded bottom, or if you have a wok ring.

If you have a glass top or electric stove, you might consider a sturdy, flat-bottomed nonstick wok instead (Korean-made ones are my go-to). Carbon steel woks can warp over time and then lose full contact with the electric element, and you won't be able to get good heat transfer. I have a video on my website that talks about the pros and cons of various types of woks, and also one on how to take care of your carbon steel wok.

 Which Kind of Wok Should You Buy?

Salad mortar and pestle

Stone mortar and pestle

Carbon steel wok

Multitiered steamer

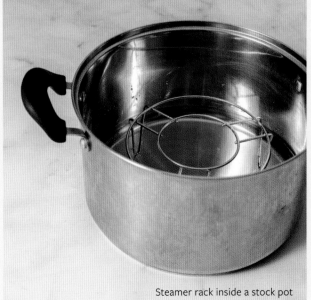

Bamboo steamer

Steamer rack inside a stock pot

Composing a Well-Balanced Thai Meal

What Exactly Are We Balancing?

After years of teaching Thai cooking, I'm beginning to feel like a broken record whenever I say that Thai food is all about *balance*.

But people sometimes misunderstand and think that this means each dish has to have a balance of sweet, salty, sour, and spicy. This is not true; if it did, everything would taste the same! In each dish, you've got a flavor "target" to hit. For some dishes it'll be sweet and salty, for others it might be salty and sour, and for some it'll be a little bit of everything. Each dish has its own flavor identity. But the balance has to happen at the level of the whole meal.

Thai food is usually served family style, with multiple dishes on the table shared by everyone. (I say "usually" because some dishes are meant to be served on their own.) So, on the family-style table, the choice of which dishes to serve together makes a big difference to the overall experience of the meal. I'm happy to know that many people are aware of this, because I have received many messages asking what dishes they should serve together.

In my first book, I discuss the issue of balance from the perspective of what kinds of dishes you should have on the table. But after speaking to many fans and followers of my YouTube channel, I realize that many people plan their Thai meal based on the one or two dishes that they want to make. So the question is usually worded something like "I want to make X. What else should I serve that would go well with X?" And in the same way, as you browse through this book, you'll probably find yourself drawn toward a particular dish you want to try. So here are some guiding questions to help you build a well-balanced meal around that dish.

The Dish You Want to Make, Is It . . .

RICH? If so, have something light and refreshing, such as a salad or brothy soup, on the table.

SOUPY? This includes anything with lots of liquid, whether it's a soup, a stew, or a curry. If so, serve a "dry" dish with it, like something grilled or deep-fried, or a stir-fry that's not too saucy.

MEAT-CENTRIC? If so, make sure you've got lots of vegetables to lighten it up and provide different textures.

SPICY? If so, make sure you have something not spicy on the table. I know some people will say "But I love spicy food!" Yes, I do too, but having something not spicy to provide contrast will make the spicy dish even more satisfying.

SOFT? This is something like a tender steamed fish, an eggplant stir-fry, or a curry with potato. If so, also have something crisp or crunchy on the table.

OPPOSITE OF THE ABOVE? Then simply reverse it.

What Is the Prominent Taste of This Dish? Is It . . .

SWEET? Some Thai dishes have a sweeter flavor profile, like the Instant Pot (or Not) Massaman Curry Chicken (p. 79), and if you've got that on the table, it's important to also have something that's tart and bright, to keep the sweetness from becoming cloying. Salty foods don't cut sweetness nearly as well as acidic foods do. Most Thai salads are sour and fresh-tasting, so that's always an easy solution to turn to.

SOUR? We love our limes and our tamarind in Thailand, so many dishes are prominently sour, whether they're salads, soups, or (even) curries. You can balance sour with sweet or salty dishes, but another great way to do it is with heavy, starchy foods. It's not a coincidence that many Thais love *laab*, including Beef Laab (p. 48), a lime-heavy dish, with dense and chewy sticky rice. Heavy noodles also work; we sometimes serve papaya salad with a rice noodle stir-fry, such as the Minimalist Pad Thai (p. 195). Rich and creamy dishes such as my coconut milk–based Quick Yellow Curry with Beef (p. 71) can help give more substance to acidic foods which tend to be light.

SALTY? Saltiness seems to be the most neutral of the tastes, in the sense that all savory dishes have to have some saltiness as the base seasoning, just to bring out the flavors of all the ingredients in the dish. And when saltiness is the prominent taste (think salty fried chicken), the need to

balance it with something else isn't as strong. Having said that, I think a salty dish can only be elevated when paired with something sweet and/or sour. This is why our go-to dipping sauce for salty fried foods like fried chicken is the sweet and vinegary chili sauce that lines just about every supermarket shelf these days!

Whoa, That's a Lot to Think About!

I know it sounds like a lot, but trust me, it's actually intuitive, especially once you become familiar with several Thai dishes. It's second nature for most Thais, and every time I'm with friends and family in Thailand ordering food

at a restaurant, it's an interesting dynamic to observe. It starts with a couple of people ordering something based on their wants, and from that point on, you can see the wheels turning for everyone else, using those first dishes as a base for ordering the rest of the meal. I don't think most people even realize that's what they're doing, but it becomes clear that balance is on everyone's minds when you hear people veto suggestions with "Too many soupy things already" or "We already have two deep-fried dishes." One point that's often brought up when my friends and I order food is "We don't have any vegetables yet." Seems like we often forget about vegetables when faced with tantalizing meat and seafood options!

Tips for Fast and Efficient Cooking

If you want to cook *sabai-sabai* on a weeknight, you'll need to be efficient in the kitchen so that cooking the dishes don't end up being more time-consuming than necessary. Here are some tips:

Make Your Own Meal Kits

If you're not yet proficient with cooking Thai food, it may take you a bit longer, as you will still need to read recipes and don't yet have the muscle memory for the dishes. On the weekend or whenever you have time, you can do a lot of advance prep to cut down on the amount of time it takes on the day-of. Here are a few things you can do:

MAKE THE SAUCES. There are very few sauces I can think of that will not last in your fridge for at least 1 week and usually much longer. Curry sauces, stir-fry sauces, and dips can all be made in advance, then you can add meat and vegetables on the day-of. You can make curry sauces in bulk and freeze them in portions, and sauces or dressings that contain salty ingredients, like fish sauce and soy sauce, will last a long time in the fridge. But if anything contains lime juice, save the lime juice for adding on the day you're serving the dish, as it tastes best when freshly squeezed.

MAKE THE WHOLE DISH. Can the whole thing be done in advance and just reheated? Curries, soups, and stews are all great for this and will taste even better the next day. Just be sure to save fresh herbs, delicate vegetables, fresh lime juice, and anything that can easily overcook for when you reheat before serving.

CHOP STURDY VEGETABLES. Chopped non-leafy, sturdy veg like carrots, bell peppers, and cauliflower will last in the fridge for up to 1 week.

CUT MEAT. If your meat is fresh, you can cut it into pieces 1 to 2 days in advance and keep it in the fridge, but seafood should be cooked as fresh as possible.

Bulk Process

Some ingredients need the same thing done to them every time, and instead of doing this a little at a time, do it all at once. Here are some examples specific to Thai cooking:

CHOP PALM SUGAR. Chopping palm sugar a few tablespoons at a time as you need it is one of the most annoying things, especially because you need to do it on a clean board, since you may have to put half of the puck back in the cupboard. Chop a bunch at once, then keep it in an airtight container. Fresh palm sugar is softer and easier to chop than when it is old and dried out, anyway.

TOAST SPICES. You can toast any whole spice, but coriander and cumin seeds in particular benefit from toasting, and they are the ones used most often in Thai cooking. Toasting them will help the aroma come out more fully, but trust me, you don't want to toast them a teaspoon at a time! Toast them all at once, and keep in an airtight jar in a cool, dry place. And on that note, never pre-grind coriander seeds, as they do not maintain their aroma well. I use whole spices whenever I can.

TOAST RICE. If you want to regularly prepare Thai recipes that use toasted rice powder, such as laab (p. 48) or BBQ chicken with *nam jim jeaw* (p. 149), you can toast the rice in advance, but do not grind it. Toasted rice will maintain its aroma in an airtight container for at least 1 month, but once ground, it loses its aroma quickly. Toasting a large amount of rice can get a bit smoky, so make sure the kitchen is well ventilated. Keep pre-toasted rice in an airtight container in a cool, dry place or in the fridge.

TRANSFER OYSTER SAUCE TO A SQUEEZE BOTTLE. It is a royal pain to try to pour a measured amount of oyster sauce out of a glass bottle. Transferring it takes time, but at least you'll feel annoyed only once and it'll be a dream to use going forward. Make sure the oyster sauce is not cold when transferring or it will be even harder to pour. You can also do this with any other liquid ingredients that come in containers and are not easy to regulate when poured; I have vanilla extract, white vinegar, cooking oil, maple syrup, and a few other ingredients in squeeze bottles too.

MAKE TAMARIND PASTE IN BULK. Homemade tamarind paste is miles better than store-bought, and many people in Thailand make tamarind a little at a time every time they need some. But it's much more efficient to make it all at once, as it lasts a while in the fridge and can also be frozen, and you can even can it, for long-term room temperature storage. See page 266 for how to make tamarind paste.

PREWASH YOUR HERBS AND VEGETABLES. I know that when you're tired from grocery shopping, all you want to do is stuff the produce in the fridge and be done. But washing and drying your produce before you put it away means you don't have to do it each time you cook, and you don't have to deal with cutting wet vegetables. Not to mention that delicate herbs like cilantro will last longer if you wash off dirt and surface bacteria before storing.

Is There Any Idle Cooking Time Involved?

Doing all the prep before you start can help keep things organized, and that certainly feels good, but it's not necessarily the most efficient thing to do. Before you prepare any recipe, read the instructions and see if there is any hands-off time. It might be 10 minutes of simmering, or 30 minutes of roasting. Then do only as much prep as needed to get to that stage, and use the idle time to prep for the rest of the dish. If cooking multiple dishes, these idle times are also golden opportunities to get another dish started. And if nothing else, clean.

Plan Your Chopping

One of the things that adds unnecessary time to cooking is having to wash and dry your knife and cutting board in between chopping certain ingredients. So if there are a bunch of items to chop that don't need to be cut in any specific order, I try to start with those that will leave my board the cleanest, so that I can move on to the next one without having to wash it or the knife.

Scraps Bowl on the Counter

"No idle moment, no wasted movement" was one thing I learned when working under pressure in professional kitchens. If you have to move or, heaven forbid, open the cabinet door to get to your compost or garbage bin, your prep session isn't as efficient as it might be. I keep a bowl handy on the counter, next to my cutting board, so I don't have to take even one step just to throw something away. Think about other inefficiencies in your kitchen: What else can you do to minimize movement when you cook?

APPETIZERS

Ahaan Riek Nam Yoi | อาหารเรียกน้ำย่อย

Dishes Not Served With Rice

I have said many times that Thai people eat everything with rice. Well, there are some exceptions, such as the recipes in this chapter. These dishes might be considered "appetizers" in the West, but because we do not eat in courses, they are served in various ways. In Thailand, these dishes are considered any of the following:

SNACKS | *KONG KIN LEN* | ของกินเล่น The Salad Rolls (p. 40) are the perfect example of a *kong kin len*, something we eat when we're hungry between lunch and dinner. Many of these are sold by street vendors or at supermarkets where people can grab-and-go after work or school.

DRINKING FOOD | *GUB GLAM* | กับแกล้ม These are the salty, fried, and munchy things that go great with beer, such as the Fish Sauce Wings (p. 27) and the Laab Bites (p. 30). And, yes, in Thailand our beverage of choice is usually a light beer or something ice-cold, not wine.

APPETIZERS | *AHAAN RIEK NAM YOI* | อาหารเรียกน้ำย่อย Foods that are served before the main dishes arrive. Wait, didn't I just say Thai people don't eat in courses? Yes. But at get-togethers in restaurants, these are the dishes early guests enjoy while they wait for everyone else. And with traffic in Thailand . . . the wait can be long!

DIP PLATTERS | *KREUANG JIM* | เครื่องจิ้ม I know I said that these are dishes that are not served with rice, but actually in Thailand dip platters are served with rice as part of the main meal! I've included one dip platter recipe, the Coconut Tuna Dip (p. 34), because it is mild and makes a great stand-alone appetizer. Most of our other dips are spicy, strong, and definitely need some rice to tame them.

Fish Sauce Wings

Peek Gai Tod Nam Pla | ปีกไก่ทอดน้ำปลา

This method is hands-down my favorite way to cook wings at home. These wings look far too simple to be anything special, but the amount of flavor they deliver will surprise you as you find yourself going back for more. The secret is in the salty umami of the fish sauce, so it's important to use good-quality fish sauce here. By using only wing flats, as is usually done in Thailand, I can shallow-fry and still have the crispy golden-brown skin you'd find in deep-fried wings. You can also throw them on the grill or deep-fry them, and several of my YouTube viewers have reported great success with air-frying, though I've never personally tried it. These are the perfect food to go with a summer beer, and to make it a meal, a side of sticky rice is all you need.

***

Put the wings in a large zip-top bag or a casserole dish large enough to hold them in one layer. Add the fish sauce and toss well. Let the wings marinate for 20 to 30 minutes, flipping the bag over (or the wings themselves, if in a dish) halfway through.

Use tongs to remove the wings from the marinade and place them on a paper towel–lined baking sheet in one layer. Pat the tops of the wings dry with more paper towel.

Sprinkle the pepper all over the wings and press it onto the skin to stick.

If shallow- or deep-frying, sift the rice flour through a fine-mesh sieve evenly but thinly over the wings, then flip the wings and repeat on the other side. Put the wings into the sieve and toss a few times to remove excess flour; you want the wings to be entirely coated with a thin layer of flour. If grilling, you do not have to flour them.

(Continued)

SERVES 4

COOKING TIME: 20 minutes, plus 20 to 30 minutes of marinating

2 pounds (1 kg) chicken wing flats (see note)

3 tablespoons (45 ml) fish sauce

Freshly ground white or black pepper, to taste

½ cup (50 g) rice flour or cornstarch (omit if grilling), plus more as needed

Oil for frying (optional)

Sticky rice (p. 238), for serving (optional)

***

Do-ahead: The wings can be marinated 1 day in advance, but drain off excess marinade after 30 minutes.

Note: Using flats gives you the option to shallow-fry and still get crispy skin, but you will need a splatter guard, as oil tends to jump during shallow-frying. If you want to use drumettes, I recommend deep-frying, grilling, or air-frying them.

To shallow-fry, place a 12-inch (30 cm) skillet over medium-high heat and add ¼ inch (6 mm) of oil. Once the oil is hot, add the wings in one layer, thick-skin side down. The oil should sizzle excitedly as you put the wings down; if it doesn't, wait for the oil to get hotter. You should be able to put exactly 1 pound (450 g) wing flats in a 12-inch (30 cm) skillet. Cover with a mesh splatter guard (the oil tends to jump during shallow-frying) and fry without moving them until golden brown on the underside, about 4 minutes. Then flip and fry the other side just until cooked through, 2 to 3 minutes more. Repeat with the second batch.

To deep-fry, heat at least 1 inch (2.5 cm) of oil in a pot to 375°F (190°C) and fry the wings for 4 to 5 minutes, until golden brown and cooked through. Do this in batches and don't crowd the pot.

To grill, preheat the grill on high heat, then place the wings thick-skin side down and grill with the lid open until the skin is golden brown. Move them around as needed to get even browning. Flip and cook on the other side until the wings are cooked through; it should take a total of 8 to 10 minutes.

Serve the wings on their own or with a side of sticky rice and a cold fizzy beverage.

Laab Bites

Laab Tod | ลาบทอด

SERVES 6 AS AN APPETIZER, OR 4 AS A MAIN

COOKING TIME: 35 minutes if deep-frying or pan-frying; 45 minutes if baking

3 tablespoons (45 ml) uncooked Thai glutinous rice or jasmine rice

1 makrut lime leaf (optional)

1 pound (450 g) lean ground pork

¼ cup (30 g) minced shallots

3 tablespoons (24 g) all-purpose flour

2 tablespoons (12 g) finely chopped lemongrass, from bottom half only

½ teaspoon (2 ml) roasted chili flakes, store-bought or homemade (p. 263), or to taste

3 tablespoons (45 ml) lime juice

2 tablespoons (30 ml) fish sauce

¼ cup (6 g) finely julienned mint leaves (see note)

Oil for frying (optional)

SERVING SUGGESTIONS

Mint leaves

Butter or romaine lettuce leaves

Roasted peanuts

Sticky rice (p. 238)

Do-ahead: The mixture can be made 1 day in advance, but add the mint right before cooking.

Note: If the mint leaves are large, cut them lengthwise so you don't get long pieces.

Laab is a northeastern ground meat salad, but a modern rendition now exists that turns the spicy, sour, and toasty flavors into fried meatballs. Brilliant, I know! If frying doesn't sound quick and easy to you, I have included options for baking and pan-frying. You might be surprised when trying these for the first time, because they are sour, to keep the spirit of the original salad that inspired them. But the acid cuts the grease, which makes these very hard to stop eating. To make it a meal, add a side of sticky rice and a pounded Thai salad, such as the Vegetarian Pounded Corn & Cucumber Salad (p. 62).

———

If baking, preheat the oven to 400°F (200°C).

Make the toasted rice powder by placing the rice and makrut lime leaf in a small dry skillet over medium-high heat. Cook, stirring constantly, until the rice is dark brown and the lime leaf is crisp. It might get a bit smoky, so make sure the kitchen is well ventilated. Pour onto a plate to cool slightly, then grind both the rice and the lime leaf with a mortar and pestle or a coffee grinder until it's mostly a fine powder, but still with some larger bits for texture.

Make the meatballs by combining the pork, shallots, flour, toasted rice powder, lemongrass, chili flakes, lime juice, and fish sauce in a mixing bowl; mix with your hands until well blended. Add the mint and mix just until combined.

Form the mixture into meatballs. If deep-frying or baking, make 1½-inch (4 cm) balls—about 1 rounded tablespoon (15 ml)—and pack them tightly. If you want to pan-fry, make patties about 2 inches (5 cm) in diameter and ½ inch (1.2 cm) thick.

To deep-fry, heat 1½ inches (4 cm) of frying oil in a medium pot or wok and heat it to 350°F (180°C). Add the meatballs one at a time. Depending on how big your pot is, you may need to fry in two or three batches. Cook the meatballs for 4 to 5 minutes, until well browned on the outside and cooked through on the inside. You want these quite dark, not a golden brown, to ensure a crispy exterior. Scoop them out and drain on paper towel.

To bake, arrange the meatballs on a baking sheet lined with parchment paper and bake for about 20 minutes, until cooked through and browned. If you want, you can brown them further under the broiler: transfer the cooked meatballs onto a fresh baking sheet and place

them under the broiler, about 5 inches (12.5 cm) from the element or flame. Broil on high for about 3 minutes, until browned to your liking.

To pan-fry, heat the largest skillet you have over medium heat and add enough oil to thoroughly coat the bottom. Once hot, add as many patties as will fit, and cook without moving them for 2 to 3 minutes per side, until they are well browned. Remove from the pan and rest them on a paper towel–lined plate.

Serve the meatballs either on their own, or with a side of crisp lettuce and mint leaves, for a little bite-sized lettuce wrap. To make it a meal, serve alongside some Thai sticky rice.

To Fry, to Bake, or to Pan-Fry?

In Thailand, deep-frying at home is quite common because most homes have outdoor kitchens, so we can fry without the house smelling like a fast-food joint afterward! For this recipe, pan-frying is absolutely fine, but I generally prefer deep-frying because it gives the meatballs the crispiest exterior, and I find it much less finicky than having to monitor and flip each piece individually. But for maximum convenience, baking is great because you can do it all in one batch, though you compromise on the crispiness of the exterior. So if you have time, the extra broiling step really helps. And yes, you can air-fry these.

Eggs & Herb Salad

Yum Kai Tom | ยำไข่ต้ม

A fresh, citrusy, and spicy herb salad brings humble boiled eggs to life. You wouldn't guess by how beautiful these are, but this is one of those "desperate dishes" my grandma likes to make when she can't think of anything else. Because, like most people, we always have eggs, and all other ingredients in this recipe are the most basic staples of a Thai kitchen. So when all else fails, we can always make a *yum kai tom*. We usually serve this with rice as part of a Thai meal, but it works well as a plated appetizer, and also goes incredibly well with plain rice porridge (p. 245) for breakfast.

———

Bring a pot of water to a full boil, then slowly lower the eggs into the water and boil for 8 minutes. Cool the eggs in a large bowl of cold water, then peel and set aside. You want the yolks to be set but still moist.

Grind the dried shrimp in a clean coffee grinder until fine and fluffy. Alternatively, soak them in hot water for a few minutes to soften, then finely chop or pound with a mortar and pestle until shredded. (If using bonito flakes, crumble the flakes with your fingers to break them down a bit further.) Set aside.

For the dressing, pound the chilies into a paste with a mortar and pestle, then add the palm sugar and pound to dissolve it into a thick paste. Add the lime juice and fish sauce, and swirl with the pestle until the sugar is completely dissolved. Stir in the shallots, lemongrass, and half of the dried shrimp.

Sprinkle some sliced lemongrass on the serving plate to prevent the eggs from sliding around. Then cut the eggs in half lengthwise and place them on the plate cut side up.

When ready to serve, mix the cilantro and green onions into the dressing, then top each egg with some of this mixture. Finish with a sprinkle of the remaining dried shrimp.

Serve as an appetizer or with jasmine rice.

SERVES 4

COOKING TIME: 25 minutes

5 large eggs

1 heaping tablespoon (10 g) dried shrimp (see note)

1 to 2 Thai chilies

2 teaspoons (10 ml) finely chopped palm sugar, packed

2 tablespoons (30 ml) lime juice

1 tablespoon (15 ml) fish sauce

2 tablespoons (15 g) finely chopped shallots

2 inches (5 cm) lemongrass from bottom half, thinly sliced, plus extra for plating

3 sprigs cilantro, chopped (see note)

1 small green onion, chopped

Jasmine rice, for serving (optional)

Do-ahead: Boil the eggs up to 2 days in advance.

Notes: *If you are allergic to shrimp, substitute 3 tablespoons (45 ml) Japanese bonito flakes.*

Don't sweat it if you don't have all the herbs, but I'd say it's important to have at least two types. Mint and dill would work well too.

Duck or Chicken?

Chicken eggs are great in this dish, but we often use duck eggs, which are much more commonly consumed in Thailand than in the West. In dishes where medium-cooked eggs are the goal, duck eggs are preferred because they have yolks that can be cooked to the perfect gooey-but-not-runny stage, which chicken eggs never really achieve. If you want to try it, look for duck eggs at larger Asian supermarkets or farmers' markets.

Coconut Tuna Dip

Lohn Pla Tuna | หลนปลาทูน่า

SERVES 4 TO 6

COOKING TIME: 10 minutes

½ to ¾ cup (125 to 185 ml) coconut milk

¼ cup (25 g) finely julienned shallots

1 can tuna in water, drained (4 ounces/115 g drained weight)

2 to 3 Thai chilies, cut in large chunks on a diagonal, plus extra for garnish

3-inch piece (15 g) lemongrass, from bottom half, thinly sliced

2 teaspoons (10 ml) fish sauce

2 teaspoons (10 ml) tamarind paste, store-bought or homemade (p. 266)

1 teaspoon (5 ml) finely chopped palm sugar

3 to 4 sprigs cilantro, chopped, plus extra for garnish

SERVING SUGGESTIONS

Plain rice crackers

Dipping veggies

Crispy pork rind

Jasmine rice

Do-ahead: The dip can be made in advance and keeps in the fridge for at least 1 week.

I am passionate about *lohn* because it's such a hidden gem of Thai cuisine and I think more people need to know about it. It's a type of dip made from simmering some type of protein with coconut milk, seasoned to be a little bit of everything: salty, sweet, and tart, with just a hint of spiciness. Unlike our other dips, which tend to be fiercely spicy, *lohn* is creamy and mild, making it the first kind of dip I could enjoy as a kid. People make *lohn* with all kinds of finely chopped or ground meat, and it works surprisingly well with canned tuna too, which is so convenient! We typically serve *lohn* and other dips with veggies and rice as part of a meal, but it works great as an appetizer as well.

———

Place ½ cup (125 ml) coconut milk and shallots in a small pot and bring to a boil over medium heat. Let it boil for a few minutes, until reduced by about half.

Add the tuna, chilies, lemongrass, fish sauce, tamarind paste, and sugar; stir to mix well, breaking up any chunks of tuna. Turn the heat down to low and simmer for about 2 minutes, until the flavors are combined.

If the dip is too thick, add more coconut milk so there is some pooling liquid, but the mixture should still have a dip-like consistency. Taste and adjust the seasoning with more fish sauce, tamarind paste, or sugar as needed, then remove from the heat.

Just before serving, stir in the chopped cilantro and pour into a bowl. Garnish with more cilantro, chilies, and a splash of coconut milk, if desired. Serve with rice crackers, dipping veggies, and crispy pork rind. Or serve with jasmine rice as part of a meal.

Pork & Peanut Dip with Rice Crackers

Kao Tung Na Tung | ข้าวตังหน้าตั้ง

I absolutely adored this dip when I lived in Thailand, but we didn't have it often because it's traditionally served with homemade deep-fried rice crackers—not something one whips up at home, and rice crackers weren't sold at the store. So it was always a real treat whenever I got to eat it at a restaurant. The dip itself couldn't be easier, though, so when I noticed rice crackers for sale at just about any store in Canada, I wondered if they would work even though they look quite different from those in Thailand. Well, it turns out, they work *perfectly* and I was only sad that I didn't think to try them earlier! The flavor of this dip is so uniquely Thai—the salty-sweet-spicy combo, the creamy coconut milk, and the toasty peanuts . . . it never fails to bring me home.

———

Grind the chili in a coffee grinder into a powder.

Grind the peanuts in a small food processor or with a mortar and pestle until mealy, but don't turn them into peanut butter. If using a mortar and pestle, remove the peanuts from the mortar and set aside.

Cut the cilantro sprigs in half, separating the parts with leaves from the stems alone. Chop both parts but keep them separated.

Grind the peppercorns into a powder with a mortar and pestle. Add the garlic and then the cilantro stems and pound into a fine paste. Add the ground dried chili and pound to mix.

Heat a medium pot over medium heat, then add the oil and the garlic-chili paste and sauté for 2 to 3 minutes, until aromatic. Deglaze with half of the coconut milk, scraping the bottom of the pot if anything is stuck.

Add the ground pork and stir to break it up; it's important there are no big chunks, for the right dip consistency. Cook until no longer pink. Add the remaining coconut milk, peanuts, tamarind paste, sugar, and fish sauce; simmer for a few minutes, until reduced to a thick, dippable consistency.

Stir in the shallots and turn off the heat. Taste and adjust the seasoning as needed; it should have a good balance of salty and sweet, with just a hint of acidity to keep it bright.

When ready to serve, stir in the cilantro leaves. Serve with plain rice crackers.

SERVES 4 TO 6
COOKING TIME: 20 minutes

1 (5 g) guajillo chili or equivalent weight of another chili

⅓ cup (50 g) roasted peanuts

8 sprigs cilantro

¼ teaspoon (1 ml) white peppercorns

4 cloves (20 g) garlic

1 tablespoon (15 ml) neutral oil

½ cup (125 ml) coconut milk, divided

½ pound (225 g) ground pork

2 tablespoons (30 ml) tamarind paste, store-bought or homemade (p. 266)

1½ tablespoons (18 g) finely chopped palm sugar, packed

1½ tablespoons (22 ml) fish sauce

¼ cup (30 g) thinly sliced shallots

Plain rice crackers, for serving

Do-ahead: The dip can be made in advance; it will keep in the fridge for at least 1 week.

No Pork? No Problem.
In Thailand, this dip is often made with a combination of ground pork and ground shrimp. No, they don't sell ground shrimp at the store, but you can grind your own by finely chopping it (a Chinese cleaver is great for this). You can also use ground chicken or turkey, but I would suggest using dark meat, so that it will not be too lean. For a vegan version, use crumbled extra-firm or pressed tofu, and sub soy sauce for fish sauce. I would not use ground beef, as it has a strong taste that would mess with the flavor profile of this dish.

Tomato Coconut Salsa

Yum Makeua Ted | ยำมะเขือเทศ

I created this recipe several years ago when I needed to bring snacks to a potluck, and being who I am, I felt the need to make it at least a little bit Thai. So I got the idea to make a Thai version of chips and salsa, which simply meant that I would make a Thai salad, or a *yum*, with diced tomatoes (see p. 47 for more on *yum*). I decided to go with a more elaborate *yum* by adding coconut milk, Thai chili paste, toasted coconut, and peanuts to make it richer, and so that it wouldn't just taste like a pico de gallo with fish sauce . . . not that that would be bad. It turned out to be a hit, which meant that it warranted sharing. It's a delightful change from the usual chips and salsa, and you can even serve it over fish or chicken for dinner!

————

Dice the tomatoes into about ¼-inch (6 mm) pieces, then place in a strainer set over a bowl to remove excess liquid; let drain for at least 15 minutes. Do not discard the liquid.

Make the dressing by boiling the coconut milk in a small pot over medium-high heat for a few minutes, until it's thick; you should be able to run your spatula through it and leave a trail that doesn't go away. Remove from the heat and add the chilies, 2 tablespoons (30 ml) lime juice, chili paste, fish sauce, and sugar; stir to mix.

Toast the shredded coconut by putting it in a dry skillet and stirring it over medium-high heat until it's a deep golden brown; this takes just a few minutes, so stir constantly—do not walk away. You can make it darker for a toastier flavor. Remove from the pan and add to a small mixing bowl.

Grind the peanuts until mealy, using either a food processor or a mortar and pestle; there should not be any big chunks, but don't turn them into peanut butter. Add the peanuts to the coconut, then add the drained tomatoes and shallots.

Pour the dressing over and mix well. The mixture may look a bit thick right now, but the tomatoes will soon release some liquid. Taste and adjust the seasoning with more lime juice as needed.

When ready to serve, if the salsa still looks too thick, add in some of the reserved tomato liquid. Stir in the chopped cilantro, and serve with tortilla chips or rice crackers, or use as a sauce to serve with fish or chicken.

SERVES 4 TO 6
COOKING TIME: 25 minutes

2 tomatoes (about 9 ounces/250 g)

3 tablespoons (45 ml) coconut milk

2 Thai chilies, minced

2 to 3 tablespoons (30 to 45 ml) lime juice

1 tablespoon (15 ml) Thai chili paste, store-bought or homemade (p. 258)

1 tablespoon (15 ml) fish sauce

½ teaspoon (2 ml) granulated sugar

2 tablespoons (12 g) unsweetened dried shredded coconut

¼ cup (35 g) roasted peanuts (optional, see note)

2 tablespoons (15 g) small-diced shallots

3 to 4 sprigs cilantro, chopped

Plain rice crackers or tortilla chips, for serving

Do-ahead: Make the dip up to 1 day in advance, adding cilantro just before serving.

Note: The peanuts can be omitted if you want a lighter dip. Or, if you're allergic to peanuts, you can substitute cashews.

Salad Rolls with Spicy Garlicky Dip
Salad Rolls | สลัดโรล

MAKES 28 PIECES
COOKING TIME: 30 minutes

SPICY GARLICKY DIP

1 clove (5 g) garlic

½ to 1 Thai chili

¼ + ⅛ teaspoons (1.5 ml) table salt

¼ cup (60 ml) mayonnaise

1½ tablespoons (22 ml) sweetened condensed milk

1½ tablespoons (22 ml) lime juice

SALAD ROLLS

7 sheets of 8-inch (20 cm) round Vietnamese rice paper

4 to 5 cups (70 to 90 g) baby salad greens

14 (3-inch/8 cm long) strips of protein of your choice (see note)

1 cucumber, cut in 3-inch (8 cm) sticks

1 carrot, thinly julienned (I use a julienne peeler)

Any other veggies or herbs you like (bell peppers, avocado, beets, sprouts, cilantro, mint, Thai basil)

Do-ahead: The dip can be made up to a few days in advance. The salad rolls can be made a few hours in advance and kept well wrapped with plastic wrap or in an airtight container at room temp.

Note: For the protein, my favorites are ham, roast chicken, shrimp, imitation crab, and firm or pressed tofu (especially the marinated kind). Anything that you like in a sandwich will work here. Cut them into sticks about 3 inches (8 cm) long, and about the thickness of a thick-cut french fry.

Salad Roll Wrapping

I generally don't like eating raw vegetables, but the first time I tried these salad rolls in Thailand, I could not stop eating them. It's all in the creamy, garlicky, spicy dip that is nothing like any salad roll dipping sauce you've ever had, not to mention the unique wrapping technique that produces cute little bouquets of greens. These are a new style of snacks that became popular among Thailand's many grab-and-go food vendors, and my mom used to bring them home after work for a healthy snack. I haven't seen them served at any Thai restaurants overseas, nor sold at touristy spots in Thailand, so it's a real hidden gem of the locals. It's a lot easier to understand how the rolling works by seeing it in action in the video accessed via the QR code below.

FOR THE DIPPING SAUCE

Using a mortar and pestle, pound the garlic, chili, and salt into a fine paste. Add the mayo, condensed milk, and lime juice; stir until combined. Taste and adjust the seasoning as needed. The sauce will keep in the fridge for at least 1 week.

FOR THE SALAD ROLLS

Cut a rice paper circle in half with scissors. Prepare a large bowl of hot tap water (as hot as you can stand dipping your hands in).

Dip a piece of halved rice paper in the water for 8 to 10 seconds, then put it on a clean work surface, the flat edge facing either to the left or right. Let it sit for another 10 to 15 seconds, until it has absorbed all the water around it and the sheet has softened. Fold about 1 inch (2.5 cm) of the rounded side toward the center, so that you now have two straight sides.

In your hand, stack about 4 leaves of baby salad greens, with the stems facing the same direction. Lay the salad stack on the rice paper, about 2 inches (5 cm) above the edge closest to you, making sure the tops of the leaves are sticking out about ½ inch (1.2 cm) over the left side of the rice paper. Repeat with another stack of greens, placing it on the right side of the paper in the same way.

Place the protein and all the other vegetables on top of the greens, centering them horizontally so that they will cut evenly when you cut the salad rolls in half.

Pick up the edge closest to you, fold it over the filling, and roll it away from you, keeping the salad roll as tight as you can. You will end up with a salad roll with two open ends. Cut the roll into two pieces and place each piece, cut side down, on a serving plate. Repeat with the remaining rice paper circles, greens, protein, and vegetables.

Serve the salad rolls at room temperature with the dipping sauce. If not serving right away, keep them well wrapped with plastic wrap or in an airtight container, to prevent drying.

Too Lazy to Wrap?

Serving a lot of people and don't want to spend time wrapping? I am with you 100%. You can make your guests do the work by setting out the ingredients and a couple of bowls of hot water for a "make your own salad rolls" party. Or you can do even less work and serve the sauce as a dip for a veggie platter—the best part is the sauce, anyway!

Flaky Roti with Yellow Curry Dip

Roti Jim Gaeng Garee | โรตีจิ้มแกงกะหรี่

In Thailand, curry is most commonly served with rice, but sometimes certain curries are served with roti. And when Thai people say "roti," we're talking about the flakey, crispy, chewy, fried flatbread that are also referred to as roti canai or roti paratha, depending on where you are. Yellow curry chicken is one of those curries that is sometimes paired with roti, but instead of making a whole curry, you can just make the sauce and serve it as a dip. My trouble here was trying to get the chicken flavor into the dip without having to use any chicken. Turns out, chicken bouillon cube was the perfect solution. The tomatoes are my own addition, as I think it's satisfying to have a little pop of acidity in each bite.

Into a small pot, pour about ¼ cup (60 ml) coconut milk and bring to a boil over high heat. Add the curry paste and onions, stirring to mix. Once the mixture starts to thicken, turn the heat down to medium and keep stirring until the curry is very thick and the onions are very soft.

Add the remaining coconut milk, ⅛ teaspoon (0.5 ml) bouillon, and sugar, and bring to a boil, then turn the heat down to low and simmer for 5 minutes.

Stir in the tomatoes and turn off the heat. Taste and add the fish sauce to taste, or if you want a stronger chicken flavor, and there's room for more salt, you can add a touch more bouillon.

When ready to serve, cook the roti. Heat a skillet over medium-high heat, add the oil, and, once the pan is hot, place a frozen roti in the pan. Fry until nicely browned, 2 to 3 minutes, then flip and cook the other side until browned. Rest the cooked roti on a piece of paper towel. If you want, you can fluff the roti by placing your hands on either side of the paper towel and "clapping" to scrunch and separate the layers. Rotate the roti ninety degrees and fluff it one more time. (This doesn't work quite as well with frozen Chinese pancakes.) Repeat with the remaining roti.

To serve, tear the roti into big, shaggy chunks if you want to serve it finger-food style, or leave them whole, for people to tear themselves. Serve while the roti is still hot, along with the warm curry dip.

SERVES 6
COOKING TIME: 25 minutes

1 cup (250 ml) coconut milk, divided

1 tablespoon (15 ml) yellow curry paste, store-bought or homemade (p. 257)

¼ cup (30 g) finely minced onion

⅛ to ¼ teaspoon (0.5 to 1 ml) chicken bouillon cube, paste, or powder (see note)

1 tablespoon (12 g) finely chopped palm sugar, packed

¼ cup (50 g) diced fresh tomatoes

1 to 2 teaspoons (5 to 10 ml) fish sauce

1 tablespoon (15 ml) neutral oil

1 package frozen roti paratha (see note)

Do-ahead: *The curry dip can be made in advance and refrigerated for up to 1 week.*

Notes: *In Thailand, Knorr is the most popular brand of bouillon cubes, and that's the brand I use for this. You can use another brand, but start with just ⅛ teaspoon (0.5 ml), then taste and adjust from there.*

If you cannot find roti paratha, you can use frozen Chinese scallion pancakes, but if there is a version without scallions available, that would be preferable.

Repurposing Leftover Curry

If you make a coconut-based curry and you've eaten it all except for just that little bit of sauce that's left, save it and use it as a dip for roti, for a near-instant appetizer. You don't need a lot, even just ¼ cup (60 ml) sauce will be enough for two people. Any curry sauce will work, but most commonly we serve green, *massaman*, or yellow curry with roti. Depending on the curry, you may need to reduce the sauce a bit so it'll be thick enough to cling to the roti.

SALADS

Yum, Tum, Pla, Laab | ยำ ตำ พล่า ลาบ

Thai Salads

How to Eat a Thai Salad

Salads in Thai cuisine are treated very differently than are salads in the West. First, they are not a first course. Salads are served alongside a multi-dish Thai meal, and they act as the bright, tart, fresh element of the meal that helps balance richer dishes.

Salads are also not meant to be eaten on their own. You do not sit with a bowl of Thai salad and eat it for lunch at your desk. It is always served with rice, sticky rice, or even rice porridge, depending on the salad. The flavors of Thai salads are strong, spicy, and tart and are meant to be accompanied by more neutral carbs. The exception to this are some noodle salads, including the Mama noodle salad (p. 51), which can be eaten alone.

Thai Salad Dressing 101

As you browse these salad recipes, you will quickly realize that the dressings are all very similar to each other. Lime juice, fish sauce, chilies, and sugar are the core ingredients of Thai salad dressing. We don't use vinegars or oils. So this means that once you learn how to make a basic dressing, you can make many types of Thai salads simply by changing up the meat, veggies, and herbs, and adjusting the dressing slightly as needed to better match your mix of ingredients.

Types of Thai Salads

There is no one word in Thai that means salad. But we do have a few types of dishes that would be classified as a salad in the English sense of the word, meaning that ingredients are tossed together with a dressing.

YUM | ยำ: This is the most basic, and most generic, kind of salad. A *yum* can be made of any ingredients, though most of the time it is protein-centric. The dressing is made of at least the basic four: lime juice, fish sauce, fresh chilies, and sugar, but more ingredients can be added, such as Thai chili paste or even coconut milk.

TUM | ตำ: *Tum* means to pound with a mortar and pestle, which is how this type of salad is made. Pounding a salad might sound bizarre, but it's only the dressing that's actually pounded, and other ingredients are more gently crushed or simply tossed. Our famous green papaya salad is made in this manner.

LAAB | ลาบ: This northeastern specialty is much more specific than a *yum*. To be a *laab*, it has to contain toasted rice powder, mint, fish sauce, lime juice, and roasted chili flakes. The main ingredient is traditionally ground or finely chopped meats, though nowadays people have gotten very creative and make *laab* from just about anything. *Nam tok* is a similar type of salad, but the meat is grilled and sliced rather than ground.

PLA | พล่า: Probably the least common of all the salads. It started out as our version of ceviche, where proteins such as shrimp and beef are cooked with the acid of lime juice. Nowadays, people have stopped this practice because of the risk of food poisoning, so most of the time that you see a *pla*, it is very much like a *yum*, but with a lot of lemongrass and mint, and often Thai chili paste.

Beef Laab

Laab Neua | ลาบเนื้อ

SERVES 4
COOKING TIME: 20 minutes

3 tablespoons (30 g) uncooked jasmine or glutinous rice

1 makrut lime leaf (optional)

¾ pound (340 g) ground beef

2 tablespoons (30 ml) fish sauce

⅓ cup (35 g) julienned shallots

1 stalk lemongrass, bottom 5 to 6 inches (12.5 to 15 cm) only, thinly sliced

2½ to 3 tablespoons (37 to 45 ml) lime juice

1 to 2 teaspoons (5 to 10 ml) roasted chili flakes, store-bought or homemade (p. 263)

2 green onions, chopped

10 sprigs cilantro, or 6 to 7 leaves sawtooth coriander, chopped

1 cup (8 g) mint leaves, torn if large, plus small ones for garnish

FOR SERVING

Fresh veggies, such as sliced English cucumber and romaine lettuce leaves

Sticky rice, but jasmine rice will do in a pinch

Transforming Leftover *Laab*

I often find myself with a little bit of *laab* left over—not really enough for another full meal, and not ideal to eat on its own because all the herbs are wilted and the toasted rice has absorbed all the dressing. Over the years I have used it up in many delicious ways: in an omelet, on top of avocado toast, or—my current favorite—tossed with rice and topped with a fried egg. How would you transform *your* leftover *laab*?

First of all, it is *laab*, not *laRb*. Now that that's out of the way, *laab* is the epitome of *Isaan*, or northeastern Thai, food. Spicy, salty, sour, and loaded with fresh herbs, this rustic dish doesn't make for pretty eating, as the flavors will have you unabashedly using your hands to stuff your mouth with sticky rice. If you don't eat beef, no worries; as I always say, you can *laab* anything, and even some of the herbs are optional. There are a few ingredients without which it is no longer a *laab*, though, so make sure you have toasted rice powder, lime juice, chili flakes, and mint.

———

Make toasted rice powder by placing the rice and makrut lime leaf in a small dry skillet over medium-high heat. Cook, stirring constantly, until the rice is dark brown and the lime leaf is crisp. It might get a bit smoky, so make sure the kitchen is well ventilated. Pour onto a plate to cool slightly, then grind both the rice and the lime leaf in a coffee grinder or mortar and pestle until it is mostly a powder, with a few larger pieces for texture.

Place a large pot over high heat and add the ground beef and fish sauce (no oil needed). Stir constantly, breaking up any chunks, until the beef is fully cooked. It may look like a large pot is overkill for this amount of beef, but a smaller pot would trap too much liquid and make the mixture too soupy. You could use a skillet, but it's a lot easier to stir and break up the beef in a pot.

Remove the pot from the heat and add the shallots, lemongrass, lime juice, and chili flakes. Let the mixture cool for a few minutes before stirring in the toasted rice powder, green onions, cilantro, and mint (this prevents the fresh herbs from wilting in the heat and the toasted rice powder from absorbing too much liquid too soon). Mix well. Taste and adjust the seasoning with more fish sauce or lime juice as needed. The flavor should lead with the tartness of the lime and be plenty spicy.

Transfer to a serving plate and garnish with mint leaves. Serve with fresh veggies and sticky rice or jasmine rice. If you have lettuce leaves, you can make lettuce wraps.

Warm Mama Noodle Salad

Yum Mama | ยำมาม่า

This is a warm noodle salad that is substantial enough to be a whole meal. Mama is Thailand's favorite brand of instant noodles, so much so that the word "mama" has come to simply mean instant noodles. We love it so much, we commonly use it as an ingredient, and even some noodle soup vendors offer mama as one of the noodle options. As much as I'd like to say you can substitute another brand, you really can't. Thai instant noodles have a unique flavor and texture that are key to the identity of this dish, so you really need them for the full effect.

———

Bring a pot of water to a boil to make the noodles.

Make the dressing by combining the chilies, sugar, and 2 tablespoons (30 ml) lime juice in a large mixing bowl. Stir until most of the sugar is dissolved.

Place a 10-inch (25 cm) skillet on high heat, and add the ground pork and fish sauce. Cook for 2 to 3 minutes, stirring to break up any chunks. Once the pork is cooked, add the cabbage and the seasoning from the packets that came with the noodles. Stir for another minute, just to cook the cabbage down slightly. Pour the pork and cabbage into the bowl with the dressing.

Break the noodle blocks into quarters and cook in boiling water, stirring occasionally, just until they are fully loosened from the block shape, about 2 minutes. Drain the noodles very well, shaking off as much liquid as possible, and add them to the pork mixture.

Add the onions, tomatoes, and celery stalks and leaves and toss well, then taste and adjust the seasoning with more lime juice as needed. Top with the cilantro and serve warm.

SERVES 4 AS AN APPETIZER, OR 2 AS A MAIN
COOKING TIME: 20 minutes

1 to 2 Thai chilies, minced (optional)

1½ tablespoons (18 g) finely chopped palm sugar, packed

3 tablespoons (45 ml) lime juice, divided

½ pound (225 g) ground pork or ground dark chicken meat

2 teaspoons (10 ml) fish sauce

1 cup (85 g) diced cabbage

2 (2 ounce/55 g) packages pork- or chicken-flavored Mama instant noodles (see note)

⅓ cup (35 g) thinly julienned red onion

¾ cup (100 g) halved cherry tomatoes

1 stalk celery, sliced, plus a handful of celery leaves

8 to 10 sprigs cilantro, chopped

Do-ahead: Make the dressing and cook up to the point where the pork and cabbage are done, and keep both components in the fridge up to 1 day in advance. When ready to serve, warm the pork mixture slightly before proceeding.

Notes: The noodles come with a small packet of chili powder, but to make this dish extra spicy, you can add the fresh chilies.

You can find Mama brand at most Asian grocery stores, and even at some non-Asian stores. Pork or chicken are good neutral flavors for this dish, but you can experiment with the tom yum or beef flavors as well. Make sure you're buying the classic wheat noodles, as some Mama flavors come with rice or glass noodles, so check the label for the type of noodles used.

Thai Tuna Salad

Yum Pla Tuna | ยำปลาทูน่า

SERVES 4 AS AN APPETIZER, OR 2 AS A MAIN

COOKING TIME: 5 minutes

DRESSING

1 to 2 Thai chilies, minced

1½ tablespoons (22 ml) lime juice

I tablespoon (15 ml) fish sauce

1 tablespoon (12 g) finely chopped palm sugar, packed

2 teaspoons (10 ml) neutral oil (omit if the tuna is packed in oil)

SALAD

1 can tuna, drained (4 ounces/115 g drained weight)

1 stalk lemongrass, bottom 4 inches (10 cm) only, thinly sliced

1-inch piece (12 g) ginger, finely julienned, plus extra for garnish

3 to 4 makrut lime leaves, finely julienned (optional)

3 tablespoons (20 g) finely julienned shallots

6 to 7 sprigs cilantro, chopped

1 teaspoon (5 ml) fish sauce (if needed)

¼ cup (35 g) roasted cashews

FOR SERVING

Jasmine rice or plain rice porridge (p. 245)

Butter or romaine lettuce leaves (optional)

Do-ahead: Make the dressing up to 1 day in advance and keep in the fridge. You can chop and combine all the salad ingredients in advance, then toss with the dressing just before serving.

Throw away any ideas you have of a tuna salad, as this salad is nothing like that. No mayo, no mush. This salad is light, bright, and bursting with fresh Thai herbs. Eating it with plain rice like any other Thai salad is great, but my favorite way to eat *yum pla tuna* is either with rice porridge (p. 245) or as a bite-sized lettuce wrap, with a whole cashew in every bite.

———

In a small mixing bowl, make the dressing by combining the chilies, lime juice, fish sauce, sugar, and oil; stir until most of the sugar is dissolved. If there are stubborn chunks of sugar, mash them with the back of a spoon.

Add the tuna to the dressing, then add the lemongrass, ginger, makrut lime leaves, shallots, and cilantro and mix well. Taste and adjust the seasoning as needed; depending on how salty the tuna is, you may need to add more fish sauce.

Plate and top with roasted cashews and extra julienned ginger. You can eat it with jasmine rice or plain congee, or use lettuce leaves to make bite-sized wraps.

Dressing It Up

This simple dish cleans up nicely as an hors d'oeuvre for a fancy meal. Use Belgian endive or the inner leaves of romaine lettuce as a "boat" and put a spoonful of the tuna salad in it, topped with chopped roasted cashews. To make it a bit more substantial, add a little bundle of Vietnamese rice vermicelli to each piece. It's also fantastic as a filling for cucumber cups, and a dot of mayo at the bottom of each cup would not be out of place if you wanted it to be a little creamy.

Vegan Soft Tofu & Herb Salad

Yum Taohu Yen | ยำเต้าหู้เย็น

You'll be hard-pressed to find Thai salads that are vegan, because most of them are centered on animal protein, and the dressing *always* contains fish sauce. So when I was asked to demo a Thai salad recipe at a vegan food show, I needed to come up with something nontraditional. Inspired by the Japanese chilled tofu dish *hiyayakko,* I came up with a Thai spin. Cold soft tofu topped with a Thai herb salad is one of the most refreshing things you can eat in the summer. I love adding three or four types of herbs for complexity, but if you only have one or two of those listed, it'll still be great. I'm breaking one of the rules of Thai salads and choosing not to add any chilies to this, because I really want to maximize the cold effect. If you serve this with jasmine rice, like most Thai salads, the contrast of hot and cold makes it even more spectacular, but it's great on its own as well.

──────

Make the dressing by combining the soy sauce, lime juice, and sugar in a small bowl; stir until the sugar is mostly dissolved. If there are stubborn sugar chunks, let them sit for a minute to soften, then mash them down with the back of a spoon.

Add the cucumber, bell peppers, shallots, chopped herbs, and sesame seeds; stir to mix.

Unmold the tofu onto a serving dish with some depth to hold the sauce; most of the time the tofu pops out if you turn the container upside down and squeeze. But if it won't come out, run a knife around the edges and try again. For a more elegant presentation, trim the edges of the tofu to make it neat. You can leave it whole or cut it into 4 to 6 pieces for easy serving.

Spoon the salad on top of and around the tofu, letting the sauce run over. Serve with jasmine rice, if desired.

SERVES 4
COOKING TIME: 5 minutes

2 tablespoons (30 ml) soy sauce (see note)

2 tablespoons (30 ml) lime juice

1½ tablespoons (18 g) finely chopped palm sugar, packed

½ cup (65 g) small-diced English cucumber

¼ cup (30 g) small-diced red bell pepper

2 tablespoons (16 g) finely diced shallots

⅓ cup (80 ml) chopped herbs (cilantro, mint, green onions, or lemongrass, or a combination)

1 teaspoon (5 ml) toasted black or white sesame seeds (optional)

1 (10.5 ounce/300 g) package soft tofu

Jasmine rice, for serving (optional)

Do-ahead: Cut the vegetables and make the dressing up to 1 day in advance, but do not combine them until serving.

Note: If you eat fish, try the recipe using fish sauce instead of soy sauce, for a more authentic Thai salad flavor.

Don't Make the Tofu Cry

It's important not to unmold the tofu too long before you are ready to serve it, otherwise it will "cry." Soft tofu is not a stable gel, and if you let it sit out "naked," you will soon see water pooling around the tofu. This is water that was in the tofu slowly leaking out. This happens even faster if you cut the tofu, creating more surface area. This is why, when you store leftover tofu, you want to keep it in water—so that it retains its moisture.

Chinese Sausage Salad

Yum Goonchiang | ยำกุนเชียง

SERVES 4
COOKING TIME: 15 minutes

SALAD

5 ounces (150 g) Chinese sausage, sliced ¼-inch (6 mm) thick on a diagonal (see note)

3.5 ounces (100 g) sliced English cucumber, about 1 cup (250 ml)

½ stalk celery, plus a handful of leaves (optional; add more cucumber if not using)

2 tablespoons (15 g) finely julienned shallots

7 to 8 sprigs cilantro, chopped

Jasmine rice or plain rice porridge (p. 245) for serving

DRESSING

1 to 2 Thai chilies, minced

2 tablespoons (30 ml) lime juice

1½ tablespoons (22 ml) fish sauce, divided

1 teaspoon (10 ml) granulated sugar

Do-ahead: The dressing can be made 1 day in advance and kept in the fridge. Vegetables and sausages can also be prechopped.

Note: *It's important to choose a good brand of sausage. I like to go for an all-pork one with an ingredient list that doesn't include too many additives. Some brands are too salty, so if you find that to be the case with yours, cut down on the fish sauce. Also, even though they may look like pepperoni sticks, do not eat Chinese sausages raw! They have to be fully cooked first.*

This is one of my favorite things to eat with *kao tom*, or plain rice porridge (see page 245). Think oatmeal, but it's rice, with no seasoning at all. We love it for breakfast, or as a comforting, homey meal. The porridge is plain and soft, so it is usually paired with a strongly flavored dish that has lots of textures, which is exactly what this salad is. The Chinese sausages are chewy, sweet, and salty, while the dressing is tart and spicy, and the crunchy cucumber gives some freshness, so there is a little bit of everything going on here.

——

Place the Chinese sausage pieces in a 10-inch (25 cm) skillet in a single layer. Add enough water to come three-quarters of the way up the sausages, then turn the heat to high and bring the water to a boil. Let the sausages cook until the water evaporates, flipping them halfway through. Meanwhile, line a plate with a couple of layers of paper towel.

Once the water has almost all evaporated, turn the heat down to medium, and once it dries up completely, allow the sausages to fry in the rendered fat until the underside is browned—this happens very quickly, within 1 minute or so, because of the sugar in the sausages, so watch them carefully. Turn the sausages over and let the second side brown for 30 seconds to 1 minute, then remove from the heat. Drain the sausages on the paper towel and let cool slightly.

Make the dressing by combining the chilies, lime juice, half of the fish sauce, and sugar in a small bowl; stir until the sugar is mostly dissolved.

To the dressing, add the sausages, cucumber, celery, shallots, and cilantro; toss to mix. Give it a taste, and add more fish sauce as needed; how much fish sauce you need will depend on the saltiness of the sausage. Serve with jasmine rice or plain rice porridge. This doesn't look like a lot of food, but it's an intensely flavored dish and you won't need much of it.

> **Water-Frying**
> The cooking technique that we commonly use for Chinese sausage is quite brilliant. We call it water-frying, and while it's a two-step process, it all happens in one pan. First, the sausages are boiled in water, which cooks, hydrates, and softens them, and renders out some of the fat. Then we let the water dry up, allowing the rendered fat to now fry and brown the sausages. For some dishes, like fried rice, you can just pan-sear the sausages, but the boiling, as I say, hydrates and softens them, which makes them better for when they are the bulk of the dish, as with this salad.

Shrimp Salad with Lemongrass & Mint

Pla Goong | พล่ากุ้ง

Originally, the word *pla* referred to salads made with proteins that are cooked by the acid of lime juice, much like a ceviche. Nowadays, people prefer to cook the protein with heat, but they still keep the abundance of thinly sliced lemongrass and mint that's characteristic of a *pla*. Most Thai people blanch the shrimp in water, but I prefer to sear it, to maximize the flavor from browning. I've given you the option to add sour mango should you have some—it's a trick I learned from Unchai, my go-to Thai restaurant in Vancouver, and the extra fruitiness really elevates the dish.

——

Dry the shrimp thoroughly with paper towel; it's important to do this to minimize any oil splattering and maximize browning.

Place a large skillet over high heat and add the oil; wait until it's very hot before proceeding. Use tongs to lay the shrimp in the pan in one layer, and sear without moving them until browned on the underside and the shrimp are about two-thirds cooked. Once browned, they should release easily from the pan. Flip and cook on the other side just until they are done. Place the shrimp in a bowl to cool while you make the dressing.

Make the dressing by combining the Thai chili paste, lime juice, fish sauce, ½ teaspoon (2 ml) sugar, and chilies in a small mixing bowl; stir until the chili paste and sugar have fully dissolved.

Use tongs to transfer the shrimp into the dressing, leaving behind any collected juices for now, and toss to coat. Add the mango, shallots, mint, lemongrass, and makrut lime leaves. Toss gently until combined, then taste and add more sugar as needed. Also, if the dressing can stand to be slightly diluted, add some of the reserved shrimp juice; this juice adds good flavor, but if you add a lot it could dilute the dressing too much.

Plate and garnish with more mint leaves, if desired. Serve with jasmine rice.

SERVES 4
COOKING TIME: 10 minutes

12 ounces (340 g) medium to large shrimp, peeled and deveined, thawed if frozen

2 tablespoons (30 ml) neutral oil

1½ tablespoons (22 ml) Thai chili paste, store-bought or homemade (p. 258)

2 tablespoons (30 ml) lime juice

1½ tablespoons (22 ml) fish sauce

½ to 1 teaspoon (2 to 5 ml) granulated sugar (see note)

1 to 2 Thai chilies, minced

½ cup (65 g) julienned mango, preferably sour (optional)

¼ cup (25 g) julienned shallots

½ cup (7 g) mint leaves, torn if large, plus extra for garnish

1 stalk lemongrass, bottom half only, thinly sliced

2 to 3 makrut lime leaves, finely julienned (optional)

Jasmine rice, for serving

Note: *The amount of sugar you need depends on how sweet your chili paste and mango are, so start out with ½ teaspoon (2 ml) and add more as needed.*

Leftover Anything Laab

Laab Kong Leua | ลาบของเหลือ

SERVES 1 TO 2
COOKING TIME: 20 minutes

1 tablespoon (15 ml) uncooked jasmine or Thai glutinous rice

5 ounces (150 g) leftover meat and/or vegetables

1 tablespoon (15 ml) fish sauce

1 tablespoon (15 ml) lime juice

Pinch of granulated sugar

Roasted chili flakes, store-bought or home-made (p. 263), to taste

3 tablespoons (22 g) finely julienned shallots

A big handful of mint and any other fresh herbs (see note)

FOR SERVING

English cucumber, sliced

Sticky rice or jasmine rice

Romaine or butter lettuce, if making lettuce wraps

Note: *In addition to the mint, other good options are cilantro, green onions, and dill, but feel free to experiment with other herbs you have on hand.*

Taste and Adjust

Writing a recipe for leftovers can be only so specific because the main ingredient is unknown. I always tell people to taste and adjust no matter what, but it's especially important to do that here. This recipe is a basic formula that works with most simply seasoned foods without any sauces, like roast chicken, pork chops, or roasted veggies. If your leftovers come to the table already with strong seasoning, especially if they're quite salty, start with half the amount of fish sauce and lime juice, and taste and adjust from there.

I have often said you can *laab* anything. And in "anything" I include bits of leftover meats and vegetables. Tart, spicy, and fresh, this treatment is guaranteed to "fix" any dry Thanksgiving turkey, or the ends of roast beef. I've even *laab*-ed roasted squash and cut-up pieces of omelet. *Laab* is usually served with sticky rice, but you can serve it with jasmine rice, wrap it in lettuce, or serve it with fresh cucumber. Note: I have provided a small base recipe here because it's meant for using up bits and bobs in the fridge; scale up to whatever quantity of leftovers you have.

———

Make the toasted rice powder by placing the rice in a small dry skillet over medium-high heat. Cook, stirring constantly, until the rice is dark brown. It might get a bit smoky, so make sure the kitchen is well ventilated. Pour onto a plate to cool slightly, then grind into a powder with a mortar and pestle or a coffee grinder, leaving some pieces a bit larger for texture.

Thinly slice, chop, or shred your leftovers into small pieces; you can decide how best to process the item depending on what it is. For poultry, I like to shred it by hand; beef, I thinly slice; and veggies, I coarsely chop. The key here is small pieces.

Heat the leftovers up slightly so they are warm or room temperature; you can do this in the microwave or give them a quick sauté in the skillet.

Make the dressing by combining the fish sauce, lime juice, sugar, chili flakes, and shallots in a mixing bowl; stir until the sugar is mostly dissolved.

Add the leftovers, toasted rice powder, and fresh herbs to the dressing; toss until well combined. Taste and adjust the seasoning as needed.

Serve with cucumber and sticky rice or jasmine rice, or with lettuce leaves if making wraps.

Vegetarian Pounded Corn & Cucumber Salad

Tum Tang Kaopoad Mungsawirat | ตำแตงข้าวโพดมังสวิรัติ

Green papaya salad, or *som tum*, is Thailand's most famous salad, but it's just one of many types of *tum*, or pounded salads. Corn is my favorite non-papaya ingredient in a *tum* because the sweetness of the corn matches perfectly with the tart and spicy dressing. A *tum* usually contains fish sauce and dried shrimp, but I've made this one vegetarian, and it is just as fantastic. If you eat eggs, try it with the salted duck eggs, which add pops of creamy saltiness that I absolutely love.

——

Bring a large pot of water to a boil, then add the corn and cook for 6 to 7 minutes. Allow it to cool enough to handle, then slice off the kernels with a knife, keeping them in large pieces as much as possible.

IF USING A MORTAR AND PESTLE

In a large salad mortar and pestle, pound the garlic and chilies into a fine paste. Add the palm sugar and pound until it's dissolved into a thick paste.

Add about half of the peanuts and pound a few times to crush them a bit. Then add the tomatoes and crush gently to release some of their juices.

Add the lime juice and soy sauce, throwing in the rind of the juiced limes as well, if you wish. Use a large spoon to stir until it's all well mixed and the sugar has completely dissolved into the dressing. At this point, if you are using a small mortar and pestle, transfer the salad to a mixing bowl. Otherwise finish mixing in the mortar.

Add the corn and cucumber and toss gently to mix, then transfer to a serving plate. Top with the remaining roasted peanuts, and serve with wedges of salted duck eggs, if desired.

(Continued)

SERVES 4
COOKING TIME: 20 minutes
SPECIAL TOOL: Mortar and pestle (see note)

1 large 8-inch (20 cm) ear of corn (about 8 ounces/225 g kernels, thawed if frozen)

2 cloves (10 g) garlic

1 to 2 Thai chilies, to taste

1½ tablespoons (18 g) finely chopped palm sugar, packed

¼ cup (35 g) unsalted roasted peanuts, divided

1 medium (125 g) tomato, cut in bite-sized wedges

2½ tablespoons (37 ml) lime juice, rinds reserved (see note)

2 tablespoons (30 ml) soy sauce

1 heaping cup (150 g) julienned cucumber

1 cooked salted duck egg, cut into wedges (optional, see sidebar p. 64)

Notes: After juicing the limes, reserve the rinds and cut them into a few wedges. We like to add the rind to the salad for the extra aroma that comes from the skin; it is not meant to be eaten.

Traditionally, we use a special mortar and pestle for pounded salads (see p. 18 for more info), but I have provided alternate methods if you have only a small one or none at all. If you don't have a mortar and pestle, follow the method as specified.

IF YOU DO NOT HAVE A MORTAR AND PESTLE
Make the dressing by adding the palm sugar to a small bowl. Add the lime juice and soy sauce, stirring to mostly dissolve the sugar. Don't worry about a few stubborn chunks; they'll have dissolved by the time you need the dressing. Finely grate the garlic and mince the chilies and stir them into the dressing.

Chop the peanuts coarsely and add half of them to a large mixing bowl, then add the tomatoes and crush them gently with a wooden spoon to release some of their juices. Stir in the corn and cucumber.

If the dressing still has some undissolved sugar, use a spoon to push down on any remaining chunks and they should crush pretty easily. Pour the dressing over the salad and toss everything together.

Plate, top with the remaining roasted peanuts, and serve with wedges of salted duck eggs, if desired.

> **Don't Peel the Eggs!**
> Make sure you buy cooked salted duck eggs so you don't have to boil them yourself. Also, don't peel them! Salted duck egg shells are so brittle, it would be incredibly tedious to peel the eggs. Just cut the eggs in half right through the shell, then use a thin spoon to scoop out each half, as with an avocado. You can then cut each half into wedges. You can find salted duck eggs at most Asian grocery stores in the section where all the other eggs are sold.

Pounded Cabbage Slaw

Tum Galum Plee | ตำกะหล่ำปลี

In the early '80s, my parents spent some time in the United States, and back then, Thai ingredients were not nearly as available as they are now. One of the first substitutions my mom made in her cooking was to use cabbage instead of green papaya for *som tum*, our famous green papaya salad. She was so surprised by how well it worked that decades later she remembered to tell me about it when I left Thailand. I wasn't in a rush to try it, because I can get green papaya here in Vancouver, but when I finally did, I was surprised too. It's like coleslaw, but better! I immediately thought this should replace all slaws in pulled-pork sandwiches and tacos. Light, crunchy, tart, and spicy, this salad can be served with anything rich and meaty, especially barbecue.

――――

IF USING A MORTAR AND PESTLE

In a large mortar and pestle, pound the garlic and chilies into a fine paste, then add the palm sugar and pound until it's dissolved into a thick paste.

Add about half of the peanuts and pound a few times to crush them a bit. Then add the tomatoes and crush them gently to release some of their juices.

Add the fish sauce, lime juice, and tamarind paste, throwing in the rind of the juiced limes as well, if you wish. Use a large spoon to stir until the sugar has dissolved into the dressing. At this point, if you are using a small mortar and pestle, transfer the dressing to a large mixing bowl; otherwise you can finish the salad in the mortar.

If you're using a mixing bowl, add the cabbage and carrots and toss, using a spoon, to mix well.

If you're using the salad mortar, add the cabbage and carrots, then use the pestle to pound the salad gently three or four times. Use a large spoon to flip the salad from bottom to top. Repeat the pound-and-flip process a few times until everything is thoroughly mixed. Taste and adjust the seasoning as needed.

Transfer to a serving bowl, then top with the remaining peanuts.

(Continued)

SERVES 4

COOKING TIME: 5 minutes

SPECIAL TOOL: Mortar and pestle (see note)

2 cloves (10 g) garlic

1 to 3 Thai chilies, to taste

2 tablespoons (24 g) finely chopped palm sugar, packed

¼ cup (35 g) unsalted roasted peanuts, divided

1 medium (125 g) tomato, cut in bite-sized wedges

2 tablespoons (30 ml) fish sauce

2 tablespoons (30 ml) lime juice, rinds reserved (see note on p. 63)

1 tablespoon (15 ml) tamarind paste, store-bought or homemade (p. 266), or ½ tablespoon (7 ml) lime juice

2 cups (170 g) shredded red or green cabbage

¾ cup (65 g) julienned carrot

Do-ahead: Make the salad without the cabbage and carrots, and keep in the fridge for up to 1 day. Mix everything before serving.

Traditionally, we use a special mortar and pestle for pounded salads (see p. 18 for more info), but I have provided alternate methods if you have only a small one or none at all. If you don't have a mortar and pestle, follow the method as specified.

Make the dressing by adding the palm sugar to a small bowl. Add the fish sauce, lime juice, and tamarind paste and stir to mostly dissolve the sugar. Don't worry about a few stubborn chunks; they'll have dissolved by the time you need the dressing. Finely grate the garlic and mince the chilies; stir into the dressing.

Chop the peanuts coarsely and add half of them to a large mixing bowl, then add the tomatoes and crush them gently with a wooden spoon to release some of their juices. Stir in the cabbage and carrots.

If the dressing still has some undissolved sugar, use a spoon to push down on any remaining chunks; they should crush pretty easily. Pour the dressing over the cabbage and toss everything together.

Plate the salad, then top with the remaining peanuts.

The Pound and Flip

The idea of pounding a salad might seem a bit strange. But most of the heavy pounding happens at the beginning, to make a paste out of the garlic, chilies, and sugar. Once the delicate ingredients go in, you need to be a bit gentler. The final step of pounding and flipping allows flavors to meld quickly as ingredients are gently mixed and brought together. Scan the QR code for a video showing this technique.

The Pound-and-Flip Technique

CURRIES, SOUPS & STEWS

Gaeng, Tom | แกง ต้ม

Thai Curries, Soups, and Stews

Curries, soups, and stews are your best friend on a weeknight because they can be made entirely in advance and then reheated. These dishes play an important role in a Thai meal, as they serve as the liquid, giving moisture to a meal that might otherwise be too dry. We never have a Thai meal without some sort of dish that has been simmered in a pot.

How to Eat a Thai Curry

Thai curries are always eaten with rice. And although some of the curries might seem quite soupy, you still pour it over your rice on a plate. This is why we eat jasmine rice in Thailand—it has just the right amount of stickiness and fluffiness to hold the curry sauce. Short-grain or basmati rice would not work as well because they do not absorb sauce as readily.

Also, don't feel like you have to cover all your rice with the curry. In a Thai meal, where multiple dishes are served, people take a little bit of food at a time and go back for more as needed. You'd start with a couple of spoonfuls of curry on one corner of your rice, keeping the rest of the rice plain to eat alongside the other dishes.

How to Eat a Thai Soup or Stew

Soups and stews are also served with rice, but they differ from curries in that they tend to be brothy (though some curries can be brothy too, but that's for another day). When there is soup or stew in a Thai meal, you are given a little bowl. You fill your bowl with some soup from the table, then you can choose to attack it however you want.

If it's a more substantial stew, such as Grandma's Spareribs & Vegetable Stew (p. 90), I spoon it over my rice. If it's a lighter, slurpable soup like Coconut Galangal Mushroom Soup (p. 101), I eat it on its own as I enjoy the meal, or add a bit of rice to the bowl and eat it like a rice soup. If the stew is the only thing I'm serving, I put it in a big bowl with some rice and eat it like a rice soup.

A Note About Store-Bought Stocks

For the most part I am okay with you using store-bought stock for a weeknight Thai meal, even though they tend to have different flavors from what we use in Thailand. But for some dishes, such as the Glass Noodle Soup with Pork Meatballs (p. 98) and most noodle soups in the One-Dish Meal chapter (pp. 177–207), homemade stock *really* makes a difference because the stock basically *is* the dish. This is one reason to always have some frozen stocks in the freezer! See page 265 for how to make a Thai-style pork or chicken stock.

Quick Yellow Curry with Beef

Gaeng Garee Neua | แกงกะหรี่เนื้อ

For years I thought of beef curry as a dish that required simmering chunks of stew beef for hours until tender. But for a weeknight, I wondered if there was a way to do it quickly and without a pressure cooker. Then I remembered my days working at a quick-service Thai restaurant, where we churned out pots of fork-tender beef curry in 45 minutes. The secret was using thinly sliced beef and choosing a flavorful but not-too-tough cut so it would not take a long time to tenderize. The restaurant used flank, which was great but a little lean for my liking. I found chuck top blade to be the perfect choice in terms of flavor and fat content, and it only takes about 20 minutes of simmering to become fork-tender.

———

Slice the steak into ⅛-inch (3 mm) pieces, removing any silver skin on the exterior (the little strip of connective tissue running through the middle of the steak is fine to leave).

Place the beef in a medium pot and add just enough water to submerge it. Add the salt and 1 tablespoon (15 ml) curry paste and stir to mix; bring to a simmer over high heat. Turn the heat down to low and simmer for 20 to 25 minutes, until fork-tender. The timing will vary if you use a different cut of meat. Skim off any scum that floats to the top.

While the beef cooks, make the curry sauce. In a medium pot, bring ¾ cup (185 ml) coconut milk to a boil over medium-high heat, then add the remaining curry paste and stir to mix well. Turn the heat down to medium and stir frequently until the mixture is very thick and the coconut oil separates from the paste, about 5 minutes (the oil may not separate depending on the coconut milk you're using; this is okay).

Add the remaining coconut milk, sugar, 1 tablespoon (15 ml) fish sauce, and the tamarind paste to the curry. Stir to mix, then bring to a boil over medium-high heat.

(Continued)

SERVES 4

COOKING TIME: 45 minutes

1½ pounds (675 g) chuck top blade steak (see note)

1 teaspoon (5 ml) table salt

5 to 6 tablespoons (75 to 90 ml) yellow curry paste, store-bought or homemade (p. 257), divided

2 cups (500 ml) coconut milk, divided

1½ tablespoons (18 g) finely chopped palm sugar, packed

1 to 2 tablespoons (15 to 30 ml) fish sauce

1 tablespoon (15 ml) tamarind paste, store-bought or homemade (p. 266) (see note)

10.5 ounces (300 g) waxy potatoes, such as new or red-skinned potatoes, cut into 1½-inch chunks

½ medium (120 g) yellow onion, julienned

¾ cup (100 g) halved cherry tomatoes

Jasmine rice, for serving

Do-ahead: *The whole curry can be made up to 3 days in advance and reheated. If reheating, be sure to not overcook the potatoes—or add them when serving.*

Notes: *If you can't find chuck top blade, you can choose other cuts of beef that are flavorful but not too tough. Most inexpensive steaks sold for marinating and grilling fit this bill, and if possible, choose one that is not too lean. If you have time to cook, you can choose any stewing beef and increase the cooking time accordingly.*

If you don't have tamarind paste, no need to buy or make it just for this recipe. We just need a little bit of acid to brighten up the sauce, so a few dashes of Worcestershire sauce or a squeeze of lime at the end will also do.

Add the potatoes and onions, and simmer for 5 minutes, then remove from the heat while you wait for the beef to be done; the potatoes should not be fully cooked at this point.

Once the beef is tender, use a slotted spoon to transfer only the beef into the curry. Then add only as much of the beef cooking liquid as needed to keep everything barely submerged. Taste the sauce and adjust the seasoning with more fish sauce, tamarind, or sugar as needed.

Turn the heat to medium and simmer the curry for another 5 to 10 minutes, until the potatoes are fully cooked.

Stir in the tomatoes, turn off the heat, and allow the tomatoes to soften in the residual heat for 1 to 2 minutes. Serve with jasmine rice.

Cooking Beef Out of the Curry

Why not just simmer the beef in the curry itself, you ask? The technique used in this recipe is one that's commonly used in Thai cuisine when cooking with beef, for a couple of reasons. When you simmer the beef, you will notice a lot of brown scum in and on top of the liquid, which would discolor the otherwise beautiful curry sauce. As well, many Thai people don't like the strong beef flavor that would be in the curry if it were all cooked together, especially because beef in Thailand can be quite gamey. And, in our weeknight-friendly case, it also saves time so that we can make the rest of the sauce while the beef is doing its thing.

Pan-Seared Prawns in Red Curry Sauce

Choo Chee Goong | ฉู่ฉี่กุ้ง

Choo chee is a term for a simple dish of seafood served in a red curry sauce. Most commonly, *choo chee* is made with Thai short mackerel, whose firm flesh and strong flavor holds up well to the spicy and robust sauce. But at nice seafood restaurants you'll find versions made with pricy seafood, such as large river prawns. Unlike our regular curries, *choo chee* is meant to be *kluk klik*, which means saucy but not soupy.

———

Pull off the center ribs from larger makrut lime leaves and discard. Stack the leaves and julienne them with a sharp knife as thinly as you can. Set aside a little pinch for garnish.

Place a large skillet on high heat and add the oil. Once hot, add the prawns in one even layer. Cook without moving them until browned on the underside and the prawns are about two-thirds cooked, about 2 minutes. Flip and sear the other side just until they are cooked through. Remove from the pan and set aside.

Make the curry sauce. In the same pan, turn the heat down to medium and add ¼ cup (60 ml) coconut milk; bring it to a simmer. Add the red curry paste and stir frequently, about 2 minutes, until it's very thick and you can see oil sizzling out of the paste (the oil may not separate depending on the coconut milk you're using; this is okay).

Add the remaining coconut milk, lime leaves, and sugar, and simmer on low heat for about 3 minutes to allow the flavors to mingle.

Add the prawns to the sauce and toss to coat and to warm back up for about 1 minute. If the sauce feels a little too thick to easily coat the prawns, add a splash of water to thin it out.

Taste and add fish sauce as needed; it's important to taste first, as different curry pastes have different salt levels.

Plate the *choo chee* in a shallow bowl or a plate with a bit of depth, then drizzle with coconut milk to garnish, and top with the reserved julienned makrut lime leaves. Serve with jasmine rice.

SERVES 4
COOKING TIME: 20 minutes

4 to 5 makrut lime leaves

2 tablespoons (30 ml) neutral oil

1 pound (450 g) large prawns (16/20 count), peeled and deveined, patted dry (see note)

1¼ cups (310 ml) coconut milk, divided, plus extra for garnish

2 to 3 tablespoons (30 to 45 ml) red curry paste, store-bought or homemade (p. 255)

1 tablespoon (12 g) finely chopped palm sugar, packed

Fish sauce, as needed

Jasmine rice, for serving

Note: If buying frozen prawns, be sure to buy about 25% more to account for the weight of the ice glaze.

For Special Occasions

I love *choo chee* because it can be so luxurious, yet the preparation is simple. If you have a lobster tail or big scallops, *choo chee* is the perfect treatment. For a more elegant presentation, don't toss the seafood with the sauce; simply pour the sauce onto a nice platter and arrange the seafood on top of it so you can showcase the catch. Use only meaty seafood, as delicate items like crab or tender fish would be overpowered by the sauce.

Green Curry Chicken with Winter Melon

Gaeng Kiew Waan Gai Sai Fak | แกงเขียวหวานไก่ใส่ฟัก

SERVES 4

COOKING TIME: 30 minutes

1¾ cups (435 ml) coconut milk, divided

1½ cups (22 g) Thai basil leaves, plus an optional 10 to 15 leaves (see note)

3 to 4 tablespoons (45 to 60 ml) green curry paste, store-bought or homemade (p. 256)

1 pound (450 g) boneless, skinless chicken thighs, cut in bite-sized strips

1 cup (250 ml) unsalted or low-sodium chicken stock

12 ounces (340 g) winter melon, peeled and cut in 1½-inch (4 cm) cubes

6 to 7 makrut lime leaves

1 tablespoon (12 g) finely chopped palm sugar, packed

½ red bell pepper, julienned

1 to 2 tablespoons (15 to 30 ml) fish sauce

Jasmine rice, for serving

Note: *The optional basil is for boosting the green color of the curry. The green in the curry paste comes from green chilies, which means that if you add more curry paste because you want the dish to look prettier, it'll also be spicier. Adding blended green basil leaves is a way to get around that.*

People often ask me if they can use a different vegetable or meat in this curry instead. And my answer is always: Of course! While that is true, in Thailand there are some common curry-meat-veggie combinations, and this trio of green curry, chicken, and winter melon is a real classic. Winter melon has almost no flavor of its own, but it absorbs flavor like a sponge. When cooked, it becomes translucent and so soft that it disintegrates in your mouth, and you wonder how it ever held its shape in the curry. The melon can grow to a pretty massive size, so it's often sold at Asian supermarkets pre-cut into chunks. If it's not available, zucchini makes a great substitute.

_____

Place ¾ cup (185 ml) coconut milk in a medium pot over medium heat and reduce until very thick, about 5 minutes.

Optional step for a more vibrant color: While the coconut milk is reducing, julienne 10 to 15 basil leaves and pound them with a mortar and pestle until fine, then add the curry paste and pound to mix. (Alternatively, you can blend the basil in a blender with just enough of the remaining coconut milk until smooth.)

Add the curry paste to the reduced coconut milk and stir frequently for 2 to 3 minutes, until the mixture is very thick and the coconut oil separates from the paste (the oil may not separate depending on the coconut milk you're using; this is okay). If the paste sticks to the bottom of the pot, deglaze with a bit of coconut milk.

Add the chicken and stir to coat it with the paste, then add all the remaining coconut milk (including the basil-blended coconut milk), stock, and winter melon. Twist the makrut lime leaves to bruise them and release their aroma before tearing them into big chunks and adding to the pot, removing any big center stems. Stir in the palm sugar and simmer gently for about 15 minutes, until the chicken is fork-tender.

Stir in the bell peppers and cook for 2 minutes to soften.

Taste the broth, then add fish sauce to taste. How much fish sauce you need depends on how salty your curry paste is, so it's important to taste first. You want this to be strongly seasoned, as it will be served with plain rice.

Turn off the heat and stir in the 1½ cups (22 g) basil. Serve with jasmine rice.

Using Chicken Breasts

Even though I always recommend using chicken thighs for curry, I know some of you are going to insist on using boneless, skinless chicken breasts. So here's a tip for making sure it's still going to be delicious. You don't want to stew it for a long time, as you do with thighs, or you will get dry, overcooked chicken. The two meats do not behave the same way when cooked. For breasts, you want to cook them minimally, so add the strips at the end along with the bell peppers and simmer for 2 to 3 minutes, just until they're cooked through. To compensate for the time the breasts won't have to absorb flavor from the sauce, you'll want to marinate them in 2 teaspoons (10 ml) fish sauce for at least 10 minutes beforehand.

Instant Pot (or Not) Massaman Curry Chicken

Gaeng Massaman Gai | แกงมัสมั่นไก่

Unlike other Thai curries, *massaman* is always paired with slow-braised meats, so it usually takes a long time to cook, but the flavor reward is well worth it. You can buy *massaman* curry paste, but it's not always available and, quite frankly, not always good. Fortunately, it's easy to turn red curry paste, whether store-bought or homemade, into *massaman*, since both pastes use the same base. All you need are some spices, most of which you probably already have. I usually make *massaman* chicken on the stovetop because it doesn't require too much cooking time, and I do feel that the chicken tastes better with a longer braising time to allow the flavors to absorb, but it works well using a pressure cooker if you have one and want it even faster.

FOR THE CURRY PASTE

Place all the spices in a dry skillet and toast over medium-high heat, moving them constantly, until the cumin seeds have darkened slightly and the spices are aromatic.

Transfer the spices to a plate and cool slightly. Grind into a powder using a coffee grinder or mortar and pestle.

Mix all the spices with the red curry paste and shrimp paste until combined—I find it's easiest to mix them by pounding with a mortar and pestle.

FOR THE CURRY

Place ½ cup (125 ml) coconut milk in a large pot and bring to a boil over medium heat. You can also use an Instant Pot, and bring to a boil on the medium sauté mode.

Add the curry paste and stir to mix well, and let the mixture thicken, stirring frequently, until the mixture is very thick and the coconut oil separates from the paste, about 5 minutes (the oil may not separate depending on the coconut milk you're using; this is okay). If the paste sticks to the bottom of the pot, deglaze with a bit of coconut milk.

(Continued)

COOKING TIME: 45 minutes in the Instant Pot, or 65 minutes on the stovetop

QUICK MASSAMAN CURRY PASTE

4 whole cloves, or ¼ teaspoon (1 ml) ground cloves

2 pods green or white cardamom, or ¼ teaspoon (1 ml) ground cardamom

1 teaspoon (5 ml) coriander seeds

1 teaspoon (5 ml) cumin seeds

1 teaspoon (5 ml) ground cinnamon, or 2 inches (5 cm) cinnamon stick

⅛ teaspoon (0.5 ml) freshly grated or ground nutmeg

4 to 5 tablespoons (60 to 75 ml) red curry paste, store-bought or homemade (p. 255)

1 teaspoon (5 ml) fermented shrimp paste (optional, see note p. 80)

CURRY

2 cups (500 ml) coconut milk, divided

5 to 6 tablespoons (75 to 90 ml) *massaman* curry paste

3 tablespoons (36 g) finely chopped palm sugar, packed

2 to 3 tablespoons (30 to 45 ml) tamarind paste, store-bought or homemade (p. 266)

2 to 3 tablespoons (30 to 45 ml) fish sauce

2 pounds (1 kg) chicken thighs, bone-in, skin-on

10.5 ounces (300 g) waxy potatoes, such as new or red-skinned potatoes, cut in 1-inch (2.5 cm) chunks

½ large yellow onion, cut in ½-inch (1.2 cm) strips

¼ cup (35 g) unsalted roasted peanuts

Jasmine rice, for serving

Do-ahead: *The whole curry can be made in advance and reheated. If reheating, be sure not to overcook the potatoes, or add them when serving. The curry paste can be frozen.*

Note: *Add shrimp paste only if the red curry paste doesn't already contain it.*

Add the remaining coconut milk and stir to mix, scraping the bottom to make sure no curry paste is stuck. Add the palm sugar, 2 tablespoons (30 ml) tamarind paste, and 1 tablespoon (15 ml) fish sauce. Stir to mix well, then taste the sauce and add more fish sauce as needed. You will need to adjust the seasoning again after it's done, but it's important that the chicken is cooking in a well-seasoned sauce.

For the Instant Pot: Add the chicken and cook it under high pressure for 5 minutes. Allow the Instant Pot to naturally release for 10 minutes before releasing the remaining pressure.

For the stovetop: Add the chicken to the sauce and simmer gently over low heat, partially covered, for 35 minutes.

Add the potatoes, onions, and peanuts; if there is not enough liquid to keep the potatoes and onions barely submerged, top it up with more coconut milk or water (using coconut milk will make a richer curry). Cook the potatoes over medium heat, or on the medium sauté mode, for about 10 minutes, until they are fully cooked.

Taste and adjust the seasoning with more fish sauce or tamarind paste as needed. Serve with jasmine rice.

My Thoughts on the Instant Pot

I have an Instant Pot, but I don't use it often. As a chef, I like to be able to see how my food is doing so that I can make adjustments as it cooks. I feel an unnerving loss of control when I put things into a completely enclosed machine that I can't check on until it's done. However, there are a few things that I like the Instant Pot for, and one is for making stocks. It's freeing to not have to worry about topping my stock up with water or keeping an eye on the time, and I *love* not having to turn the annoyingly loud hood fan on for hours. I also don't mind it for making braised beef dishes, because beef can take 2 to 3 hours to tenderize, so the time saved is significant. But for many dishes that don't take as long, by the time I factor in the preheat, the cool down, and any parts of the dish that require me to cook it in regular sauté mode, I'm not saving much time in the end.

Southern Turmeric Crab Curry

Gaeng Pu Bai Chaploo | แกงปูใบชะพลู

Simple luxury. Good crabmeat may be expensive, but it can be a ready-to-eat protein that requires no prep, so it's a wonderful way to treat yourself to a fine meal even when you're short on time. This dish is the epitome of southern Thai food, which is known for seafood and its liberal use of turmeric. You can make southern Thai curry paste, or *prik gaeng tai*, from scratch, but I've shared a shortcut method here using store-bought red curry paste as a base and just adding to it the ingredients that make it "southern." Red curry is the basic paste containing ingredients common to most curries, so it's super versatile in this way.

Make the curry paste by pounding the black peppercorns with a mortar and pestle until fine. If using fresh turmeric, add it to the peppercorns and pound into a fine paste. Add the red curry paste, ground turmeric (if using), and shrimp paste; pound to mix.

Place ⅓ cup (80 ml) coconut milk in a medium pot and bring to a boil over medium heat. Add the curry paste and keep stirring until it is very thick and coconut oil starts to separate from the paste, 4 to 5 minutes (the oil may not separate depending on the coconut milk you're using; this is okay).

Add the remaining coconut milk, stock, and sugar, and simmer for 5 minutes to allow the flavors to mingle.

Taste the sauce and add fish sauce as needed; how much depends on how salty your curry paste is, so it is important to taste first. If you want a stronger turmeric flavor, you can also add more; if using fresh turmeric, simply pound it into a paste or finely grate before adding.

Add the greens and cook just until wilted, about 30 seconds, then gently stir in most of the crabmeat, setting aside a little for garnish. Once the crab is heated through, another 30 seconds or so, remove the pot from the heat.

Ladle the curry into a serving bowl and top with the reserved crabmeat. Serve with jasmine rice or rice vermicelli.

See photo on page 82

See photo on page 82

SERVES 4

COOKING TIME: 10 minutes

QUICK SOUTHERN CURRY PASTE

½ teaspoon (2 ml) black peppercorns

2 inches (10 g) fresh turmeric, or ½ teaspoon (2 ml) ground turmeric

3 to 4 tablespoons (45 to 60 ml) red curry paste, store-bought or homemade (p. 255)

1 to 2 teaspoons (5 to 10 ml) fermented shrimp paste (see note)

CURRY

2 cups (500 ml) coconut milk, divided

½ cup (125 ml) unsalted chicken stock or water

2 teaspoons (8 g) finely chopped palm sugar, packed

2 to 3 teaspoons (10 to 15 ml) fish sauce, to taste

4 cups (90 g) wild betel leaves, cut in ¾-inch (2 cm) ribbons (see note)

10.5 ounces (300 g) fresh crabmeat

Jasmine rice or rice vermicelli, for serving (see sidebar, p. 83)

Do-ahead: *The curry paste and curry sauce can be made in advance and frozen. Or make the curry sauce a few days in advance and store in the fridge. Add the crabmeat and greens just before serving.*

Notes: *Use only 1 teaspoon (5 ml) shrimp paste if the curry paste already contains some.*

Traditionally, we use wild betel leaves or bai chaploo (not to be confused with the psychoactive betel leaves). You can find them at some Vietnamese stores, sometimes labeled la lot. You can use any other dark leafy greens you like, such as Chinese broccoli, yu choy, or kale.

Crab Curry Noodles

Although you absolutely can serve this dish with rice, southern crab curry is unique in that it is often served with rice vermicelli. There are a few different products on the market labeled "rice vermicelli"—some are thread-thin, while others are round and a little thicker; you can use whichever you prefer. You can serve it like a bowl of pasta, with the sauce poured over the noodles, or you can also serve it family style, along with other dishes. If that's case, after you have cooked the noodles, dunk them into a big bowl of cold water to cool, then grab a small bunch and coil them into little bundles. Then you can take a little bundle to eat with the curry, while still enjoying the rest of the meal with rice.

Pineapple & Shrimp Red Curry

Gaeng Kua Subparod Goong | แกงคั่วสับปะรดกุ้ง

SERVES 4

COOKING TIME: 30 minutes

2 tablespoons (15 g) dried shrimp (optional)

1 (14 ounce/398 ml) can pineapple chunks, drained, or 1¾ cups (435 ml) chopped fresh pineapple (see note)

1½ cups (375 ml) coconut milk, divided

3 to 4 tablespoons (45 to 60 ml) red curry paste, store-bought or homemade (p. 255)

½ to 1 cup (125 to 250 ml) water or unsalted chicken stock

7 to 8 makrut lime leaves

1 to 2 tablespoons (15 to 30 ml) fish sauce

2 to 3 teaspoons (8 to 12 g) finely chopped palm sugar, packed

1 to 2 tablespoons (15 to 30 ml) tamarind paste, store-bought or homemade (p. 266)

½ red bell pepper, julienned

1 pound (450 g) shrimp, size 26/30 or larger, peeled and deveined, thawed if frozen

Jasmine rice, for serving

Note: Be sure to buy canned pineapple packed in pineapple juice, not in syrup.

At the beginning of the Covid-19 lockdown, I found myself at the grocery store faced with half-empty shelves, and I started to panic. Next thing I knew, I was grabbing all sorts of canned and dried goods I don't even normally buy, and that is how I ended up with canned pineapple, something I never buy because I find it so flavorless. After staring at the cans every time I looked in the cupboard, I finally realized after a few months that this curry is the perfect use for them. Red curry has such a strong flavor that it doesn't really matter if your pineapple is disappointing. The most important trick in this recipe is squeezing the juice out of the pineapple to make room for the curry sauce to penetrate it—this allows the flavors of the curry and the pineapple to coalesce, rather than it tasting like curry in one bite and pineapple in another.

_____

Finely chop the dried shrimp or grind them into "fluff" in a coffee grinder.

Place the pineapple chunks in a bowl and squeeze them with your hands so they give up some of their juice. You want them to have room to absorb the curry sauce. Leave both the juice and the pineapple in the bowl.

In a medium pot, bring ½ cup (125 ml) coconut milk to a boil over medium heat, then add the red curry paste and stir to mix. Cook, stirring frequently, until the mixture is very thick and the coconut oil separates from the paste, about 5 minutes (the oil may not separate depending on the coconut milk you're using; this is okay). If the paste sticks to the pot, deglaze with a bit of coconut milk.

Add the remaining coconut milk, ½ cup (125 ml) water, the dried shrimp and the pineapple and all the juice you squeezed out, but not the juice from the can. Twist the makrut lime leaves to bruise them and release their aroma before tearing them into big chunks and adding to the pot, discarding any big center stems. Simmer on low heat for 5 minutes.

Add 1 tablespoon (15 ml) fish sauce, 2 teaspoons (10 ml) sugar, and 1 tablespoon (15 ml) tamarind paste. Stir to dissolve the sugar, then taste and adjust the seasoning. How much of the seasonings you need will depend on the flavor of the pineapple and also the curry paste— you want the sauce to be a little sweet and a little tart, with a good amount of saltiness as a base.

Add the bell peppers and cook for 1 minute. Then add the shrimp and cook for 30 seconds to 1 minute, or just until they are done. Turn off the heat and do a final taste. Serve with jasmine rice.

Yellow Curry vs. Yellow Curry
Store-bought yellow curry paste is not usually that spicy, but after having a few people report to me that their yellow curry was unexpectedly incredibly spicy, I realized that there are *two* Thai yellow curry pastes on the market. The "wrong" paste to use in this recipe is the one for yellow *sour* curry, or *gaeng leuang*, a southern Thai water-based curry that is indeed exceedingly spicy. It is actually the "true" yellow curry, because *gaeng leuang* literally means "yellow curry." So, when shopping, make sure the label does not say "sour," or look for the word *garee* (sometimes spelled *karee*).

Yellow Curry with Roasted Potato & Cauliflower

Gaeng Garee Dok Galum | แกงกะหรี่ดอกกะหล่ำ

This dish is inspired by one of my favorite Indian dishes, *aloo gobi*, a delightful mix of potatoes, cauliflower, and lots of spices. The turmeric, spices, and potatoes in *aloo gobi* have always reminded me of Thai yellow curry. So, while it's not traditional to put cauliflower in yellow curry, the brilliance of this combination cannot be denied. Since there is no meat, the trick here is roasting the vegetables to add more robustness to the curry. While you could drop raw veggies into the sauce, roasting them develops that delicious "browned" flavor. Just think about how much better roasted potatoes are than boiled—*that* is the difference.

———

Preheat the oven to 450°F (230°C) and set two racks in the oven, spaced apart evenly.

Toss the potatoes in ⅛ teaspoon (0.5 ml) salt and 1 tablespoon (15 ml) oil. Spread them on a baking sheet, cut side down, and roast for 20 to 25 minutes, until browned on the underside.

Toss the cauliflower in ⅛ teaspoon (0.5 ml) salt and 1 tablespoon (15 ml) oil. Spread the florets on a baking sheet, cut side down, and roast for about 15 minutes, until browned on the underside.

While the vegetables roast, make the curry sauce. Place ¾ cup (185 ml) coconut milk in a medium pot and bring to a boil over medium-high heat. Stir in the curry paste, mixing well, then turn the heat down to medium and stir constantly until the mixture is very thick and the coconut oil separates from the paste, about 5 minutes (the oil may not separate depending on the coconut milk you're using; this is okay). If the paste is sticking to the pot, deglaze with a bit of coconut milk.

Stir in the remaining coconut milk, 1 tablespoon (15 ml) fish sauce, 1 tablespoon (15 ml) tamarind paste, and sugar. Simmer over low heat for at least 5 minutes, until the vegetables are done roasting.

Add the roasted vegetables and the onions to the curry sauce, then add just enough of the stock to submerge everything. Simmer the vegetables for about 5 minutes to allow them to absorb the curry flavor.

Stir in the tomatoes and turn off the heat, allowing them to soften in the residual heat for a few minutes. Taste and adjust the seasoning, adding more fish sauce, tamarind paste, or sugar as needed. Serve with jasmine rice.

SERVES 4
COOKING TIME: 35 minutes

- 12 ounces (340 g) waxy potatoes, such as new or red-skinned potatoes, cut in 1½-inch (4 cm) chunks

- ¼ teaspoon (1 ml) table salt, divided

- 2 tablespoons (30 ml) neutral oil, divided

- 12 ounces (340 g) cauliflower florets, about 1 medium head

- 2 cups (500 ml) coconut milk, divided

- 5 to 6 tablespoons (75 to 90 ml) yellow curry paste, store-bought or homemade (p. 257)

- 1 to 2 tablespoons (15 to 30 ml) fish sauce or soy sauce

- 1 to 1½ tablespoons (15 to 22 ml) tamarind paste, store-bought or homemade (p. 266) (see note)

- 1½ tablespoons (18 g) finely chopped palm sugar, packed

- ½ medium (120 g) yellow onion, cut in strips

- 1½ cups (375 ml) unsalted chicken or vegetable stock

- ¾ cup (100 g) halved cherry tomatoes

- Jasmine rice, for serving

Note: If you don't have tamarind paste, no need to buy or make it just for this recipe. We just need a little bit of acid to brighten up the sauce, so a few dashes of Worcestershire sauce or a squeeze of lime at the end will also do.

Panang Curry Chicken

Panang Gai | พะแนงไก่

Everyone needs a go-to recipe that elevates basic boneless, skinless chicken breasts. Look no further, this is it. *Panang* is the fastest curry to make because it's the simplest. Instead of being soupy, like other Thai curries, *panang* sauce is thick, rich, and concentrated, making it ideal for lean, mild-flavored meats. Because the chicken doesn't spend much time in the sauce, a quick marinade ensures that the meat itself will not be bland. A little water in the marinade is my trick for creating a mini brine, which adds juiciness to lean meats and builds a bigger buffer against overcooking.

———

Marinate the chicken. Combine all the ingredients in a bowl and mix well. Let sit at room temperature for 15 minutes.

Make the curry paste. Grind the coriander and cumin seeds until very fine, using a coffee grinder or mortar and pestle. Add the roasted peanuts and grind until fine, but don't turn them into peanut butter. If using a coffee grinder, transfer the peanuts and spices into a small mixing bowl and mix in the red curry paste and shrimp paste until combined; otherwise, add the curry paste and shrimp paste to the mortar and pound to mix.

Bring ¾ cup (185 ml) coconut milk to a boil in a wok or large skillet over medium-high heat. Stir in the curry paste, then turn the heat down to medium and stir constantly until the mixture is very thick, 5 to 7 minutes. You may see coconut oil separate from the paste. If the paste sticks to the pan, deglaze with a bit of water.

Add the torn makrut lime leaves, palm sugar, and 1 teaspoon (5 ml) fish sauce and cook for about 1 minute, until the sugar is dissolved.

Add the chicken strips and toss with the curry paste. Once the chicken is halfway cooked, about 1 minute, add the remaining coconut milk and stir for another minute or just until the chicken is fully cooked. If it looks too dry, you can add a splash of water to create more sauce.

Stir in most of the bell peppers and turn off the heat, allowing them to soften just slightly in the residual heat. Taste and adjust the seasoning with the remaining fish sauce and sugar as needed.

Garnish with the julienned makrut lime leaves, the remaining bell peppers, and a splash of coconut milk, if desired. Serve with jasmine rice.

SERVES 4

COOKING TIME: 20 minutes

QUICK-MARINATED CHICKEN

1 pound (450 g) boneless, skinless chicken breasts, cut in ½-inch (1.2 cm) thick strips

2 tablespoons (30 ml) water

2 teaspoons (10 ml) fish sauce

½ teaspoon (2 ml) granulated sugar

QUICK PANANG CURRY PASTE

2 teaspoons (10 ml) coriander seeds, toasted

1 teaspoon (5 ml) cumin seeds, toasted

3 tablespoons (28 g) unsalted roasted peanuts

3 to 4 tablespoons (45 to 60 ml) red curry paste, store-bought or homemade (p. 255), to taste

1 teaspoon (5 ml) fermented shrimp paste (see note)

CURRY

1½ cups (375 ml) coconut milk, divided

10 makrut lime leaves (7 roughly torn, 3 finely julienned)

2 tablespoons (24 g) finely chopped palm sugar, packed

1 to 2 teaspoons (5 to 10 ml) fish sauce, to taste

½ medium (80 g) red bell pepper, julienned

Jasmine rice, for serving

Note: *Add the shrimp paste only if the red curry paste doesn't already contain it.*

Grandma's Spareribs & Vegetable Stew

Jub Chai | จับฉ่าย

SERVES 4

COOKING TIME: 50 to 60 minutes

6 cups (1.5 L) water

1½ pounds (675 g) chopped pork spareribs (see note)

3 (15 g) dried shiitake mushrooms, rinsed

8 ounces (230 g) peeled daikon, cut in 1-inch (2.5 cm) chunks (about 2 cups/500 ml)

6 cloves (30 g) garlic, smashed

½ teaspoon (2 ml) ground white pepper

2 tablespoons (30 ml) soy sauce

2 tablespoons (30 ml) oyster sauce

½ tablespoon (7 ml) Thai seasoning sauce

½ to 1 teaspoon (2 to 5 ml) black soy sauce (optional)

1 medium carrot (100 g), cut into bite-sized pieces

2 cups (150 g) bite-sized green cabbage pieces

2 cups (100 g) coarsely chopped Chinese broccoli (*gai lan*, see note)

Jasmine rice, for serving

Do-ahead: *Jub chai is known for being better the next day, so if possible, make this the night before.*

Notes: *Chopped spareribs are split and cut across the bones into 1- to 2-inch (2.5 to 5 cm) cubes; they're commonly available at Asian markets. You can buy a full rack and split the ribs apart, but you'll end up with bigger pieces, which are a bit unwieldy in soups. Some pieces of spareribs are all meat with no bones, meaning the meat is much thicker than when on the bone; make sure you chop these into pieces no larger than ½-inch (1.2 cm) or they will take much longer to tenderize.*

Instead of Chinese broccoli, or gai lan, you can use bok choy, yu choy, or another leafy green, such as Swiss chard.

There are a few dishes that make me think of my grandmother, and this is one of them. Actually, I associate *jub chai* with grandmothers in general, as though one isn't truly qualified to make it until they become a grandma. So, despite being too young to make this well, I think my version is (almost) as good as my grandma's. Using pork ribs is key, as it results in a rich broth without needing to use a drop of stock, and the daikon adds sweetness without needing a drop of sugar. It takes a bit of time to cook, but the fantastically unfussy prep makes it a fine candidate for a weeknight meal.

———

Bring the water to a rolling boil in a large pot over high heat. Add the pork ribs, shiitake mushrooms, daikon, garlic, pepper, soy sauce, oyster sauce, Thai seasoning sauce, and just enough black soy sauce to darken the mixture's color slightly. Simmer gently over medium-low heat, partially covered, for about 30 minutes, until the meat is fork-tender.

Remove the mushrooms from the soup and set aside to cool slightly. Then add the carrots, cabbage, and Chinese broccoli; simmer for another 10 minutes, or until the veggies are tender.

While the veggies are cooking, remove and discard the mushroom stems. Thinly slice the caps and return them to the soup.

Taste and adjust the seasoning with more soy sauce as needed. Serve with jasmine rice.

If You Have Time

The spirit of this dish is no-fuss—it's a throw-everything-into-a-pot kind of dish. But if you have time, there are opportunities for maximizing flavor by browning the pork and sautéing the garlic and pepper. Start by putting a little neutral oil in the pot and searing the pork ribs on high heat until browned. Remove the ribs, turn the heat down to low, and sauté the garlic and pepper in the same oil until aromatic, about 2 minutes. Add the ribs back in, then add the water and proceed with the recipe.

Chicken Wing Tom Yum Soup

Tom Yum Peek Gai | ต้มยำปีกไก่

Tom yum soup can be made with any kind of meat or seafood, but the version with shrimp is the most popular outside Thailand, probably because it has an intense, rich flavor thanks to the Thai chili paste. The chicken version, however, has a simpler, cleaner-tasting broth, and it is one of the most soul-soothing dishes we have to offer. You can use boneless chicken, but I love using chicken wings in this because they have an extremely high bone-to-meat ratio, which means that in 20 minutes the wings will turn plain water into chicken stock that's richer and tastier than any stock you can buy. Wings also don't require any chopping, and I'm *all* about less cleanup any time!

Bring the water to a boil in a large pot over high heat. Add the chicken drumettes, shallots, 3 tablespoons (45 ml) fish sauce and 2 teaspoons (10 ml) sugar. Simmer for about 20 minutes, until the chicken is fork-tender.

While the chicken is cooking, char the dried chilies for additional smoky flavor. Place the chilies in a dry skillet over medium-high heat and stir them for a few minutes, until they develop charred spots and smell smoky. Keep an eye on them and don't walk away! Once charred, set aside.

When the chicken is tender, add the dried chilies (keep them whole for a milder soup, break them up for a spicy soup), lemongrass, galangal, and mushrooms. Twist the makrut lime leaves to bruise them and release their aroma before tearing them into big chunks and adding to the pot, discarding any big center stems. Simmer for 5 to 7 minutes.

Add the tomatoes and cook for about 2 minutes, or just until the tomatoes are soft but still hold their shape. Turn off the heat and stir in 3 tablespoons (45 ml) lime juice. Taste and adjust the seasoning with more fish sauce, sugar, or lime juice as needed. You want it to lead with sour and salty. The sweetness is there for balance, but the soup should not taste distinctly sweet. Before serving, you can remove the herbs, as they are not meant to be eaten, though they are traditionally left in the soup. I like to remove only half to make it a little easier to eat while keeping the traditional look. Be sure to remind your guests not to eat them!

Garnish the soup with cilantro and serve with jasmine rice. The meat should be super tender and easy to pry off the bones with a spoon.

SERVES 4

COOKING TIME: 30 minutes

5 cups (1.25 L) water

1½ pounds (675 g) chicken drumettes (see note)

½ cup (60 g) coarsely chopped shallots

3 to 4 tablespoons (45 to 60 ml) fish sauce

2 to 3 teaspoons (10 to 15 ml) granulated sugar

5 spicy dried chilies, such as Thai chilies or chiles de árbol, or more to taste (see note)

2 stalks lemongrass, bottom halves only, smashed and cut in 2-inch (5 cm) pieces

10 thin slices (25 g) galangal

10 makrut lime leaves

3.5 ounces (100 g) shimeji or oyster mushrooms

1½ cups (200 g) halved cherry tomatoes

3 to 4 tablespoons (45 to 60 ml) lime juice

7 to 8 sprigs cilantro, chopped

Jasmine rice, for serving

Note: Drumettes are easier to eat in soups than whole wings. If you've got the whole wings, save the flats for Fish Sauce Wings (p. 27).

Boneless Chicken Tom Yum

If you don't want to navigate chicken bones while eating soup, I get it. You can opt to use 1 pound (450 g) bite-sized pieces of boneless chicken thighs instead, but then you must use unsalted chicken stock instead of water. Without the bones, the meat will not give a rich enough broth and the soup will not be nearly as good.

Turmeric Fish Soup

Pla Tom Kamin | ปลาต้มขมิ้น

SERVES 4
COOKING TIME: 15 minutes

3 cups (750 ml) unsalted chicken or fish stock

½ cup (60 g) coarsely chopped shallots

3-inch piece (16 g) turmeric, thinly sliced (see note)

8 thin slices (18 g) galangal

5 cloves (25 g) garlic, smashed

5 makrut lime leaves, torn into chunks

2 to 3 dried or fresh Thai chilies, halved on a diagonal

1 stalk lemongrass, bottom half only, smashed and cut in 2-inch (5 cm) pieces

1 pound (450 g) fish fillet, cut in 2-inch (5 cm) chunks (see note)

2 tablespoons (30 ml) fish sauce

2 tablespoons (30 ml) tamarind paste, store-bought or homemade (p. 266)

1 teaspoon (5 ml) granulated sugar

7 to 8 sprigs cilantro, chopped (optional)

Jasmine rice, for serving

Note: I much prefer fresh turmeric to ground in soups because the powder settles at the bottom. It's also easy to overdo ground turmeric, which will make the soup taste medicinal. If you cannot find fresh, start with ½ teaspoon (2 ml) ground turmeric and add more as needed.

Any mild white fish will work, such as cod, sea bass, or tilapia. In Thailand, mackerel is used if something firmer and with a stronger flavor is preferred.

This is a comforting soup from southern Thailand, where turmeric is used much more often than in the rest of the country. With the broth being so light and loaded with herbs, it's the kind of soup that feels therapeutic. It's perfect for when you've got a cold (add extra chilies if that's the case) or when you just feel like you deserve a bit of tasty self-care.

———

In a medium pot, combine the stock, shallots, turmeric, galangal, garlic, makrut lime leaves, chilies, and lemongrass, and bring to a boil over high heat. Turn the heat down to medium and simmer for 5 minutes to allow the herbs to infuse.

Add the fish, fish sauce, tamarind paste, and sugar, and simmer for 1 to 2 minutes, just until the fish is cooked. Remove from the heat, then taste and adjust the seasoning with more fish sauce, tamarind paste, or sugar as needed. Before serving, you can remove the herbs, as they are not meant to be eaten, though they are traditionally left in the soup. I like to remove only half to make it a little easier to eat while keeping the traditional look. Be sure to remind your guests not to eat them!

Stir in the chopped cilantro, if desired, and serve with jasmine rice.

> **Removing Turmeric Stains**
> If you don't want a yellow cutting board, put down a piece of paper towel or some other kind of barrier when you cut the turmeric, to avoid staining. Also, don't use a wooden spoon to stir the soup unless you want it to turn yellow as well. It's a good idea to wash anything that touches turmeric as soon as you're done with it so that the color doesn't have time to sink in. But if you do end up with yellow kitchen tools, putting them out in the sun for a day will help fade the stain. Otherwise, think of it as adding character!

Coconut Galangal Salmon Soup

Tom Kha Pla Salmon | ต้มข่าปลาแซลมอน

This dish is a bit reminiscent of a seafood chowder, except with the iconic herbs that are common to many Thai soups. The citrusy herbs and the subtle hint of lime make this dish pair beautifully with any fish, but I particularly love using salmon for the color it brings to an otherwise white dish. Use chicken stock for an easy version, or if you have an extra 15 minutes, make a quick fish stock for a pronounced seafood flavor (my preferred option).

⸻

FOR THE QUICK FISH STOCK

Bring the water to a boil in a medium pot over high heat. Add the bones and lemongrass, then turn the heat down to medium-low; simmer for at least 15 minutes. If you have 45 minutes, even better. You may need to top it up with more water to keep the bones submerged.

Remove the bones, and if there's lots of meat left on them, pick it off to add back into the soup. Strain the stock; you should have about 2 cups (500 ml); if you have less, add water to make up for the shortfall.

FOR THE SOUP

Bring the stock to a boil and add the coconut milk, lemongrass, galangal, and chilies. Twist the makrut lime leaves to bruise them and release their aroma before tearing them into big chunks and adding to the pot, discarding any big center stems. Simmer over medium heat for 5 minutes.

Add the mushrooms, fish sauce, and salt, bring back to a simmer, and cook for about 2 minutes, until the mushrooms look wilted. Taste and adjust the seasoning with more fish sauce or salt as needed.

Add the salmon and stir to separate the pieces. If you're using an electric stove, turn it off immediately and let the residual heat gently cook the salmon through in the next 3 minutes or so. If using a gas stove, keep the heat on for another 15 seconds before turning it off. The soup will remain hot enough to cook the salmon for a while, so this is a technique for making sure the fish does not overcook.

Stir in 1 tablespoon (15 ml) lime juice, then taste, and if you prefer a tarter soup, you can add the remaining lime juice. Before serving you can remove the herbs, as they are not meant to be eaten, though they are traditionally left in the soup. I like to remove only half to make it a little easier to eat while keeping the traditional look. Be sure to remind your guests not to eat them! Stir in chopped cilantro and serve with jasmine rice.

SERVES 4

COOKING TIME: 20 minutes, plus 30 minutes if making fish stock

QUICK FISH STOCK

3 cups (750 ml) water

12 ounces (340 g) fish bones, cut in 2-inch (5 cm) chunks

Top half of lemongrass, smashed and cut in 2-inch (5 cm) pieces

SOUP

2 cups (500 ml) unsalted chicken or fish stock

1½ cups (375 ml) coconut milk

1 stalk lemongrass, bottom half only, smashed and cut in 2-inch (5 cm) pieces

15 thin slices (35 g) galangal

1 to 2 Thai chilies, smashed until broken

6 to 7 makrut lime leaves

3.5 ounces (100 g) oyster or shimeji mushrooms

1½ tablespoons (22 ml) fish sauce

½ teaspoon (2 ml) table salt

12 ounces (340 g) salmon fillet, or another fish of your choice, cut in 1-inch (2.5 cm) cubes

1 to 2 tablespoons (15 to 30 ml) lime juice

6 to 7 sprigs cilantro, or 1 green onion, chopped

Jasmine rice, for serving

Glass Noodle Soup with Pork Meatballs

Gaeng Jeud Woonsen Moo Sub | แกงจืดวุ้นเส้นหมูสับ

SERVES 4

COOKING TIME: 30 minutes

1.4 ounces (40 g) dried glass noodles (bean threads)

1 tablespoon (15 ml) neutral oil

5 cloves (25 g) garlic, chopped

4 cups (1 L) unsalted homemade pork or chicken stock (p. 265)

5 cups (200 g) bite-sized napa cabbage pieces

1 tablespoon + 1 teaspoon (20 ml) soy sauce

2 teaspoons (10 ml) fish sauce

½ teaspoon (2 ml) granulated sugar

1 to 2 green onions and/or 7 to 8 sprigs cilantro, chopped

Freshly ground white pepper, to taste

Jasmine rice, for serving

MEATBALLS

10.5 ounces (300 g) ground pork

1 tablespoon (15 ml) soy sauce

½ tablespoon (7 ml) fish sauce

1 teaspoon (5 ml) granulated sugar

¼ teaspoon (1 ml) ground white pepper

Gaeng jeud literally means "bland curry," but this one is anything but bland. The term refers to a family of clear soups that are seasoned simply and are never spicy, in contrast to more strongly flavored curries. It's the epitome of simple Thai home cooking, and every Thai household makes some version of this dish regularly, especially if there are kids. One could say it's our chicken noodle soup. This recipe features glass noodles, which is one of the most popular versions, but it is not served on its own like ramen or pho. It is served with rice like all our other soups. Yes, carb on carb at its best!

———

Soak the glass noodles in room temperature water for 7 to 10 minutes to soften, then cut them into sections, about 3 inches (8 cm) long.

Pour the oil into a medium pot over medium heat, then add one test piece of chopped garlic. Once the garlic is bubbling, add the remaining garlic, stirring constantly until the pieces are light golden, about 5 minutes. Do not let the garlic turn brown or it will be bitter. Turn off the heat and use a slotted spoon to remove the garlic, leaving the oil in the pot. Put the garlic in a small bowl.

To the same pot, add the stock and bring to a boil over high heat.

Meanwhile, combine all the ingredients for the meatballs in a mixing bowl and mix just until combined.

Once the stock is boiling, use two spoons or a small disher to scoop and drop bite-sized chunks of the meatball mixture into the stock. They're supposed to be rustic, so no need to make them pretty.

Once all the meatballs are in the pot, add the napa cabbage, soy sauce, fish sauce, and sugar, and bring the soup back to a boil. If serving right away, add the glass noodles and cook for 3 minutes before removing from the heat. If not serving right away, turn off the heat for now, and then closer to serving time bring it back to a boil to add the noodles.

Taste and adjust the seasoning with fish sauce or sugar as needed, then stir in green onions and/or cilantro to taste. Transfer to serving bowls and top with the fried garlic and pepper. Serve immediately with jasmine rice.

Coconut Galangal Mushroom Soup

Tom Kha Hed | ต้มข่าเห็ด

One of my all-time favorite soups, and the first dish I made to cure my homesickness after moving to Canada, is *tom kha gai*. It's a heart-warming coconut soup with chicken and mushroom, infused with what I call the "Thai trinity"—lemongrass, galangal, and makrut lime leaves. For years I resisted veganizing *tom kha gai* because, to me, the chicken is core to this soup. But now that you can get so many types of Asian mushrooms at most Asian markets, plus my realization that mushrooms are quite rich in umami, I thought it was time I gave the no-chicken version a go, replacing it with a fun mix of mushrooms. The verdict? It's so good I didn't miss the chicken at all! Just one rule: no button mushrooms in this, please.

Make a quick vegetable stock. Place the water in a medium pot, then add the onions, garlic, daikon and/or celery, and pepper, and bring to a boil over high heat. Turn the heat down to medium and simmer for 15 minutes.

Strain the stock into a liquid measuring cup—you should have about 2 cups (500 ml). If you have less than that, add water to make up for the shortfall. Pour the measured amount of stock back into the pot.

Twist the makrut lime leaves to bruise them, then tear them into big chunks and add them to the stock, discarding any big center stems. Then add the lemongrass, galangal, chilies, and coconut milk, and bring to a simmer over high heat. Turn the heat down to medium-low and simmer for 5 to 7 minutes.

Add the mushrooms, soy sauce, sugar, and salt, and cook for 2 to 3 minutes, until the mushrooms are cooked through.

Add the tomatoes and simmer for 1 minute to soften, then turn off the heat. Add 1 tablespoon (15 ml) lime juice, then taste and add the remaining lime juice and more salt as needed. Before serving you can remove the herbs, as they are not meant to be eaten, though they are traditionally left in the soup. I like to remove only half to make it a little easier to eat while keeping the traditional look. Be sure to remind your guests not to eat them!

Garnish with chopped cilantro and/or green onions to taste. Serve with jasmine rice.

SERVES 4
COOKING TIME: 35 minutes

QUICK VEGETABLE STOCK

3 cups (750 ml) water

¼ medium yellow onion, small-diced

3 cloves (15 g) garlic, chopped

½ cup (65 g) diced peeled daikon and/or 1 stalk celery, small-diced

½ teaspoon (2 ml) ground white pepper

SOUP

5 makrut lime leaves

1 stalk lemongrass, bottom half only, smashed and cut in 2-inch (5 cm) pieces

15 thin slices (35 g) galangal

3 to 4 Thai chilies, smashed

1½ cups (375 ml) coconut milk

10.5 ounces (300 g) mixed Asian mushrooms, cut in bite-sized pieces (see note)

1½ tablespoons (22 ml) soy sauce or fish sauce

1 tablespoon (12 g) finely chopped palm sugar, packed

½ teaspoon (2 ml) table salt

¾ cup (100 g) halved cherry tomatoes (see note)

1½ to 2 tablespoons (22 to 30 ml) lime juice

8 to 10 sprigs cilantro and/or 1 to 2 green onions, for garnish

Jasmine rice, for serving

Notes: *Choose a few types of any of these mushrooms: shimeji, oyster, straw, maitake, fresh shiitake, enoki, and king oyster.*

Tomatoes are not traditionally added to tom kha, *but without chicken it's good to have another vegetable in the soup besides the mushrooms, and I have always loved the combination of tomatoes and coconut.*

The Asparagus Bend-and-Snap

In Thailand, lotus stems are often used in *tom gati*, but I find asparagus to be a great substitute. You've probably heard that you should bend asparagus until it snaps and discard the tough bottom piece, but I find that this way, perfectly tender parts often end up wasted. I simply chop off about 1½ inches (3.5 cm) and it has worked for me so far.

Coconut Mackerel Soup

Tom Gati Pla Too | ต้มกะทิปลาทู

Tom gati is one of those basic, old-school dishes that are commonly eaten in Thai homes, but you rarely see it outside Thailand, maybe because it's not pretty, or is too simple, or perhaps the shrimp paste funk makes it a bit of an acquired taste. Whatever the reason, I think it's such a hidden gem (and the funk is super subtle!). In Thailand, *tom gati* is most commonly made with shrimp or Thai short mackerel, but here I use regular mackerel, which works fantastically. The key salting agent in *tom gati* comes from fermented shrimp paste, but if you don't have it or don't like it, you can use fish sauce instead and cut out the salt.

———

Cut off 1½ inches (3.5 cm) **from the bottom of the asparagus** to remove the woody ends. Cut the trimmed spears into 2-inch (5 cm) pieces.

To sear the mackerel fillets, place a 12-inch (30 cm) skillet over high heat and add enough oil to coat the bottom. Pat the fish dry, then once the oil is hot, sear the fish without moving it until browned and cooked through, 2 to 3 minutes per side. Remove from the pan and let cool.

Make the herb paste by pounding the peppercorns into a powder with a mortar and pestle, then adding the shallots and shrimp paste and pounding into a rough paste.

Place the coconut milk and water in a medium pot and bring to a simmer over medium heat. Stir in the herb paste and simmer gently for 3 to 4 minutes. If using fish sauce instead of shrimp paste, add it at this step.

Meanwhile, remove all the bones and fins from the mackerel, then tear the fillets into big chunks. The skin is edible, but you don't have to put it in if you don't like it. You can also leave one fillet whole and place it on top for a more elegant presentation.

Taste the broth and add more shrimp paste, fish sauce, or salt as needed. Add the asparagus, 2 teaspoons (10 ml) tamarind paste, and sugar. Cook for 1 to 2 minutes, depending on the thickness of the asparagus.

Add the mackerel pieces and simmer for just 30 seconds to heat through. Taste and adjust the seasoning with more tamarind paste as needed.

Garnish with chopped chilies and/or cilantro, and serve with jasmine rice.

SERVES 4
COOKING TIME: 20 minutes

½ pound (225 g) asparagus

2 to 3 tablespoons (30 to 45 ml) neutral oil

2 mackerel fillets (9.5 ounces/275 g total)

½ teaspoon (2 ml) white peppercorns

½ cup (60 g) chopped shallots

1 to 2 teaspoons (5 to 10 ml) fermented shrimp paste (see note)

1¼ cups (310 ml) coconut milk

½ cup (125 ml) water

2 to 3 teaspoons (10 to 15 ml) tamarind paste, store-bought or homemade (p. 266)

2 teaspoons (8 g) finely chopped palm sugar, packed

Chopped Thai chilies and/or chopped cilantro, for garnish

Jasmine rice, for serving

Do-ahead: The mackerel can be fried a few days in advance and stored in the fridge until ready to use. This is also a great dish to make with leftover fish.

Note: If you're a shrimp paste novice, add 1 teaspoon (5 ml) at first, then taste the soup and add more if desired. If you're happy with the shrimp paste flavor, use salt to adjust seasoning. If you don't like shrimp paste, use 2 tablespoons (30 ml) of fish sauce instead.

STIR-FRIES

Pad | ผัด

Mastering Thai Stir-Fries

Stir-fries are a staple of weeknight cooking. By definition they are fast, and often simple and forgiving. Stir-fries are what I call my "desperate" meal, meaning if I can't think of anything to cook, I take whatever is in the fridge and I stir-fry it. I now keep a jar of my Universal Stir-Fry Sauce (p. 261) in the fridge for extra speed, and it makes just about anything delicious.

How to Eat a Thai Stir-Fry

As with most things, stir-fries are always eaten with rice. The sauce for our stir-fries is never thickened with starch, so it'll be loose, but that's where the jasmine rice comes in. The fluffy, slightly sticky grains absorb this sauce perfectly well. I don't recommend basmati or short-grain rice with Thai stir-fries, as they do not absorb the loose sauce quite as well.

Some stir-fried noodles and fried rice dishes are eaten on their own as a one-dish meal, and they are not included here because they have their own chapter (pp. 177–207). Everything in this chapter, including the noodle dishes, is meant to be served with rice.

Tips for Successful Stir-Frying

Stir-fries are easy, but they're not without their issues, and to make a really epic one, you do need some technique.

NEVER CROWD A WOK. Too much food means the moisture in the food will get trapped at the bottom of the wok and doesn't have a way to evaporate, so you end up with a soupy dish. This is especially important to remember when cooking noodles, as they can become soggy and mushy with too much liquid. I never cook more than two portions of noodles at a time, and only one for delicate fresh rice noodles.

IF YOU NEED TO COOK A LARGE PORTION, COOK THE MEAT SEPARATELY. Fans of my show know I always cook the meat separately because I want precise control over how long it cooks, but it also works to prevent soupy stir-fries, which can happen if you are cooking a big batch. Stir-fry all the meat first, then remove it from the pan. Cook the rest of the stir-fry and add the meat back in once the vegetables are done.

HAVE ALL YOUR INGREDIENTS READY TO GO AT ARM'S REACH. Stir-frying moves quickly, so don't turn the heat under the wok on until you've got everything lined up.

Ginger Soy Chicken

Gai Kem | ไก่เค็ม

My grandmother is from Hainan, China, and in the Chinese culture, there are a few occasions where we offer foods to our ancestors. For Chinese Thais, a must-have on the offering table is a plain, boiled whole chicken. After the ceremony, we are left with a cold, bland bird, and this is where the magic begins. My grandmother chops up the meat, then stir-fries it with garlic, ginger, soy sauce, and other seasonings. The precooked, dried-out meat absorbs all the salty-sweet flavors, especially the little shreds of chicken that tear off during the chopping—they become extra flavorful. When my grandma cooks *gai kem* without an occasion, it's never quite the same, and we always joke that the ceremony really makes the chicken taste better. This recipe is my quick way to savor the flavor of Grandma's *gai kem* without having to cook a whole chicken. And even though it will never be as good, because my chicken hasn't done its ceremonial duties, it's still got the right flavor that takes me home.

────

Cut the chicken crosswise into bite-sized, ½-inch (1.2 cm) thick strips and place in a mixing bowl. Add the soy sauce and seasoning sauce, and mix well; marinate for at least 15 minutes or up to 30 minutes at room temperature, or cover and refrigerate for up to 1 day.

Using a mortar and pestle, pound the peppercorns until fine, then add the garlic and ginger and pound into a rough paste.

Place a wok or large skillet over high heat and add enough oil to coat the bottom. Once the oil is very hot, add the chicken and spread it out in one layer. Let the chicken cook without stirring for 2 to 3 minutes, until the underside has developed some browning and the chicken is at least halfway cooked. Toss the chicken, and stir-fry until it's fully cooked. Turn off the heat and remove the chicken from the pan, leaving behind all the juices.

With the heat still off, add the garlic-ginger paste to the wok, then turn the heat to medium and sauté for 2 to 3 minutes, until all the chicken juices have dried up and the garlic starts to turn golden.

(Continued)

SERVES 4

COOKING TIME: 25 minutes

1 pound (450 g) boneless, skinless chicken thighs

1½ tablespoons (22 ml) soy sauce

1 tablespoon (15 ml) Thai seasoning sauce

¼ teaspoon (1 ml) white or black peppercorns

5 cloves (25 g) garlic

2 tablespoons (15 g) chopped ginger, plus extra julienned for garnish

2 to 3 tablespoons (30 to 45 ml) neutral oil

1½ tablespoons (18 g) finely chopped palm sugar, packed

½ to 1 teaspoon (2 to 5 ml) black soy sauce

5 to 6 sprigs cilantro, chopped, plus extra for garnish

FOR SERVING

Jasmine rice or plain rice porridge (p. 245)

Side of vegetables

Do-ahead: Marinate the chicken up to 1 day in advance. Or, if you want to make the precooked version, poach the chicken 1 day in advance (see p. 109).

Put the chicken back in, add the sugar, and turn the heat up to high. Toss constantly until the sugar is dissolved.

Add the black soy sauce, ¼ teaspoon (1 ml) at a time, until the desired color is reached. Turn off the heat, then taste and adjust the seasoning with more soy sauce or sugar as needed (if you want it sweeter, use granulated or brown sugar, which dissolve quickly).

Toss in the cilantro and plate the stir-fry, garnishing with more cilantro, if desired. Serve with jasmine rice or plain rice porridge, and a side of vegetables.

Getting Closer to the Real Gai Kem

If you have the time and want to experience something closer to the "real" *gai kem*, it's not too hard to make—and you do not have to offer it to your ancestors first. The key is starting with cooked chicken. Simply poach the chicken in lightly salted water until cooked through; a combination of dark and white meat will mimic the original dish made from a whole chicken. Chop or tear the meat into small bite-sized pieces. Then follow this recipe, but skip the chicken searing and, instead of marinating, just add all the seasoning when you add the chicken. Stir-fry until it's completely dry, with all the sauce absorbed into the chicken.

Dry Green Curry with Fish Balls & Eggplant

Gaeng Kiew Waan Look Chin Pla Pad Hang | แกงเขียวหวานลูกชิ้นปลาผัดแห้ง

SERVES 4

COOKING TIME: 20 minutes

9 ounces (250 g) Japanese or Chinese eggplant, about 1 large eggplant

2 to 3 tablespoons (30 to 45 ml) neutral oil

1 cup (250 ml) coconut milk, divided

2 to 3 tablespoons (30 to 45 ml) green curry paste, store-bought or homemade (p. 256)

6 to 7 makrut lime leaves (optional)

9 ounces (250 g) Asian-style fish balls, thawed if frozen, halved (see note)

⅓ cup (50 g) frozen peas (see note)

½ tablespoon (7 ml) granulated sugar

1 cup (15 g) Thai basil leaves

1 to 2 teaspoons (5 to 10 ml) fish sauce (optional)

Small handful julienned red bell pepper, for garnish (optional)

Jasmine rice, for serving

Notes: *You can find Asian-style fish balls in the freezer section or at the fresh seafood counter at Asian grocery stores. There are many kinds, but all will work; you could even get the assorted pack.*

Use pea eggplants instead of peas for a more traditional version. They are a bit bitter, though, so I prefer peas.

Thai-style fish balls are traditionally made by pounding clown feather-back fish meat into a sticky paste with a mortar and pestle. It's then formed into rough balls and boiled. The results are bouncy delicious-ness that are one of the most popular pairings with green curry. For a weeknight version, using store-bought fish balls is perfectly accept-able, even if the texture is slightly bouncier than that of homemade ones. Here I put fish balls in a "dry" green curry, i.e., a green curry stir-fry, but you can most certainly put them in a regular green curry as well. Thai eggplants are traditional, but I prefer the texture of Japanese eggplants, not to mention the fact that they're much easier to find!

———

Cut the eggplant into ½-inch (1.2 cm) thick slices on a diagonal, then cut each slice in half.

Place a 12-inch (30 cm) skillet over high heat, and add just enough oil to thinly coat the bottom. Once hot, add the eggplant in one layer; you may need to do this in batches. Cook the eggplant without moving it until browned on the underside, about 1 minute, then flip and cook the other side briefly, just until it has some brown spots. The second side won't brown as well because the oil will have all been absorbed, but that's okay. Turn off the heat and transfer the partially cooked eggplant to a bowl.

Add about ½ cup (125 ml) coconut milk to a wok and bring to a boil over medium heat. Stir in the curry paste. Twist the makrut lime leaves to bruise them and release their aroma before tearing them into big chunks and adding to the wok. Stir for 2 to 3 minutes, until the mixture is very thick.

Add the remaining coconut milk, fish balls, peas, and sugar; toss for about 1 minute, just until the fish balls are heated through. Add the eggplant and toss gently for about 1 minute.

Turn off the heat and fold in the basil just until wilted. Taste and add fish sauce as needed. Depending on the saltiness of the curry paste and how much you use, you may not need to add any fish sauce at all.

Plate and sprinkle with julienned bell peppers. Serve with jasmine rice.

Salt & Chili Shrimp

Goong Pad Prik Gleua | กุ้งผัดพริกเกลือ

Here, juicy shrimp are tossed in a salty, slightly sweet, subtly spiced seasoning. This is a surprisingly delicious dish given how simple it looks. *Pad prik gleua* is one of the few preparations in Thai cuisine that uses salt as the main seasoning rather than fish sauce or soy sauce. The five-spice powder is not always used, but I love adding just a touch of it for a hint of warm, sweet flavor that just makes you wonder, "Hmm, what is that?" Typically, the shrimp are deep-fried instead of seared (because Thai people don't pan-sear anything), so feel free to do that if you are so inclined.

––––

In a small bowl, combine the salt, sugar, five-spice powder, and white pepper.

Pat the shrimp very dry with a paper towel to prevent them from splattering in the hot oil. Then place a large 12-inch (30 cm) skillet on high heat and add enough oil to coat the bottom. Once the oil is very hot, lay the shrimp down in one layer; you may need to do this in batches. Sear the shrimp without moving them until browned on the underside and at least halfway cooked, about 2 minutes. Flip and sear the other side until cooked through. Turn off the heat and use tongs to transfer the shrimp to a bowl, leaving all the oil behind.

With the heat still off, add the garlic, cilantro stems, and chilies, then turn the heat to medium and stir until the garlic is golden.

Add the bell peppers and shrimp, leaving behind any liquid that collected as the shrimp rested. Sprinkle the dry seasoning over the shrimp and toss for a few seconds, just until all the seasoning is evenly distributed.

Turn off the heat and toss in half of the green onions. Plate and sprinkle more green onions on top. Serve with jasmine rice.

SERVES 4
COOKING TIME: 20 minutes

½ teaspoon (2 ml) table salt

½ teaspoon (2 ml) granulated sugar

¼ teaspoon (1 ml) five-spice powder, store-bought or homemade (p. 263)

¼ teaspoon (1 ml) ground white pepper

1 pound (450 g) large shrimp, at least 16/20 count, peeled and deveined, thawed if frozen

2 to 3 tablespoons (30 to 45 ml) neutral oil

8 cloves (40 g) garlic, chopped

6 cilantro stems, chopped (optional)

1 to 2 Thai chilies, chopped

½ cup (60 g) small-diced red and/or green bell pepper

1 to 2 green onions, chopped

Jasmine rice, for serving

Garlic Pepper Chicken

Gai Pad Gratiem Priktai | ไก่ผัดกระเทียมพริกไทย

SERVES 4

COOKING TIME: 25 minutes

1 pound (450 g) boneless, skinless chicken breasts or thighs

1 tablespoon (15 ml) water

1 tablespoon (15 ml) oyster sauce

2 teaspoons (10 ml) soy sauce

2 teaspoons (10 ml) fish sauce

1½ teaspoons (7 ml) granulated sugar

½ teaspoon (2 ml) ground white or black pepper

3 tablespoons (45 ml) neutral oil

8 cloves (40 g) garlic, chopped

¼ teaspoon (1 ml) black or dark soy sauce, plus more as needed (optional)

7 to 8 cilantro sprigs, chopped, plus extra for garnish

FOR SERVING

Jasmine rice

Side of vegetables

Do-ahead: Marinate the chicken and/or make the fried garlic 1 day in advance.

This is one of the most basic items you can get at a *raan kao gaeng,* a type of restaurant in Thailand where an array of ready-to-eat dishes are laid out on big trays and in pots, and you choose a couple of things to go on top of your rice. Chicken (or pork) is marinated in the ultimate Thai trinity of umami sauces: oyster, soy, and fish. It's stir-fried in garlic oil, with enough pepper to give it a little heat without it being spicy, then topped with golden, crispy fried garlic. It's super kid-friendly as well, not having any pesky vegetables to pick out and whatnot. You'll want to have a side of veggies or a soup to go with it, for a complete meal.

_____

Slice the chicken into ½-inch (1.2 cm) thick strips, and once you get to the thick part of the breast, cut each piece horizontally in half to even out the size. Place the chicken in a mixing bowl and add the water, oyster sauce, soy sauce, fish sauce, sugar, and pepper. Marinate for at least 15 minutes or up to 30 minutes at room temperature, or cover and refrigerate for up to 1 day.

While the chicken marinates, fry the garlic. Place a small pot on medium-low heat, then add the oil and one "test" piece of chopped garlic. Once the garlic is bubbling, add the remaining garlic, then turn the heat down to low. Fry gently, stirring frequently, until the garlic is golden but not browned, about 5 minutes—browning will cause the garlic to become bitter. Strain the garlic through a metal sieve, reserving the oil.

Place a wok or large skillet over high heat and add the garlic oil. Once the oil is very hot, add the chicken and spread it into one layer, letting it sear without moving it until starting to brown on the underside and at least halfway cooked, about 2 minutes. Toss the chicken and stir-fry until fully cooked. At this point, if you want, you can add the black soy sauce, ¼ teaspoon (1 ml) at a time, until the desired color is reached.

Turn off the heat, then toss in half of the fried garlic and chopped cilantro to taste. Plate and top with the remaining fried garlic and more cilantro, if desired. Serve with jasmine rice and a side of vegetables.

Using Delicate Fish

If you've ever ordered a fish stir-fry from an Asian restaurant, you may have noticed that the fish is always battered and deep-fried before being tossed in the wok. That is because the fried batter becomes a sort of "shell" that prevents the fish from falling apart in the aggressive tossing. This is what you would need to do if you want to use delicate, flaky fish. Alternatively, you can pan-sear whole fillets and put them on a serving platter. Then cook the veggies with the sauce as per the recipe and pour it over the fish, which makes for a more elegant presentation.

Cashew Salmon

Pla Salmon Pad Med Mamuang Himapan | ปลาแซลมอนผัดเม็ดมะม่วงหิมพานต์

Before meeting me, my husband's favorite Thai takeout dish was cashew chicken. So, naturally, when I came into his life, it became his most requested Thai meal. Not wanting to make the exact same thing all the time, I changed things up by using salmon instead of chicken. It was fantastic, and it gave me a very good excuse to add more fish to our diet. The secret to making sure that the salmon doesn't break when you stir-fry is to not fully cook it, so the middle doesn't become flaky—that's what will hold the fish together. Not to mention that medium-cooked salmon is so much more moist and delicious anyway! Flavor-wise, any other fish will work, but stick to firm-flesh fish, since stir-frying delicate fish is a recipe for a broken mess. A delicious mess, mind you, but still a mess. See the sidebar for an alternative cooking method that works with delicate fish.

——

Make the sauce by whisking all the ingredients in a small bowl.

Place a well-seasoned wok or large nonstick skillet over high heat and add the oil. Once the oil is very hot, add the salmon in a single layer without crowding the pan; you may need to do this in batches. Sear the salmon until browned on the underside and about halfway cooked, 1 to 2 minutes. Flip the salmon and sear the other side for just 30 seconds, then turn off the heat and remove the salmon from the pan, leaving all the oil behind; the salmon should be slightly undercooked— this will help keep it moist and prevent breaking.

With the heat still off, add the garlic and onions to the pan, then turn the heat to medium and stir until the garlic starts to turn golden.

Turn the heat up to high and add the mushrooms and peppers, and toss for about 1 minute.

Add the salmon back in, along with any collected juices, then add the sauce, cashews, and ½ teaspoon (2 ml) sugar. Toss gently for 10 to 15 seconds, just until the salmon is evenly coated in the sauce, then turn off the heat. Taste the sauce and add more sugar if needed, as the sweetness of the chili paste can vary between brands.

Transfer the salmon and veggies to a shallow bowl and top with green onions. Garnish with more cashews, if desired, and serve with jasmine rice.

SERVES 4
COOKING TIME: 20 minutes

SAUCE

1½ tablespoons (22 ml) Thai chili paste, store-bought or homemade (p. 258)

1 tablespoon (15 ml) oyster sauce

2 teaspoons (10 ml) soy sauce

2 teaspoons (10 ml) fish sauce

2 teaspoons (10 ml) sesame oil

½ to 1 teaspoon (2 to 5 ml) roasted chili flakes, store-bought or homemade (p. 263), to taste (optional)

STIR-FRY

2 tablespoons (30 ml) neutral oil

1 pound (450 g) salmon, cut in big chunks

5 cloves (25 g) garlic, chopped

¼ large yellow onion, cut in ¼-inch (6 mm) strips

4 ounces (120 g) shimeji or oyster mushrooms

½ red bell pepper, julienned

⅓ cup (45 g) unsalted roasted cashews, plus extra for garnish

½ to 1 teaspoon (2 to 5 ml) granulated sugar

1 to 2 green onions, chopped

Jasmine rice, for serving

Do-ahead: *Make extra sauce and keep it in the fridge so you have it ready to go; it will keep indefinitely.*

No-Fry Sweet & Sour Pork

Moo Pad Priew Waan | หมูผัดเปรี้ยวหวาน

SERVES 4
COOKING TIME: 20 minutes

12 ounces (340 g) pork tenderloin

2 teaspoons (10 ml) soy sauce

2 tablespoons (30 ml) neutral oil

5 cloves (25 g) garlic, chopped

½ medium (100 g) onion, cut in ⅓-inch (8 mm) strips

1½ cups (150 g) halved, sliced Persian or Japanese cucumber

1 cup (150 g) diced fresh pineapple (see note)

1 cup (100 g) julienned bell pepper, any color

½ cup (70 g) unsalted roasted cashews, plus extra for garnish

1 to 2 green onions, chopped (optional)

Jasmine rice, for serving

SWEET & SOUR SAUCE

2 tablespoons (22 g) packed brown sugar

2 tablespoons (30 ml) white vinegar

2 tablespoons (30 ml) oyster sauce

2 tablespoons (30 ml) sriracha-style hot sauce

1 tablespoon (15 ml) soy sauce

2 teaspoons (10 ml) toasted sesame oil

Note: Using fresh pineapple makes a big difference here; I buy it pre-cut in the ready-to-eat food section at the supermarket.

When you hear "sweet and sour pork," you probably think of a Chinese takeout meal rather than a Thai dish. Rest assured, the two are very different. The Thai version is much lighter and fresher. And while you would never call the Chinese-American version a healthy meal, the Thai version makes a pretty well-balanced meal with some rice. The meat isn't breaded and deep fried, and the sauce isn't thick and syrupy sweet. Instead, the stir-fry is loaded with veggies, with a light sauce that is moderately sweet. A little heat from the sriracha keeps it interesting too. It'll change how you look at what a "sweet and sour" dish can be!

——

Remove any silver skin from the pork, then cut the tenderloin in half horizontally. Cut each half into ⅓-inch (8 mm) slices and place them in a small mixing bowl. Add the 2 teaspoons (10 ml) soy sauce and mix well to coat.

Make the sweet and sour sauce by combining all the ingredients in a small bowl; stir until the sugar is mostly dissolved.

Place a wok on high heat and add the oil. Once it's very hot, add the pork and spread it out into one layer (you may need to do this in batches). Let the pork cook without moving it until browned on the underside, 1 to 2 minutes. Toss and stir for about 30 seconds, or just until most of the exterior looks cooked; don't worry about the inside being done at this point. Place the pork in a bowl, leaving behind any oil and juices.

In the same wok on medium heat, add a little more oil if needed, then add the garlic and onions and stir until the garlic starts to turn golden.

Turn the heat up to high and add the cucumber, pineapple, bell peppers, and sauce. Toss for about 2 minutes.

Add the pork back in and stir for 30 seconds, just until heated through. Be careful not to overcook the pork, as lean meat like tenderloin becomes dry quickly. (Pork is perfectly safe to eat medium-cooked to a minimum internal temperature of 145°F/63°C). Turn off the heat and stir in the cashews and green onions.

Plate and top with more cashews and green onions, if you like. Serve with jasmine rice.

Pork Shoulder Red Curry Stir-Fry

Pad Ped Moo | ผัดเผ็ดหมู

I love introducing people to *pad ped* as a way to show them that curry pastes do not have to be used for curries. It's just a paste of herbs and spices, so you can use it anywhere you would add herbs and spices! It is such a quick and easy dish, and delivers a boatload of flavor. I also love that it can work with a lot of different meats and veggies. The basil adds a lovely floral freshness, but it's not necessary. Makrut lime leaves alone are perfectly sufficient; I always have those in the freezer, and you should too.

_____

Slice the pork shoulder into thin pieces, against the grain, no thicker than ⅕ inch (5 mm), and place in a small mixing bowl. Add the fish sauce and mix well to coat.

Place a wok or large skillet over high heat and add the oil. Once the oil is very hot, add the pork and spread into a single layer as much as you can, working in batches if needed. Cook the pork without stirring for 1 to 2 minutes, until the underside has browned a bit and the pork is at least halfway cooked. Then stir the pork for about 15 seconds, just until the exterior is no longer raw. Immediately turn off the heat and remove the pork from the pan, leaving behind all the juices. (Do not worry about cooking the pork through at this stage. It will cook through by the end.)

With the heat still off, add the red curry paste and stir to mix it with the oil. Turn the heat to medium-low and sauté the paste for about 2 minutes, deglazing with a splash of the coconut milk if it sticks or seems a bit dry.

Add the remaining coconut milk and sugar, then twist the makrut lime leaves to bruise them and release their aroma before tearing them into big chunks and adding to the pan, discarding any big center stems. Stir to mix with the sauce.

Turn the heat up to high and add the vegetables; cook until the veggies are 90% done to your liking. If the sauce is drying up, add a splash of water.

Add the pork back in, along with any collected juices, and toss for about 30 seconds to heat through. Turn off the heat, then add the basil and toss just until wilted.

Taste and add more fish sauce as needed, keeping in mind this will be served with plain rice so it should be well seasoned. How much fish sauce you need will depend on how salty the curry paste is. Serve with jasmine rice.

SERVES 4
COOKING TIME: 20 minutes

1 pound (450 g) pork shoulder

1 tablespoon (15 ml) fish sauce

2 tablespoons (30 ml) neutral oil

3 tablespoons (45 ml) red curry paste, store-bought or homemade (p. 255)

½ cup (125 ml) coconut milk

1 tablespoon (12 g) finely chopped palm sugar, packed

5 to 6 makrut lime leaves (see note)

2 cups (175 g) diced firm vegetables of your choice (see note)

1 cup (15 g) Thai basil leaves, loosely packed

Jasmine rice, for serving

Notes: If you have Thai basil, you can omit the lime leaves, and vice versa; you just want at least one herb in there.

Traditional vegetables I use are Thai eggplant and long beans, but anything firm and crunchy will work, such as sugar snap peas, green beans, or carrots. You can use a few kinds, if you wish.

> **Pork Shoulder for Stir-Fries**
> Most people in North America use pork shoulder (aka pork butt) for braising and stewing. But I'm advocating for this cut to be used for stir-frying because it is so much more flavorful than the leaner cuts people are generally tempted to use. It's got a bit more chew, but when sliced thinly against the grain and not overcooked, it's such a satisfying texture, and the abundance of fat ensures that it's never dry. Try it once and you will be hooked!

Old-School Pad Gaprao

Pad Gaprao Moo Kai Dao | ผัดกะเพราหมูไข่ดาว

SERVES 4
COOKING TIME: 10 minutes, plus 5 to
10 minutes if frying eggs

2 to 3 Thai chilies, or as many as you can
handle

⅓ cup (40 g) chopped mild red peppers
(see sidebar)

7 cloves (35 g) garlic

Oil for frying eggs (optional)

4 eggs (optional, see note)

2 to 3 tablespoons (30 to 45 ml) neutral oil

1 pound (450 g) lean ground pork

2 tablespoons (30 ml) fish sauce

2 teaspoons (10 ml) granulated sugar

1½ cups (22 g) holy basil or Italian basil leaves
(see note)

Jasmine rice, for serving

*Notes: Pad gaprao is typically paired with a fried egg
when served as a one-dish meal. If serving as part of
a multi-dish Thai meal, you can omit the egg.*

*You might be tempted to use Thai basil instead, but
Italian basil is actually the better substitute.*

More Than Just Heat

I usually say you can make things as spicy
as you want, but for the real *pad gaprao*
experience, you should make it as spicy as
you can handle! But it's not just about the
heat, as chilies also provide flavor that's
important to this dish. This is why we use
mild and hot chilies; the mild ones add
the needed chili flavor without making
the dish too spicy. Red bell pepper will
work, but preferably something smaller
and less watery. The seeds and pith can
be removed to reduce heat.

Pad gaprao, sometimes written (incorrectly) as *pad kra pao,* is a true
staple of the Thai diet. It's sold by street vendors and at fancy
restaurants, and made at home all over the country. I call this the
"old school" version because it's the old style that differs from the
newer variants that are more popular today. It's much simpler,
seasoned with only fish sauce, and has no vegetables, so the flavor of
the basil really shines. Modern variations include soy sauce, oyster
sauce, and veggies like onions and long beans. There's no wrong way
to do it, and I want to share this piece of history before it disap-
pears—and also because it's much simpler to make than modern
versions, but equally delicious!

———

Using a mortar and pestle, pound the Thai chilies until fine, then add
the mild red peppers and garlic and pound into a rough paste.

If you're making fried eggs, make them now. In a small nonstick
frying pan, heat about ⅓ inch (8 mm) of oil over medium-high heat.
Test the temperature of the oil by adding a little piece of vegetable
scrap, like the garlic or pepper, and it should bubble excitedly right
away. Once the oil is hot, add 1 egg. The white should bubble up right
away. Using a spoon to occasionally baste the top of the egg with oil
to help it cook faster, cook for about 1 minute for a runny yolk, or
2 minutes for a set yolk. You want the white crispy and browned, so if
it's not browning, turn up the heat. Remove the egg from the pan and
drain on paper towel; repeat with the remaining eggs.

Place a wok on medium heat, then add the oil and garlic-chili paste.
Stir for about 2 minutes, until the smallest bits of garlic start to turn
golden.

Turn the heat up to high, add the ground pork, then quickly toss to
mix with the garlic-chili paste. Add the fish sauce and sugar, and keep
tossing and breaking up the pork until it is fully cooked.

Turn off the heat, then add the holy basil and cook just until wilted.
Taste and adjust the seasoning with fish sauce and sugar as needed.

Plate and serve with jasmine rice. If serving as a one-dish meal, place
the rice on a plate, spoon the pork over it, and top everything with the
fried egg.

Mushroom & Tofu Holy Basil Stir-Fry

Taohu Pad Gaprao | เต้าหู้ผัดกะเพรา

This vegan version of the ever so popular *pad gaprao* was an instant hit when I first made it. My unsuspecting carnivorous husband devoured it, and was surprised when I told him it was vegan. (Not even a drop of fish sauce??) Put it on top of hot jasmine rice and it's really all you need for a simple meal, but if you eat eggs, try serving it with a runny fried egg, the way we love to do it in Thailand.

———

Crumble the tofu with your hands into rough chunks that resemble cooked ground meat, then place them on a paper towel–lined plate to absorb excess moisture.

If the shiitake mushrooms have thick stems, cut them off, then slice the caps into ¼-inch (6 mm) slices.

Using a mortar and pestle, pound the Thai chilies until fine, then add the mild red peppers and garlic and pound into a rough paste.

Make the sauce in a small bowl by combining the soy sauce, seasoning sauce, and ½ teaspoon (2 ml) black soy sauce.

If you're making fried eggs, make them now following the instructions on page 122.

Place a wok on medium heat and add the oil and garlic-chili paste. Once the garlic is bubbling, keep stirring for about 2 minutes, until aromatic and the garlic starts to turn golden.

Add the onions and mushrooms, then turn the heat up to high and cook for 1 minute, until the mushrooms are wilted. Add the tofu, sauce, and sugar, then toss for 2 to 3 minutes, until any pooling liquid in the pan has dried up. If you want a darker color, add a little more black soy sauce.

Turn off the heat and add the basil, tossing just until wilted. Taste and adjust the seasoning with soy sauce and sugar as needed.

Plate and serve with jasmine rice. If serving as a one-dish meal, place the rice on a plate, spoon the tofu over it, and top everything with the fried egg.

SERVES 4

COOKING TIME: 20 minutes, plus 5 to 10 minutes if frying eggs

12 ounces (340 g) extra firm tofu, drained

4 ounces (120 g) fresh shiitake mushrooms

2 to 3 Thai chilies, or as many as you can handle

⅓ cup (40 g) chopped mild red peppers (see sidebar on p. 122)

7 cloves (35 g) garlic

2 tablespoons (30 ml) soy sauce

2 teaspoons (10 ml) Thai seasoning sauce

½ to 1 teaspoon (2 to 5 ml) black or dark soy sauce (optional)

Oil for frying eggs (optional)

4 eggs (optional, see note)

2 tablespoons (30 ml) neutral oil

¼ large (50 g) yellow onion, diced

2 teaspoons (10 ml) granulated sugar

1½ cups (20 g) holy basil or Italian basil leaves

Jasmine rice, for serving

Note: Pad gaprao *is typically paired with a fried egg when served as a one-dish meal. If serving as part of a multi-dish Thai meal, you can omit the egg.*

Glass Noodle Stir-Fry with Eggs & Asparagus

Woonsen Pad Kai Gub Naw Mai Farang | วุ้นเส้นผัดไข่กับหน่อไม้ฝรั่ง

SERVES 4
COOKING TIME: 20 minutes

2.8 ounces (80 g) dried glass noodles

½ pound (225 g) asparagus

3 tablespoons (30 ml) neutral oil

5 cloves (25 g) garlic, chopped

4 large eggs

½ teaspoon (2 ml) ground white pepper

Jasmine rice, for serving

SAUCE

¼ cup (60 ml) water or unsalted chicken stock

1 tablespoon (15 ml) granulated sugar

1 tablespoon (15 ml) oyster sauce

1 tablespoon (15 ml) soy sauce

1 tablespoon (15 ml) fish sauce

Note: The eggs are the only protein here, though you could substitute half of them with shrimp or ground pork, which is quite commonly done. But isn't it nice sometimes to not have to deal with raw meat for dinner?

In Thailand, we have a rustic, homey dish in which glass noodles are stir-fried with eggs and a vegetable called *cha-om*, or climbing wattle. It's a delicate needle-shaped green with a distinct flavor and aroma. Unable to get *cha-om* in Canada, I decided to try this dish with another vegetable with a distinct flavor—asparagus, sliced thinly to mimic the shape and tenderness of *cha-om*. While it doesn't taste the same, and the aroma is not nearly as strong as *cha-om*, it is just as lovable.

———

Soak the glass noodles in room temperature water for 7 to 10 minutes, until soft and pliable. Drain, then use scissors to cut the noodles into 3-inch (8 cm) sections.

Cut off about 1.5 inches (3.5 cm) from the bottom of the asparagus to remove the tough parts. If the asparagus are on the thicker side, thinly slice them on a sharp diagonal so you have elongated ovals at least 1 inch (2.5 cm) long, leaving the tip intact. If they are very thin, you can cut them into 2-inch (5 cm) sections.

Make the sauce by stirring together all the ingredients in a small bowl until the sugar is dissolved.

Place a wok or large nonstick skillet over medium-high heat and add the oil and garlic. Once the garlic is bubbling, stir until it turns golden.

Turn the heat up to high, then add the eggs. Break the yolks with your spatula, then let them cook undisturbed for about 15 seconds, until the whites are set on the underside. Scramble the eggs slightly, keeping them chunky and marbled.

Once the eggs are about halfway done, add the noodles, asparagus, and pepper, then drizzle the sauce on top of the noodles and toss everything together until the sauce is evenly distributed and absorbed.

Give the noodles a taste to see if they are done to your liking, and if you prefer them softer, add a splash of water and keep tossing until they're dry again. Turn off the heat, then taste and adjust the seasoning. Plate and serve with jasmine rice.

Scrambled Eggs for Dinner

One thing I noticed shortly after moving to Canada was that eggs rarely make an appearance on the dinner table. In Thailand, eggs are a staple ingredient in all our meals. We make salads, omelets, steamed egg custards—and we also scramble them into stir-fries, like in this dish. You're probably used to seeing eggs in fried rice and maybe fried noodles, but quite often we simply stir-fry vegetables, such as cucumber or kabocha squash, and scramble some eggs in at the end. The eggs absorb the sauce and become delicious, tender morsels, and make for an easy, no-fuss protein.

STEAMED, PAN-FRIED & ROASTED

Neung, Yaang, Ob | นึ่ง ย่าง อบ

When There is No Oven

I think of these recipes as "put them in and let them go" kind of dishes. In the West, these would be things you put into the oven, but since Thai people do not cook with ovens, these are foods that we steam or grill.

The steamer is our oven. It is what we use to cook large pieces of protein, such as a whole fish, and it is how we often cook our desserts. Grilling is not often done at home, so most grilled foods in Thailand are sold by restaurants or street vendors. But luckily grilling is much more accessible here with barbecues in most backyards, and at least a broiler in the oven that can get the job done in a pinch.

Pan-frying isn't something we do much of since traditionally we only use woks. My family didn't own skillets until much later when we started venturing into Western cooking. So there aren't really any Thai dishes that are supposed to be pan-fried, but I have modified a few recipes to be made in a skillet, as there really isn't a better tool for creating a good sear.

Steaming 101

If you have only ever steamed vegetables but not meats or whole dishes, here are some pointers for success. For more on steaming implements, see page 18.

- **Always preheat the steamer.** Just like the oven, you want the food to go into a hot chamber, so before cooking, bring the water to the temperature indicated in the recipe (boil, simmer, etc.). For most dishes, the water should be boiling.
- **Keep an eye on the water.** Having all the water boiled dry and the bottom of your pot scorched is not fun, but I also don't add an excessive amount of water as it takes forever to preheat. I usually start with about 2 inches of water.
- **Beware of steam burns.** You can put a baking sheet into a 350°F oven with bare arms and the dry hot air will not burn you in that short time. But the moist heat of a steamer transfers much more efficiently, which means it can burn you in seconds. When placing food into a steamer, always use oven mitts or steamer tongs.

3-Flavor Fish

Pla Raad Prik Saam Roht | ปลาราดพริกสามรส

Saam roht means "three flavors," which in this case refers to the sauce—it's sweet, salty, and sour in equal measure. It's an easy dish that looks impressive—a simple pan-seared fish drenched in a glossy red sauce. Traditionally, we deep-fry a whole fish for this, but I find that a well-seared fish, especially with its skin, is equally satisfying. I live in Vancouver, and lingcod is my favorite local species to serve with this sauce, but you can use any white fish that's tender and flaky, as long as it's got a thick enough meat to stand up to the flavorful sauce.

_____

If you're using fish that is thicker than 1 inch (2.5 cm), preheat the oven to 350°F (175°C) in case you need to finish cooking the fish in it.

Cut the cilantro sprigs in half, separating the part with leaves from the stems alone. Finely chop the stems, and set the leafy parts aside for garnishing.

Using a mortar and pestle, pound the cilantro stems, garlic, and peppercorns into a fine paste. Add the chilies and pound to form a rough paste. Add the bell peppers and crush gently just until the pepper pieces are smashed and some juices are released.

In a small pot over medium heat, pour in 1 tablespoon (15 ml) oil and cook the pounded pepper mixture for about 3 minutes, stirring constantly. Once the mixture has lost about half of its liquid, add the palm sugar, tamarind paste, and fish sauce. Keep cooking until the sugar is dissolved, then let the sauce simmer for 3 to 4 minutes to thicken to the consistency of a thin syrup.

Turn off the heat, then taste and adjust the seasoning as needed. If it is too strong, you can add a splash of water to dilute; if it is too weak, reduce the sauce a bit longer. Remember that this sauce will go on completely unseasoned fish, so its flavor should be quite strong on its own. Cover the pot while you fry the fish.

(Continued)

SERVES 4
COOKING TIME: 25 minutes

8 sprigs cilantro

6 cloves (30 g) garlic, chopped

½ teaspoon (2 ml) white peppercorns

1 to 2 Thai chilies, or to taste

¼ (70 g) red bell pepper, finely chopped

4 tablespoons (60 ml) neutral oil, divided

⅓ cup (65 g) finely chopped palm sugar, packed

3 to 4 tablespoons (45 to 60 ml) tamarind paste, store-bought or homemade (p. 266)

3 tablespoons (45 ml) fish sauce

1 pound (450 g) white fish fillet

¼ to ½ cup (38 to 75 g) all-purpose flour or cornstarch

Jasmine rice, for serving

Do-ahead: *Make the sauce up to 1 week in advance and keep in the fridge.*

Pat the fish dry with paper towel, then generously sprinkle it with flour, coating the fish on both sides. Shake off any excess flour so you have a thin, even coating.

Heat a large nonstick skillet over medium-high heat, then pour in enough oil so the bottom is thoroughly coated. When the oil is very hot, carefully place the fish, skin side up, into the pan, letting it drop away from you. There should be a loud, excited sizzling as soon as the fish touches the pan.

Fry the fish without moving it for 2 to 3 minutes, until it is well browned and about halfway cooked. Flip and cook on the other side for another 2 to 3 minutes. If you're using a thick fillet, you may need to finish it in the oven for about 5 minutes or so. Check the doneness of the fish either by carefully cutting open the center of the fillet with a dinner knife (the flesh should flake easily and look opaque) or inserting an instant-read thermometer into the center—the internal temperature should be a minimum of 145°F (63°C).

Place the cooked fish on a serving platter that has some depth to hold the sauce. Reheat the sauce if needed, and if it has dried out while it sat, you can also stir in a splash of water. Pour the sauce over the fish.

Chop the reserved cilantro leaves and sprinkle overtop to garnish. Serve with jasmine rice.

Three Friends

Saam roht has three flavors, but there's another trio hidden in the dish called *saam glur,* or "three friends." This is the pounded mixture of cilantro roots (or stems), garlic, and white peppercorns. It's essentially the Thai mirepoix, a flavor base for so many dishes, especially marinades and sauces. When I smell *saam glur* as I'm pounding them in my mortar, that is the smell of Thailand to me.

Steamed Prawns in Garlic Lime Sauce

Goong Neung Manao | กุ้งนึ่งมะนาว

Bright, tart, garlicky, fresh, this sauce is everything you want on fresh seafood. Don't eat prawns? Substitute any seafood here and it'll be fantastic. The most common version of this dish is done with a whole fish, and in Thailand, steaming a whole fish is part of everyday cooking, as you can find whole fish just about everywhere, and every kitchen has a large steamer. Here in North America, it is not always so easy to find whole fish, and I remember being shocked that I couldn't find it at non-Asian supermarkets! So making this dish with prawns simplifies things, but it's also common to use squid. Get the largest prawns you can find (or even lobster) for an elegant presentation.

———

Set up the steamer and bring the water to a full boil over high heat.

Place the prawns in a heatproof dish with enough depth to catch the liquid that will be released during cooking; a pie plate works well (note: this will be your serving dish). You can stack the prawns if needed, but keep the height even so that they cook in the same amount of time.

Make the sauce by adding the stock to a small pot and bringing it to a boil over high heat. Turn off the heat and add the garlic and chilies; stir for 30 seconds to allow the garlic to infuse into the stock. Stir in the sugar, lime juice, and fish sauce. Taste and adjust the seasoning as needed.

Steam the prawns for 4 to 8 minutes, until fully cooked. The timing will vary depending on the size of the prawns, so it's a good idea to check them early so as to not overcook them.

Carefully remove the prawns from the steamer and place the dish on a plate lined with moist paper towel for easier handling (the paper towel keeps it from sliding). You'll notice a lot of liquid around the prawns; spoon off 3 tablespoons (45 ml) and add it to the sauce, then pour or spoon off the rest and discard (it's okay to leave a little bit behind).

Stir the celery and cilantro into the sauce and pour it over the prawns, then garnish with celery leaves and cilantro.

Serve with jasmine rice and a generous helping of sauce.

SERVES 4
COOKING TIME: 20 minutes

1 pound (450 g) large prawns, at least 16/20 count, peeled and deveined (see note on p. 75)

½ cup (125 ml) unsalted chicken stock

6 cloves (30 g) garlic, finely chopped

1 to 2 Thai chilies, minced

1 tablespoon (12 g) finely chopped palm sugar, packed

3 tablespoons (45 ml) lime juice

2½ tablespoons (37 ml) fish sauce

½ cup (60 g) small-diced celery, plus an optional handful of celery leaves, for garnish

⅓ cup (80 ml) chopped cilantro, plus extra for garnish

Jasmine rice, for serving

Steamed Black Cod with Thai Miso

Pla Hima Neung Tao Jiew | ปลาหิมะนึ่งเต้าเจี้ยว

SERVES 4

COOKING TIME: 20 minutes

1 pound, 2 ounces (510 g) black cod steaks (see note)

4 teaspoons (20 ml) soy sauce, divided

1 tablespoon (15 ml) neutral oil

4 cloves (20 g) garlic, chopped

2-inch piece (24 g) ginger, finely julienned

¼ teaspoon (1 ml) ground white pepper

½ cup (125 ml) unsalted Thai-style chicken or pork stock, store-bought or homemade (p. 265)

2 tablespoons (30 ml) fermented soybean paste

1 tablespoon (15 ml) granulated sugar

1 green onion, chopped, white and green parts separated

Jasmine rice, for serving

Do-ahead tips: The sauce can be made up to a few days in advance and stored in the fridge until ready to use, then brought to a simmer before pouring onto the fish.

Note: If black cod is not available, use any mild, tender white fish.

In my biased opinion, no one does steamed fish better than Thai people. Although we don't have a huge variety of steamed fish dishes, we have a handful of sauces that are tried and true. This one is a favorite of mine for fatty fish like black cod. The generous amount of ginger and the sharp, salty fermented soybean paste cut the fat so perfectly. You can steam a whole fish if you like, but fish steaks are great and more manageable, since they don't require such a large steamer. Fillets work too, but steaming fish bone-in keeps the meat more moist and delicious.

Set up the steamer and bring the water to a full boil over high heat.

Place the fish on a heatproof dish with some depth for the sauce; a pie plate works well (note: this will be your serving dish). Drizzle 1 teaspoon (5 ml) soy sauce evenly onto the fish and spread it around with your fingers. Steam for 7 to 8 minutes, until the fish is cooked through.

While the fish steams, make the sauce. Put a small pot or a skillet over medium heat, then add the oil, garlic, ginger, and white pepper, and sauté for about 2 minutes, until the garlic starts to turn golden. Add the stock, fermented soybean paste, sugar, and the remaining soy sauce, and simmer for about 2 minutes to allow the garlic and ginger to infuse into the sauce. Remove from the heat and add the white part of the green onions.

Once the fish is done, carefully remove it from the steamer and place the dish on a plate lined with moist paper towel for easier handling (the paper towel keeps it from sliding). Spoon or pour off most of the collected water around the fish; it's okay to leave a little bit. For some fish, such as black cod, there will be pin bones that should be visible now that the fish is cooked. Use tweezers or your fingertips to pull them out; they should slide out easily—if they're sticking, it means the fish is not yet cooked through.

Pour the sauce over the fish. Top with the green part of the onions. Serve with jasmine rice.

Self-Saucing Steamed Pork with Ginger
Moo Sub Neung Taohu | หมูสับนึ่งเต้าหู้

Thai people use ground pork a *lot*. My fridge is always stocked with ground pork, and as soon as I run out, it immediately goes on the shopping list. This dish always seems a bit magical to me because you put a mess of ground pork into a bowl, but upon opening the steamer you find a beautiful patty sitting in an incredibly flavorful sauce that you'll want to drench your rice with. The soft tofu lightens and adds creaminess, which I love, but if you're serving veggies on the side, you can skip it.

———

Set up the steamer and bring the water to a full boil over high heat.

Finely mince 3 slices of ginger. Finely julienne the remaining 2 slices for garnish, and set aside.

In a small skillet, add the oil, garlic, and minced ginger, and sauté over medium heat for 2 to 3 minutes, until the garlic starts to turn golden. Add the mushrooms and sauté for 1 minute. Turn off the heat and transfer the mixture to a mixing bowl to cool slightly.

Add the pork to the mushroom mixture, then add the soy sauce, oyster sauce, Chinese cooking wine, sugar, pepper, and the white part of the onions. Mix just until well combined.

Taste the pork by cooking up a small chunk in the microwave or in the steamer, if it's ready, then adjust the seasoning as needed.

Place the pork in a heatproof dish with some depth to catch the sauce; a pie plate works well (note: this will be your serving dish). Shape the pork into a disk, about 1 inch (2.5 cm) thick, flattening the surface.

If using tofu, use your finger to make a deep hole in the pork, then put a piece of tofu into the hole so that it's sticking out the top slightly. Repeat with the remaining tofu pieces, spacing them out evenly.

(Continued)

SERVES 4
COOKING TIME: 30 minutes

5 thin slices (12 g) ginger

1 tablespoon (15 ml) neutral oil

3 cloves (15 g) garlic, finely chopped

1.7 ounces (50 g) fresh shiitake mushrooms, large stems removed, ¼-inch (6 mm) diced

12 ounces (340 g) ground pork, preferably not lean

1 tablespoon (15 ml) soy sauce

1 tablespoon (15 ml) oyster sauce

1 tablespoon (15 ml) Chinese cooking wine (optional, see note)

1 teaspoon (5 ml) granulated sugar

¼ teaspoon (1 ml) ground white pepper

1 to 2 green onions, chopped, white and green parts separated

5 ounces (150 g) soft tofu, cut in 1-inch (2.5 cm) cubes (optional)

Jasmine rice, for serving

Do-ahead: The pork can be mixed up to 1 day in advance and steamed when ready to serve.

Note: I use salted Chinese cooking wine, which is widely available, but if you have the unsalted kind, even better. You can also substitute dry sherry or sake. No need to add salt, as the salted wine isn't very salty.

Steam for about 15 minutes, until the pork is cooked through, or until an instant-read thermometer inserted in the center of the patty registers at least 165°F (74°C).

Turn off the heat, sprinkle the julienned ginger and the green part of the onions on top of the patty, then close the steamer for 30 seconds or so, to steam the onions briefly.

Carefully remove the dish from the steamer and place on a plate lined with moist paper towel for easier handling (the paper towel keeps it from sliding). Serve with jasmine rice.

A Love Letter to Ground Pork

Ground pork is easily my favorite meat to use because of its versatility and ease of use (no chopping? I'm in!). Unlike ground beef, the flavor is mild enough that it can be used in any recipe, but unlike ground chicken, it's fatty and flavorful and generally makes for more delicious dishes. We put it into omelets, use it for meatballs, and add it to stir-fries and even salads! And it's the perfect stuffing for just about anything that can be stuffed. When I was a kid, we ground the pork by hand, mincing it with a big cleaver. It was my favorite task in the kitchen—the rhythmic sound of the cleaver hitting the butcher's block reminds me of home to this day. If you don't eat pork and want to substitute ground chicken, be sure to use ground dark-meat chicken so it isn't too lean and dry.

Thai Pork Omelet

Kai Jiew Moo Sub | ไข่เจียวหมูสับ

If I had to choose a national dish for Thailand, this would be a strong contender. In its simplest form, it requires nothing but eggs and fish sauce, and yet it manages to be so delicious and nourishing for the soul. It is our "nothing else to eat" or "dorm life" dish, which can be found in every culture, I'm sure. You can omit the ground pork for a truly basic *kai jiew*, but the meat and green onion make for a more substantial meal that doesn't seem quite as desperate. You can get fancy by adding oyster sauce, chopped onion, or white pepper, but using only fish sauce is the original formula. I've provided recipes for two versions; the two-egg is perfect for a solo meal—for one of those alone and lazy nights—and it's also much easier to flip an 8-inch (20 cm) omelet than a larger one. The three-egg version is great for two people or for sharing as part of a bigger meal.

———

In a small mixing bowl, beat the eggs with a fork until no streaks of egg whites remain. Add the ground pork, fish sauce and green onions, and mix until the pork is all broken up.

Place a nonstick skillet over high heat and add the oil; there should be enough oil to evenly and generously coat the bottom. Wait for the oil to get very hot. Test the oil temperature by dropping a small amount of egg into the oil; it should puff up excitedly right away.

Pour the eggs into the pan and quickly scramble the center of the eggs for 5 to 8 seconds; this will allow the omelet to cook more evenly. Don't stir the edges, so that you keep a nice round shape, and don't stir for too long or you'll end up with scrambled eggs.

Turn the heat down to medium and cook the omelet for about 3 minutes, until the underside is well browned and it's set enough to flip; the top will still be a bit runny, which is okay.

Flip the omelet. If you're so inclined, toss the pan to flip the omelet in one piece. (A tip: if you've never pan-flipped before, this is not the dish to experiment with!) For a "safer" flip, use your spatula to cut the omelet into 3 wedges, like a pizza, then flip them with the spatula one piece at a time.

Cook the second side for about 2 minutes, until well browned and cooked through. Serve immediately with rice and hot sauce.

See image on page 142

SERVES 1 OR 2
COOKING TIME: 10 minutes

FOR A 3-EGG OMELET (10-INCH/25 CM SKILLET)

3 large eggs (see note)

4 ounces (115 g) ground pork (see note)

2 teaspoons (10 ml) fish sauce (see sidebar, p. 143)

1 green onion, chopped (optional)

3 tablespoons (45 ml) neutral oil

FOR A 2-EGG OMELET (8-INCH/20 CM SKILLET)

2 large eggs (see note)

2.5 ounces (75 g) ground pork (see note)

1¼ teaspoons (6 ml) fish sauce (see sidebar, p. 143)

1 small green onion, chopped (optional)

2 tablespoons (30 ml) neutral oil

FOR SERVING

Jasmine rice

Sriracha-style hot sauce

Notes: *If you are using different-sized eggs, you will need to adjust the amount of fish sauce accordingly. A large egg in North America weighs about 2 ounces (56 g).*

Ground chicken or shrimp can also be used.

For a meatless omelet, use 1 teaspoon (5 ml) fish sauce for every 2 large eggs.

Eye-Balling Fish Sauce
Most of the time, if I'm cooking for myself, I eyeball the ingredients, as I'm sure many of you do. But speaking from past experience, use measurements for the Thai Pork Omelet. It is so hard to get the right number of glugs of fish sauce, and because fish sauce is so potent, half the time I'd end up with an omelet that was too salty, which is frustrating and not really fixable. After too many salty omelets, I decided to stick to a formula. The ratio in this recipe is a good one to start with, but you may need to adjust depending on the brand of your fish sauce and the size of your eggs, or if you're adding other fillings.

Steamed Tofu Deluxe

Taohu Neung Song Kreuang | เต้าหู้นึ่งทรงเครื่อง

SERVES 4
COOKING TIME: 10 minutes

SAUCE

1½ tablespoons (22 ml) Chinese cooking wine (see note on p. 139)

1 tablespoon (15 ml) soy sauce

1 tablespoon (15 ml) fermented soybean paste

1½ teaspoons (7 ml) brown sugar

¼ teaspoon (1 ml) ground white pepper

10.5 ounces (300 g) soft tofu

1 tablespoon (15 ml) neutral oil

2 cloves (10 g) garlic, chopped

¼ medium (60 g) yellow onion, julienned

1-inch piece (12 g) ginger, julienned

⅓ medium (30 g) carrot, julienned

1.7 ounces (50 g) Asian mushrooms, such as shimeji, enoki, or shiitake

8 snow peas, julienned

Jasmine rice, for serving

Tofu in a Tube

I use soft tofu that is packaged in a square container, but you can also get one that comes in a tube. In fact, when I was growing up in Thailand, soft tofu only came in tubes, so when I discovered squared packages, I thought it rather novel. To get the tofu out of the tube, simply cut it in half with a sharp knife right through the packaging and slide the tofu out. Then, for this recipe, slice the tofu into 1½-inch (4 cm) thick pieces and arrange them on the heatproof dish you're using to steam.

In Thai, the term *song kreuang* is used to describe a version of a dish that has a lot of extra ingredients added so it looks, well, deluxe. Steamed tofu sounds rather plain, but with the abundance of colorful sautéed veggies around it, this is one of the most delicious and beautiful ways to eat tofu. Soft tofu becomes creamy when steamed, but what makes this dish special is the sauce. Salty, savory, and sweet, this meal is one even a meat eater will find truly satisfying.

——

Set up the steamer and bring the water to a full boil over high heat.

Make the sauce by combining the cooking wine, soy sauce, soybean paste, brown sugar, and white pepper in a small bowl; stir to dissolve the sugar.

Unmold the tofu into a heatproof dish with some depth for the sauce; a pie plate or a pasta bowl works well (note: this will be your serving dish).

Set aside 1 tablespoon (15 ml) sauce and pour the remaining sauce over the tofu. Steam the tofu for about 8 minutes, until hot all the way through.

While the tofu steams, cook the vegetables. Place a wok or skillet on medium heat and add the oil, garlic, onions, and ginger. Sauté until the onions are wilted and the garlic is golden, 2 to 3 minutes. Add the carrots, mushrooms, snow peas, and reserved sauce and stir until the vegetables are cooked, 1 to 2 minutes. Turn off the heat but keep the veggies in the pan while you wait for the tofu to steam.

Once the tofu is done, turn off the heat and carefully remove it from the steamer. Place the dish on a plate lined with a moist paper towel for easier handling (the paper towel keeps it from sliding). You'll notice there is a lot more liquid in the tofu bowl now; use a spoon to gently stir the sauce, then give it a taste. It should be very flavorful, since the tofu is mild, but if it tastes too salty, you can add a splash of water to dilute.

Arrange the vegetables on top of and around the tofu and serve with jasmine rice.

Tom Yum Mussels

Hoi Malang Pu Tom Yum | หอยแมลงภู่ต้มยำ

I credit the idea for this recipe to my best friend, Byron, who started steaming mussels in *tom yum* broth. It's a brilliant combination. It's as if the tart and citrusy flavors, plus the slight sweetness from the chili paste, were specifically made for mussels. Even if you don't have Thai chili paste, this recipe still works with an extra touch of sugar and some added tomatoes for umami. Usually, I'd say to serve with rice, but with this dish I love soaking a toasted crusty sourdough in the broth.

——

Thinly slice 1 stalk of lemongrass and set aside. Smash the second stalk until broken, then cut into 2-inch (5 cm) chunks. (I don't slice all of it, in order to keep the broth less "cluttered.")

In a large pot with a lid, combine the stock, shallots, chunks of lemongrass, galangal, chilies, fish sauce, and 1 tablespoon (15 ml) Thai chili paste. Twist the makrut lime leaves to bruise them and release their aroma before tearing them into big chunks and adding to the pot, discarding any big center stems. Cover and simmer over medium heat for 4 to 5 minutes.

Add the reserved sliced lemongrass and the mussels, then cover the pot and cook for about 2 minutes, until the mussels open. If any are not open, cook them for another 30 seconds, and if they still do not open, discard them.

Turn off the heat, then add 3 tablespoons (45 ml) lime juice and swirl the pot around to mix. Taste the broth and adjust the seasoning with more lime juice and fish sauce as needed. If it needs more sweetness or a more robust flavor, add more chili paste. It's important to taste and adjust, because the mussels will release different amounts of liquid, so each batch will be different.

Stir in the cilantro, transfer to a serving bowl, and serve with crusty sourdough toast. You can remove the lemongrass, galangal, and lime leaves before serving, or if leaving them in, tell your guests they are not meant to be eaten.

SERVES 4

COOKING TIME: 7 minutes

2 stalks lemongrass, bottom halves only

1¾ cups (435 ml) unsalted Thai-style chicken or pork stock, store-bought or homemade (p. 265)

½ cup (50 g) julienned shallots

8 thin slices (20 g) galangal

2 to 3 Thai chilies, crushed

1½ tablespoons (22 ml) fish sauce

1 to 2 tablespoons (15 to 30 ml) Thai chili paste, store-bought or homemade (p. 258)

5 makrut lime leaves

2 pounds (1 kg) live mussels, cleaned and debearded

3 to 4 tablespoons (45 to 60 ml) lime juice

10 sprigs cilantro, chopped

Crusty sourdough toast, for serving

Baked Thai BBQ Chicken

Gai Yang Tao Ob | ไก่ย่างเตาอบ

For many Thais, no other meat on the grill hits the spot quite like *gai yang*, served with sticky rice and *nam jim jeaw* as a dipping sauce. In Thailand, the chickens are grilled whole and spatchcocked, then chopped up into parts when served. For many years in Canada, I had no grill, so I oven-roasted my *gai yang*, and I always found it perfectly satisfying because the marinade is incredible no matter how you cook the chicken. Using chicken thighs instead of a whole chicken reduces the cooking time without sacrificing any flavor. This is a recipe to prep in advance because of the marinating time, but I've included a speedy version here that involves only 30 minutes of marinating time (see sidebar, p. 150), because sometimes you just really need *gai yang* right away.

———

Cut the cilantro sprigs in half, separating the part with leaves from the stems alone. Finely chop the stems, and set the leafy parts aside for the dipping sauce.

Make the marinade by grinding the coriander seeds and peppercorns into a powder with a mortar and pestle. Add the cilantro stems and garlic, and pound into a fine paste. Add the lemongrass and pound into a rough paste. Scrape it into a small mixing bowl.

To the herb paste, add the sugar, soy sauce, fish sauce, black soy sauce, and water (omit the water if speed-marinating; see sidebar, p. 150); stir until the sugar is dissolved.

Place the chicken in a large freezer bag or a casserole dish that's just large enough to fit the chicken in one layer. Pour the marinade over the chicken and toss the pieces to coat well. Seal the bag or cover the dish and marinate for at least 2 hours or overnight, flipping the chicken halfway through to ensure even marinating.

Preheat the oven to 400°F (200°C), or 375°F (190°C) on convection, and set the rack in the middle. Line a roasting pan with aluminum foil or parchment paper for easier cleanup, and place a rack on top of it. Remove the chicken pieces from the marinade, shaking off any excess and discarding the marinade, and put them on the rack, skin side up, making sure they are not touching each other. Roast for 20 minutes, then once the skin is dry, pull them out of the oven and brush the skin with some neutral oil, which will help it brown and shine. Roast for another 15 to 25 minutes, until the internal temperature reaches 175°F (80°C).

(Continued)

SERVES 4
COOKING TIME: 40 minutes, plus at least 30 minutes of marinating

6 to 7 cilantro sprigs

2 teaspoons (10 ml) toasted coriander seeds

1½ teaspoons (7 ml) white peppercorns

5 cloves (25 g) garlic

2 tablespoons (15 g) minced lemongrass, from bottom half only

1 tablespoon (15 ml) granulated sugar

3 tablespoons (45 ml) soy sauce

2 tablespoons (30 ml) fish sauce

1 to 2 teaspoons (5 to 10 ml) black soy sauce

½ cup (125 ml) water

8 chicken thighs (2½ pounds/1.2 kg), bone-in, skin-on

1 to 2 tablespoons (15 to 30 ml) neutral oil, for brushing

Sticky rice (p. 238) or jasmine rice, for serving

JEAW DIPPING SAUCE (NAM JIM JEAW)

1 tablespoon (15 ml) uncooked jasmine rice

2 tablespoons (15 g) minced shallots

2 tablespoons (30 ml) tamarind paste, store-bought or homemade (p. 266)

1 tablespoon (15 ml) fish sauce

1 tablespoon (15 ml) lime juice

1 tablespoon (12 g) finely chopped palm sugar, packed

¼ to ½ teaspoon (1 to 2 ml) roasted chili flakes, store-bought or homemade (p. 263), or to taste

Do-ahead: *Marinate the chicken up to 1 day in advance. You can also make the dipping sauce 1 day in advance, but add the toasted rice powder and cilantro close to serving time.*

While the chicken roasts, make the dipping sauce. In a dry skillet, toast the uncooked rice over medium-high heat, moving it constantly, until the rice has a dark-brown color, about 5 minutes. Grind into a powder using a coffee grinder or mortar and pestle.

In a small bowl, combine the shallots, tamarind paste, fish sauce, lime juice, palm sugar, and chili flakes; stir until the sugar is mostly dissolved. Don't worry about a few stubborn chunks; they'll have dissolved by the time you need the sauce. When ready to serve, chop the reserved cilantro and stir it into the sauce along with the toasted rice powder.

Allow the chicken to rest for 10 minutes before serving. Serve with sticky rice and dipping sauce. Note: *Nam jim jeaw* is intense, and a little bit goes a long way. So a drizzle or a dip is sufficient; don't pour it on like gravy!

Speed-Marinating

Even though *gai yang* tastes best when you marinate it for at least 2 hours, it is possible to do it in only 30 minutes. Omit the water from the recipe to make the marinade more concentrated, and increase the fish sauce to 3 tablespoons (45 ml). With less liquid to go around, make sure you flip the chicken halfway through for even distribution. While it's marinating and roasting, you'll have plenty of time to make the sauce and the rice.

No-Skewer Chicken Satay

Gai Sa Te | ไก่สะเต๊ะ

It took a lot of self-convincing for me to include a recipe for chicken satay, because for years I've been preaching about the fact that 99% of satays in Thailand are pork, not chicken. But it occurred to me that if you're going to cook boneless, skinless chicken breasts one way or another, the satay treatment is one of the best things you can do to this otherwise unexciting protein. I've omitted the most dreaded part of satay, the skewering, which instantly makes this weeknight-friendly. Throw the chicken on the grill if you have one, or pan-sear indoors. The *ajaad*, or quick pickles, are extra but a nice contrast to a rich dish, though you can also eat this with any tart pickles you already have in the fridge.

―――――

FOR THE MARINADE

Grind the coriander seeds, cumin seeds, and peppercorns with a coffee grinder or mortar and pestle until very fine, then transfer to a mixing bowl. Add the brown sugar, salt, turmeric, cinnamon, tamarind paste, and coconut milk; stir to mix well.

Add the chicken to the marinade and mix very well to ensure all the pieces are coated. Marinate at room temperature for 20 minutes or cover and refrigerate for up to 1 day. The longer it marinates, the better—just stir it once or twice during the marinating time.

FOR THE PEANUT SAUCE

Using a mortar and pestle or a food processor, grind the peanuts until mealy. If using a machine, be careful not to turn them into peanut butter; you want texture in the peanut sauce.

Put about ⅓ cup (80 ml) coconut milk in a small pot and bring to a boil over medium heat. Add the curry paste and cook for about 3 minutes, stirring constantly until the mixture is very thick and the coconut oil starts to separate from the paste (the oil may not separate depending on the coconut milk you're using; this is okay).

(Continued)

SERVES 4

COOKING TIME: 40 minutes, plus at least 20 minutes of marinating

MARINADE

1½ teaspoons (7 ml) coriander seeds

½ teaspoon (2 ml) cumin seeds

½ teaspoon (2 ml) white peppercorns

1 tablespoon (15 ml) brown sugar

¾ teaspoon (3 ml) table salt

¾ teaspoon (3 ml) ground turmeric

½ teaspoon (2 ml) ground cinnamon

1 tablespoon (15 ml) tamarind paste, store-bought or homemade (p. 266)

½ cup (125 ml) coconut milk

2 large boneless, skinless chicken breasts (1.2 pounds/550 g), cut in long ½-inch (1.2 cm) thick strips

Jasmine rice and/or white toast, for serving (see p. 152)

PEANUT SAUCE

½ cup (70 g) unsalted roasted peanuts

1¼ cups (310 ml) coconut milk, divided

2 tablespoons (30 ml) red curry paste, store-bought or homemade (p. 255)

2 tablespoons (30 ml) tamarind paste, store-bought or homemade (p. 266)

2 tablespoons (24 g) finely chopped palm sugar, packed

1 to 2 teaspoons (5 to 10 ml) fish sauce

AJAAD—QUICK CUCUMBER PICKLE, (OPTIONAL)

½ cup (125 ml) white vinegar

¼ cup (50 g) granulated sugar

Pinch of table salt

5 ounces (150 g) cucumber

1 to 2 Thai chilies, chopped (optional)

Do-ahead: *The sauce can be made in advance and kept in the fridge for at least 1 week. The chicken can be marinated 1 day in advance, and the pickle brine made in advance.*

You Want Toast with That?

In Thailand, it is common to serve satay with a piece of white toast. While it's not necessary, I don't feel satay is complete without it, because dipping the toast in the sauce between bites of meat is my favorite part of satay. And you'll likely have some leftover sauce, so you're going to need to eat it with something! I've even tried this as an open-faced sandwich—piling the chicken, the sauce, and the pickles on top of a piece of toasted hearty bread—and it was brilliant.

Add the remaining coconut milk and stir to mix well. Add the peanuts, tamarind paste, and palm sugar, and simmer gently for 5 minutes, stirring frequently, until thickened into a dip consistency. Be sure to scrape the bottom of the pot when stirring to prevent scorching. If the sauce gets too thick before 5 minutes of cooking time is up, add a splash of water so that you can give it the full 5 minutes to develop the flavor.

Taste and add fish sauce as needed. If it tastes a little flat, add a bit more tamarind paste to bump up the acidity.

FOR THE AJAAD

In a small pot, combine the vinegar, sugar, and salt. Cook over medium heat just until the sugar is completely dissolved. Let cool completely.

Cut the cucumber in half lengthwise, then thinly slice crosswise so you get half-moon pieces. Place the cucumber and chilies in a small serving bowl and pour the cooled vinegar mixture overtop. Keep covered until ready to serve. Don't combine the cucumber with the pickling liquid more than 30 minutes before serving, as it's best when the cucumbers are still fresh and firm.

COOKING THE CHICKEN

To grill: Preheat the grill on high heat, then arrange the chicken perpendicular to the grates, discarding the marinade. Cook with the lid open for 2 to 3 minutes, then flip and cook on the other side for another 2 minutes or until cooked through. The internal temperature should reach 165°F (74°C).

To pan-fry: Place a large nonstick skillet over high heat. Pour in enough oil to thinly coat the bottom. Once hot, use tongs to lift the chicken strips one piece at a time, shaking off any excess marinade, and place them in the pan. You'll need to do this in batches so you don't crowd the pan. Turn the heat down to medium-high and let the chicken sear until well browned, 2 to 3 minutes, then flip and sear on the other side until fully cooked, about another 2 minutes. Remove from the pan and repeat with the remaining chicken, discarding the marinade.

Serve the chicken with the peanut sauce for dipping, with the pickles and jasmine rice and/or toast on the side.

Isaan Steak Dinner

Neua Yang Jim Jeaw Makeua Ted | เนื้อย่างจิ้มแจ่วมะเขือเทศ

SERVES 4
COOKING TIME: 30 minutes

4 steaks, cut of your choice

Salt and ground black pepper

Sticky rice, for serving

**ISAAN-STYLE TOMATO DIPPING SAUCE
(JEAW MAKEUA TED)**

1 tablespoon (15 ml) uncooked jasmine or
   sticky rice

2 tablespoons (15 g) minced shallots

2 tablespoons (30 ml) tamarind paste,
   store-bought or homemade (p. 266)

1 tablespoon (15 ml) fish sauce

1 tablespoon (15 ml) lime juice

1 tablespoon (12 g) finely chopped palm
   sugar, packed

¼ to ½ teaspoon (1 to 2 ml) roasted chili
   flakes, or to taste

⅓ cup (60 g) diced tomatoes

6 to 7 sprigs cilantro or mint leaves, chopped

In my house, on our low-energy days, we slap a steak on the barbecue or in the frying pan. No chopping, just salt and pepper, and done. Sound boring? That's because I haven't told you yet about the dipping sauce: *nam jim jeaw,* a classic sauce from northeastern Thailand (Isaan) that we use for all manner of grilled meat. Let me tell you, gravy's got nothing on *jeaw.* Add sticky rice and, if you're so inclined, make a pounded salad like the cabbage slaw on page 65, and you've got a perfect Isaan steak dinner. I've added fresh tomatoes to this version of *jeaw* because the tomato chunks add some freshness to each bite of steak that I really love.

———

Take the steaks out of the fridge up to 1 hour before cooking. If you've got at least 45 minutes before you need to start cooking, season the steak with salt and pepper. If you have less than 45 minutes, leave the salting until right before cooking. Salting for less than 45 minutes will draw out moisture from the steaks but it won't have time to seep back in.

To make the dipping sauce, toast the uncooked rice in a dry skillet over medium-high heat, moving it constantly, until the rice has a dark-brown color, about 5 minutes. Grind into a powder using a coffee grinder or mortar and pestle. Set aside.

In a small bowl, combine the shallots, tamarind paste, fish sauce, lime juice, sugar, and chili flakes; stir until the sugar is mostly dissolved. Don't worry about a few stubborn chunks; they'll have dissolved by the time you need the sauce.

You can cook the steaks however you usually do, to whatever doneness you like. If grilling, oil the steaks beforehand and grill on high heat, uncovered. If pan-frying, use high heat and add enough oil to generously coat the bottom of the pan, for even browning. A cook time of 5 to 6 minutes will get you to about medium doneness for a 1-inch (2.5 cm) thick steak, and I flip the steak every 1½ minutes for even cooking. Rest the steaks for at least 5 minutes before cutting, 10 minutes if the steak is large.

While the steaks rest, finish the sauce by stirring in the toasted rice powder, tomatoes, and cilantro or mint to taste.

If you want to serve the steaks Thai style, slice them into thin pieces and serve with sticky rice and the dipping sauce. Note: *Nam jim jeaw* is intense, and a little goes a long way. So a drizzle or a dip is sufficient; don't pour it on like gravy!

Seared Scallops with Tom Yum Sauce

Hoi Shell Raad Sauce Tom Yum | หอยเชลล์ราดซอสต้มยำ

SERVES 4

COOKING TIME: 10 minutes

2 to 3 tablespoons (30 to 45 ml) neutral oil

1 pound (450 g) scallops (see note)

¼ cup (30 g) julienned shallots

1 tablespoon (7 g) minced galangal (optional)

1 to 2 Thai chilies, minced

1 stalk (20 g) lemongrass, bottom half only, thinly sliced

5 makrut lime leaves

¼ cup (60 ml) unsalted chicken stock or water

1½ tablespoons (22 ml) fish sauce

1 tablespoon (15 ml) Thai chili paste, store-bought or homemade (p. 258)

1 teaspoon (5 ml) granulated sugar

1½ tablespoons (22 ml) lime juice

Chopped cilantro, for garnish (optional)

Jasmine rice, for serving

Notes: *Ideally, you want scallops that are about 16 pieces to a pound, which are about 1½ inches (4 cm) in diameter when raw. Larger ones are okay, but they will take longer to cook. Avoid small scallops, as they are not meaty enough to withstand the strong flavors of the sauce.*

A Little Less Fancy

If there are no occasions to justify scallops, this sauce works wonderfully with other seafood too, like big, juicy shrimp, pan-seared fish, or squid. Even chicken will work. In fact, once you've made the sauce, it's likely that you'll want to put it on everything!

Over the years, I have shared many a *tom yum* recipe, from various versions of the traditional soup to *tom yum* pizza. *Tom yum* is my favorite flavor for instant noodles, chips, and pretzel sticks. You might say I'm a little obsessed, but this is true of many Thai people, not just me! This dish is the most elegant *tom yum* dish I've ever made. So luxe, yet so easy and quick, perfect for a special occasion that you might not have much time to prep for, like a weeknight anniversary dinner. For a side dish pairing, I suggest some sautéed Asian mushrooms, such as oyster or shimeji. Because mushrooms are usually a must-have in a traditional *tom yum*, they would go very well together.

Place a 12-inch (30 cm) skillet over high heat and pour in just enough oil to coat the bottom of the pan. Once the oil is hot, add the scallops, one at a time, without them touching each other; they should sizzle excitedly right away. Turn the heat down to medium-high and sear the scallops until the underside is browned, about 2 minutes. Flip and cook the other side for 1 to 2 minutes, to medium doneness; looking at the scallops from the side, you should still see a small band of translucent meat in the center.

Turn off the heat and transfer the scallops to a plate; don't pile them into a bowl or they will steam each other and you'll lose that nice browned crust.

In the same pan, turn the heat to medium and add the shallots, galangal, chilies, and lemongrass. Twist the makrut lime leaves to bruise them, then tear them into big chunks and add them to the pan, discarding any big center stems. Sauté the mixture for 2 to 3 minutes, until the shallots are soft and translucent.

Deglaze the pan with the stock, then add the fish sauce, chili paste, and sugar. The scallops should have released some liquid as they sat; pour this tasty liquid into the sauce and stir to mix. Simmer the sauce for about 1 minute to infuse the flavors of the herbs into the liquid.

Turn off the heat and stir in the lime juice. Taste and adjust the seasoning as needed, and if it is too strong, add more stock or water to dilute.

Pour the sauce onto a serving plate and arrange the scallops overtop. Garnish with cilantro and serve with jasmine rice.

VEGETABLES

Pak | ผัก

Vegetables, Thai Style

The recipes in this chapter are tasty vegetable side dishes that you can add to any meal, Thai or not. They're mostly stir-fries because that's how we usually cook vegetable-only dishes in Thailand.

In addition to these recipes, I also want to share a few more ideas for cooking vegetables that you might not have thought to try, because over the years that I've lived in Canada, I've noticed many things Thai people do with vegetables that are not commonly done here.

- **Cook your cucumber.** In North America, cucumbers seem to be used either raw or pickled. I'm not sure why, because they cook up beautifully, just like their cousin, the zucchini. In Thailand they are commonly stir-fried, such as in Sweet and Sour Pork (p. 118), and added to soups. You can cook them for just a few minutes to maintain their crunch, but in soups we like to let them simmer until soft and luscious. Mini cucumbers are preferred, as those are what we use in Thailand, but English cucumber will do.

- **Cook your lettuce.** The humble green leaf and romaine lettuces can be cooked like any other leafy greens. In Asia, they're often added to soups, but they can also be quickly stir fried. Try using romaine lettuce instead of napa cabbage in the Glass Noodle Soup with Pork Meatballs (p. 98).

- **Use beansprouts as the star.** I mostly see beansprouts used as the default vegetables in noodle dishes such as *pho* or *pad thai*, but they can be the star of the dish. In my family we often make a beansprouts stir-fry with garlic and a sauce similar to my Universal Stir Fry Sauce (p. 261), with or without meat. They also don't need to be chopped, which is perfect for a weeknight!

- **Use kabocha squash more often.** The go-to squash of North America appears to be butternut squash, but I promise you that kabocha has butternut beat in every way. It is sweeter, creamier, *and* you can eat the skin which saves you time and is more nutritious. It can be roasted, stir-fried, simmered, and used in desserts. Try the Kabocha Squash Stir Fry (p. 174), or use it instead of pumpkin purée in your baking.

Green Beans Stir-Fried with Chili Paste

Tua Fak Yao Pad Nam Prik Pao | ถั่วฝักยาวผัดน้ำพริกเผา

For a long time I was searching for an easy go-to recipe for green beans, because they're always available and inexpensive, and they make a substantial veggie side to any meal. But I've always found green beans a bit unsatisfying, since they don't absorb any sauce, so most of the time they just end up tasting like . . . beans, which is hardly exciting. So my solution was to make a sauce so intense that even just a little bit that clings onto the waxy skin adds a lot of character. Thai chili paste to the rescue! In Thailand, we would use long beans, which have a nuttier flavor and are less watery than the typical green beans sold in North America, so use those if you can find them. The optional fried shallots add a fantastic crunch, and you can buy them at many Asian markets, though if you have time, homemade ones do taste better.

———

FOR THE FRIED SHALLOTS

Halve the shallots vertically through the root, then trim off the root end far enough for the layers to come apart. Slice the layers lengthwise as evenly as possible. If the shallots are very large, halve them cross-wise as well.

Line a large plate or baking sheet with paper towel and spread out the shallots in a single layer. Lightly but evenly sprinkle salt over the shallots and then let them sit for about 10 minutes; the salt will draw out moisture from the shallots, which will help them fry faster. Once the water has been pulled out and the shallots look wet, dry them off as much as possible with a paper towel. You may need to dry them twice if the first piece of paper towel gets soaked.

In a wok or pot, add just enough oil to submerge all the shallots. Turn the heat to medium and add a test piece of shallot to the oil. Once this piece has a constant stream of bubbles, add the remaining shallots and turn the heat down to medium-low.

Keep frying, stirring frequently and maintaining the heat so the bubbling is not too aggressive. The bubbling will naturally slow down as the shallots become crispy. (See sidebar on page 162.)

Once the shallots are browned and the bubbling has mostly subsided, remove them with a mesh skimmer or slotted spoon and drain on paper towels. Cool completely and, if not using right away, store in an airtight container. To ensure they stay crispy while stored, fry them until they're 100% dry.

(Continued)

SERVES 4

COOKING TIME: 8 minutes plus 20 minutes if making fried shallots

FRIED SHALLOTS (OPTIONAL)

As many shallots as you want

Table salt

Neutral oil, for frying

SAUCE

2 tablespoons (30 ml) Thai chili paste, store-bought or homemade (p. 258)

1 tablespoon (15 ml) soy sauce

2 teaspoons (10 ml) fish sauce

2 tablespoons (30 ml) neutral oil

5 cloves (25 g) garlic, chopped

12 ounces (340 g) green beans or long beans, cut in 2-inch (5 cm) pieces

3 tablespoons (20 g) fried shallots, store-bought or homemade (optional)

Jasmine rice, for serving

Do-ahead: Make the fried shallots in advance, if using, and store in an airtight container in the fridge indefinitely. The sauce can be made in bulk and kept in the fridge indefinitely.

Make the sauce by combining all the ingredients in a small bowl.

Place a wok on medium heat and add the oil and the garlic. Sauté until the garlic starts to turn golden. Turn the heat up to high, then add the beans and a splash of water. Stir for 1 minute.

Add the sauce and keep stirring until the beans are cooked to your liking, about 2 minutes. If the sauce dries up too quickly, add a splash of water. Don't add too much water, though, as you want the sauce to be thick in the end.

Turn off the heat and taste the sauce; depending on the brand of Thai chili paste you're using, you may need to add a touch of granulated sugar.

Plate and top with the fried shallots. Serve with jasmine rice.

The Secret to Crispy Shallots

The reason foods get crispy is that they are dry. So the secret to making crispy shallots is to fry them until they have no moisture left. How would you know this? The hint is in the bubbling. Foods bubble in frying oil because their moisture evaporates into steam as it is heated. If the food is no longer bubbling, there is no more moisture. This can be tricky, though, because if the heat is too high, the shallots will brown too much before they have time to crisp. If the heat is too low, too much oil will seep inside the shallots and they'll become greasy and soggy. Keeping the shallots bubbling not too aggressively and not too weakly is a good rule of thumb, but it does take practice and experience.

Garlicky Cabbage Fish Sauce Stir-Fry

Galum Plee Pad Nam Pla | กะหล่ำปลีผัดน้ำปลา

SERVES 4

COOKING TIME: 8 minutes

8 cloves (40 g) garlic

1 to 2 tablespoons (15 to 30 ml) neutral oil

6 cups (300 g) bite-sized Chinese cabbage pieces (see note)

1½ tablespoons (22 ml) fish sauce (see note)

Ground white or black pepper, to taste (optional)

Jasmine rice, for serving

Notes: While regular green cabbage will work, Chinese cabbage has more delicate leaves and a sweeter flavor. Their shape is more squat than round, and you can find them at Chinese supermar-

kets. Cut thicker parts into smaller pieces.

Use a good-quality fish sauce, such as Red Boat, Mega Chef, or Squid, for this recipe, as it is the only sauce used.

This dish went viral for a while in Thailand, and it was quite astounding because it's just a simple plate of cabbage, cooked in the most basic way. But once you try it, you'll understand the wonder. How could a plate of cabbage possibly be this delicious? I never thought cabbage could be good on its own. As a slaw drenched in a tasty dressing, sure. As a component of something more complex, sure. But as just . . . cabbage? Turns out, the magic is in my favorite ingredient: fish sauce. The chunky pieces of garlic help too, so don't skimp on that. It's a great side to any Thai meal but, honestly, just give me some hot jasmine rice with it and it's all I need for a great light lunch.

———

Lightly smash the garlic with a mortar and pestle until it breaks into large chunks. Alternatively, you can crush the cloves with the flat side of your knife and then coarsely chop into large chunks.

Place a wok on medium heat and pour in just enough oil to coat the bottom. Add the garlic right away (no need to wait for the oil to get hot), and keep stirring until the edges start to turn golden, about 2 minutes.

Turn the heat up to high and add the cabbage, then toss to get the leaves coated in oil. Drizzle the fish sauce over the cabbage, add the pepper, and keep tossing for 1 to 2 more minutes, just until the thinner leaves are wilted but the thicker parts are still crisp.

Remove from the heat, plate, and garnish with an extra sprinkling of pepper, if desired. Serve immediately with jasmine rice. Enjoy!

Bok Choy Stir-Fry with Thai Miso

Pak Gwang Toong Pad Tao Jiew | ผักกวางตุ้งผัดเต้าเจี้ยว

Do you ever get all excited about some lush greens at the store, bring them home, then every time you open the fridge, you're completely uninspired by them? Then two weeks later you end up doing something boring just to save them? This happened to me a lot with baby bok choy because they always look so cute on the shelves, but they don't really have much to offer in terms of flavor. Then I realized that I can use *pad pak boong* sauce on them, and that changed everything. *Pad pak boong* is a water spinach stir-fry that is arguably the most popular vegetable dish in Thailand, and the secret is in the salty, umami *tao jiew*, or fermented soybean paste. Oh, and lots of garlic.

———

Halve the bok choy lengthwise through the root so the leaves stay attached. If working with larger ones, you may need to quarter them. Dry them off as much as you can to prevent the stir-fry from being too watery.

Make the sauce by combining all the ingredients in a small bowl.

Pound the garlic and chilies with a mortar and pestle briefly, just until they are broken into big chunks.

Place a wok on medium heat and add the oil and the smashed garlic and chilies. Sauté gently for about 2 minutes, until the garlic is golden. Don't use high heat at this stage—you want the garlic chunks to have time to cook and soften before they brown.

Turn the heat up to high, then add the bok choy and toss for 30 seconds. Add the sauce mixture and sugar; toss for about 1 minute, or just until the bok choy are heated through and wilted. Don't cook them for too long or they will release too much water and they will continue to wilt as they sit.

Transfer the bok choy to a shallow serving bowl, top with freshly ground pepper, and serve with jasmine rice.

SERVES 4
COOKING TIME: 10 minutes

1 pound (450 g) baby bok choy

7 cloves (35 g) garlic

1 to 3 Thai chilies, to taste (optional)

2 tablespoons (30 ml) neutral oil

1 teaspoon (5 ml) granulated sugar

Freshly ground white pepper, to taste

Jasmine rice, for serving

SAUCE

1 tablespoon (15 ml) fermented soybean paste

1 tablespoon (15 ml) oyster sauce

2 teaspoons (10 ml) soy sauce

Does That Sauce Need Thickening?
When I make a stir-fry, I am sometimes asked why I don't thicken the sauce with a cornstarch slurry. It's an understandable question, given that many people are first exposed to stir-fries through Chinese cuisine, which often uses starch-thickened sauce. Thai stir-fry sauces are never thickened, and because we always serve them with rice, the sauce is absorbed by the rice and doesn't go anywhere. You might also have noticed that Thai sauces in general are rarely thick and heavy, and very few things are thickened with starch.

Vegan Five-Spice Roasted Brussels Sprouts

Galum Dao Kua Prik Gleua | กะหล่ำดาวคั่วพริกเกลือ

Growing up in Thailand, I had never seen or heard of Brussels sprouts, and when I came to Canada I was enamored with how cute these tiny cabbages are! They intrigue me because they can be so awful when cooked badly, yet so delicious when done right, and I have always enjoyed the challenge of coming up with unique ways to make them delicious. This recipe was an instant winner. The slight sweetness is key to softening the bitterness of the sprouts, and the subtle aroma of five-spice is the magic touch. The fried garlic is the real hero here, though, so don't skip that. Warning: these are hard to stop eating!

⎯⎯⎯⎯

Preheat the oven to 425°F (220°C) and set a rack in the middle.

Meanwhile, fry the garlic. Place a metal sieve over a large, heatproof mixing bowl. Place a wok on medium heat and add the oil and a small piece of garlic as your test piece. Once the garlic is bubbling, add the remaining garlic and cook, stirring frequently, until golden. Pour the garlic and oil into the sieve, letting the oil drain into the mixing bowl.

Add the Brussels sprouts to the garlic oil, add the salt, and toss thoroughly. Place the sprouts on a baking sheet, cut side down, spreading them out so they are not touching each other. Do not wash the bowl just yet.

Roast the sprouts in the oven for about 15 minutes, until they are well browned on the underside and the tenderness is to your liking. Check the tenderness by poking a sprout with a fork.

Meanwhile, stir together the sugar, five-spice powder, and pepper in a small bowl.

As soon as the sprouts are cooked, return them to the mixing bowl, then sprinkle the five-spice mixture, soy sauce, and chilies overtop; toss to mix well.

Plate the sprouts, sprinkle the fried garlic overtop, and serve.

SERVES 4

COOKING TIME: 30 minutes

3 tablespoons (45 ml) neutral oil

8 cloves (40 g) garlic, chopped

1 pound (450 g) Brussels sprouts, halved or quartered if large (see note)

½ teaspoon (2 ml) table salt

1 teaspoon (5 ml) granulated sugar

¼ teaspoon (1 ml) five-spice powder, store-bought or homemade (p. 263)

Freshly ground white pepper, to taste

2 teaspoons (10 ml) soy sauce

1 to 2 Thai chilies, chopped (optional)

Do-ahead: *Make the sauce up to 1 week in advance and keep in the fridge.*

Note: *Before cutting the Brussels sprouts, make sure they are dried thoroughly if they've been washed, to ensure good browning.*

No-Oven, Al Dente Brussels Sprouts

Roasting Brussels sprouts in the oven until they are browned will get you tender sprouts. If you want them al dente, try pan-roasting them. Pour enough oil into a large skillet to coat the bottom. Place the sprouts cut side down (you'll need to do this in two batches), then turn the heat to medium-high. The sprouts will slowly heat up and eventually sizzle. Cook without moving them for a few minutes; once the undersides are well browned, lower the heat to medium and flip them over to cook on the other side for 1 minute. If they're too al dente at this point, add a splash of water and cover the pan for 30 to 60 seconds to steam them. For this method, I would add the salt to the five-spice mixture.

Chinese Broccoli with Oyster Sauce

Kana Pad Nam Mun Hoi | คะน้าผัดน้ำมันหอย

SERVES 4

COOKING TIME: 12 minutes

SAUCE

1½ tablespoons (22 ml) oyster sauce

½ tablespoon (7 ml) soy sauce

1 tablespoon (15 ml) water

CHINESE BROCCOLI

10.5 ounces (300 g) Chinese broccoli (*gai lan*, see note)

7 cloves (35 g) garlic

2 tablespoons (30 ml) neutral oil

½ teaspoon (2 ml) granulated sugar

¼ to ½ teaspoon (1 to 2 ml) ground white or black pepper

Jasmine rice, for serving

Note: Choose younger, smaller gai lan, as they are more tender and less likely to be bitter.

Garlic Gold

I learned this trick from my mom, who loves eating big chunks of garlic in stir-fries, and I think it works exceedingly well in this simple recipe. Instead of chopping the garlic, I briefly pound the cloves until they look shredded but are still in larger pieces. Then I cook the garlic pieces gently and slowly in the oil so they soften and become sweet, while at the same time infusing the oil with maximum garlic flavor. These soft, big garlic pieces then absorb the umami oyster sauce, and finding them in the pile of greens is like finding gold.

This is a workhorse of a side dish: so easy you will want to make it regularly, and so good no one will complain. Chinese broccoli, or *gai lan*, is a staple vegetable in Asian households because it's incredibly versatile and lasts a long time in the fridge. So having a good basic recipe for *gai lan* is gold for busy weeknights. The key to success is separating stems and leaves and cooking them at different times, because the key to not having chewy leaves is to cook them minimally. Pay attention to the heat instructions carefully here, as the final key to success is to adjust the heat as the cooking progresses.

————

Make the sauce by combining all the ingredients in a small bowl.

Cut any thick Chinese broccoli stems on a sharp diagonal into thin slices. Thinner parts of the stems can be chopped into 2-inch (5 cm) pieces. Once you get to the leaves, cut them into bite-sized chunks. Keep the stems and leaves separated.

Pound the garlic cloves with a mortar and pestle, just until they break into larger pieces; you can also smash the garlic with the flat side of your knife and cut each clove into 2 to 3 large chunks.

Place a wok on medium-low heat, then add the oil and the garlic and stir for about 2 minutes, until light golden.

Turn the heat up to medium and add the Chinese broccoli stems; stir for 30 to 45 seconds.

Turn the heat up to high, then add the Chinese broccoli leaves, sauce, sugar, and pepper. Toss for 30 to 45 seconds. Immediately remove from the heat when the leaves look mostly wilted. Do not overcook—the residual heat will wilt the leaves further, and the leaves also get chewy when cooked too much.

Serve with jasmine rice.

Mixed Veggie Stir-Fry

Pad Pak Ruam | ผัดผักรวม

This basic dish unexpectedly became one of the most popular recipes on my YouTube channel. I was surprised at first, but I think it's because everyone needs a delicious-but-simple recipe for a vegetable side dish that will go with any meal. And this is it. Considering what it is, it is incredibly tasty. The suggested veggies are my "optimal mix," but you do not need six different kinds nor do you need these specific ones. Feel free to find your own optimal mix. The secret to having all the different veggies properly cooked is to stagger-add them according to how long they take to cook.

———

Make the sauce by combining all the ingredients in a small bowl.

Organize your vegetables in the order they will be cooked. In the first bowl, place the carrots and cauliflower, or other hard veggies that take the longest to cook. A second bowl should hold the cabbage, Chinese broccoli stems, snap peas, and mushrooms, or any other medium-firm veggies. A third bowl will have the Chinese broccoli leaves or any other leafy greens.

Place a wok on medium heat, then add the oil and garlic, and sauté until the smaller bits of garlic turn golden.

Add the hard veggies (bowl 1) and a splash of water, then turn the heat up to high and toss for 2 to 3 minutes, until the veggies are halfway done. Allow most of the water in the wok to dry up before adding the second set of vegetables.

Add the medium veggies (bowl 2), sauce, sugar, and pepper. Toss until the vegetables are cooked to your liking, 2 to 3 minutes.

Add the leafy greens (bowl 3) and toss just until wilted, about 15 seconds. Remove from the heat and serve with jasmine rice.

SERVES 4
COOKING TIME: 10 minutes

SAUCE

2 tablespoons (30 ml) oyster sauce (see note)

2 teaspoons (10 ml) soy sauce

2 teaspoons (10 ml) Thai seasoning sauce

1 tablespoon (15 ml) water

STIR-FRY

1 small (70 g) carrot, cut in bite-sized sticks

4.5 ounces (125 g) small cauliflower florets (about ¼ head)

3 cups (200 g) bite-sized green cabbage pieces

3.5 ounces (100 g) Chinese broccoli (*gai lan*), stems thinly sliced on a diagonal, leaves roughly chopped into chunks

10 sugar snap peas, strings removed, cut in half on a diagonal

5 fresh shiitake mushrooms, tough stems removed and caps sliced

2 tablespoons (30 ml) neutral oil

6 cloves (30 g) garlic, chopped

1 teaspoon (5 ml) granulated sugar

Ground white pepper, to taste

Jasmine rice, for serving

Note: *To make this dish vegetarian, use a vegetarian stir-fry sauce instead of the oyster sauce; it's available at many Asian grocery stores.*

Adding Protein

If you want to make this a complete meal in itself, you can add some protein. Mix 8 ounces (225 g) of bite-sized meats with 2 teaspoons (10 ml) soy sauce. Cook the meat over high heat until browned and remove from the pan. Throw it back in along with the leafy greens at the end.

Kabocha Squash & Thai Basil Stir-Fry

Pad Faktong | ผัดฟักทอง

SERVES 4

COOKING TIME: 20 minutes

SAUCE

1 tablespoon (15 ml) oyster sauce

2 teaspoons (10 ml) soy sauce

1 teaspoon (5 ml) fish sauce

⅓ cup (80 ml) water

STIR-FRY

14 ounces (400 g) chopped kabocha squash (see note)

¼ teaspoon (1 ml) ground white pepper, or to taste

2 tablespoons (30 ml) neutral oil

5 cloves (25 g) garlic, coarsely chopped

1 teaspoon (5 ml) granulated sugar

1 cup (15 g) Thai basil leaves

Jasmine rice, for serving

Note: Choose a larger squash that feels heavy for its size—it will have thicker flesh. The weight called for is for the squash already prepped as per the instructions.

There are a few dishes that instantly remind me of my childhood, and *pad faktong* is one of them. It's a simple, popular vegetable dish that's made in just about every home. Sometimes we scramble eggs into it, sometimes we add a few slices of meat, but whatever the variation, the basil is a must. Kabocha squash is, without question, my favorite squash. It's sweeter and creamier than most other winter squashes, it cooks quickly, and the skin is edible, so you don't even need to peel it unless you prefer a smooth texture. Not to mention it's great in desserts too. In Thailand, we use a variety of squash called *faktong thai,* but it tastes pretty much identical to kabocha, which are widely available in North America.

⸺

Make the sauce by combining all the ingredients in a small bowl.

To prep the squash, carefully cut the squash in half, then scoop out the seeds. Remove any woody blemishes on the skin. The rest of the skin is edible, but if you prefer a smoother texture, you can peel it, either partially or fully, with a vegetable peeler. Cut the squash into 1-inch (2.5 cm) wedges and weigh out 14 ounces (400 g); keep the remaining squash in the fridge for another use (such as Steamed Kabocha Squash Coconut Custard, p. 211). Slice each wedge crosswise into ¼-inch (6 mm) thick pieces, leaving the pointy ends thicker to even out the size.

Place a wok on medium-high heat and add the oil and garlic. Once the garlic bubbles, stir for a few minutes, until the garlic starts to turn golden at the edges.

Add the squash, sauce, and sugar and toss to mix well. Cover the wok with a lid and let the squash cook for 3 minutes. Remove the lid and toss briefly, and if the wok has dried up, add a little splash of water, being careful not to add too much, as you don't want the end result to be soupy. Cover and cook for another 2 minutes. Uncover and toss, then check doneness by piercing a piece of squash with a fork to see if it is cooked through. If it's not, let it cook a little longer, adding another splash of water as needed.

Once the squash is cooked, toss in the basil and turn off the heat, using only the residual heat to wilt the leaves. Taste and adjust the seasoning as needed, then plate. Serve with jasmine rice.

ONE-DISH MEALS (RICE & NOODLES)

Ahaan Jaan Diew | อาหารจานเดียว

Street Food at Home

"One-dish meal" is a literal translation of the Thai term for this category of dishes, *ahaan jaan diew,* because it appears in stark contrast to how we eat most other foods. These are the sandwiches of Thai cuisine—something you eat for a quick lunch, or when you're by yourself. A lot of these also happen to be street food, because street food is what most people eat when they don't have much time or when they're alone.

This is not to say these dishes are any less appropriate for an at-home dinner, but it does mean that many of these recipes have had to be simplified, because they are not things most people cook at home, with the exception of the fried rices.

Mastering Thai Noodle Soups

I've provided a few noodle soup recipes here, but I'd like you to use them as a guide or a template for making your own, changing up the meats and veggies, and experimenting with the broth.

When you make noodle soups from scratch, it can feel like there are a lot of ingredients to stay on top of, but the cooking actually goes very quickly. In Thailand, a noodle soup vendor who has all their prep done can make your bowl in less than 1 minute! In the context of home cooking, the secret is to have as much of the prep done in advance as possible. The first time you make a noodle soup meal, it might still feel a bit chaotic, but you'll get the hang of it soon.

There are two things you absolutely should do in advance: make the stock and fry the garlic. These are the only components that take time to make; everything else is pretty manageable. The stock will keep for at least 1 week in the fridge, or it can be frozen in freezer bags. If you can soak the noodles in advance then drain and keep them in the fridge, that will help too.

Tips for Perfect Thai Noodle Soups

ALWAYS, ALWAYS USE HOMEMADE STOCK. This makes all the difference. There are times when it's okay to use store-bought stocks, but this is not one of them. The stocks you buy at the store are made with Western aromatics, with ingredients like celery and thyme or other herbs, depending on the brand. This does not work in Thai noodle soups. They are also not made with many bones, so they don't have the body that a homemade stock would have. Not to mention, the most common stock we use is pork stock, which isn't usually available premade. See page 265 for a Thai-style homemade stock, but even if you just boiled bones and water without any aromatics, you'd be better off than using store-bought.

ALWAYS ADD FRIED GARLIC AND GARLIC OIL. It sounds like just a final flair that can be omitted, but these two ingredients are incredibly important. You will not find a single noodle soup in Thailand that doesn't come with fried garlic, and it makes a big difference. Get this made ahead of time (see the recipe on p. 262), and keep it in the fridge so you have it ready to go.

PRE-SOAK THE RICE NOODLES. Although you can cook rice noodles from dried, they have the best texture when rehydrated, then blanched for only a few seconds. You can soak them in advance, drain, and keep them in a sealed container in the fridge for up to a few days. In the refrigerated section of larger Asian grocery stores, you can find fresh, uncooked rice noodles specifically made for noodle soups; they do not need to be soaked and can be cooked in boiling water for only 5 to 10 seconds. Don't confuse these with the fresh *cooked* rice noodles, which are not meant for noodle soups; the uncooked ones should still be translucent and quite hard, but not dried.

GET A NOODLE STRAINER. This utensil helps a lot, especially if you have at least three mouths to feed. Asian-style noodle strainers are a cylindrical sieve with a hook that allows them to be hooked onto the edge of a pot (see photo on page 189).

To use, put one portion of noodles along with the veggies into the strainer, then jiggle it in boiling water for 5 to 10 seconds. Lift, shake off excess water, and plop the noodles and veggies right into the serving bowl. Repeat with the remaining portions.

A metal sieve could be used instead if it's the right size and can be submerged into the water, but many are awkward to use because they're too wide and shallow. Draining noodles into a colander requires you to cook all the noodles at once, which is okay to do, but separating cooked noodles is much more of a pain than separating uncooked ones.

You could fish out the noodles using a large slotted or mesh skimmer or a spider, but if you plan on cooking noodle soups again in the future, it may be worth buying a noodle strainer from your Asian grocery or kitchen supply store; it'll cost only a few dollars and will make a world of difference.

Once you've tried the noodle soup recipes in this book, check out my other noodle soup recipes on my YouTube channel:

Noodle Soup Playlist

Egg Noodles with Shrimp Gravy

Bamee Raad Na Goong | บะหมี่ราดหน้ากุ้ง

Raad na is one of the quintessential street food dishes of Thailand. It's ubiquitous at food courts around the country and a popular option for lunch. Fresh noodles topped with a light gravy, with Chinese broccoli and any kind of meat or seafood, this dish of Chinese origins has been adopted and is widely loved in Thailand. Most commonly, this is made with fresh wide rice noodles, like the ones used in the popular Thai dish, *pad see ew,* but those are harder to find and work with, so the egg noodle version is perfect for a no-fuss meal. I use the kind of egg noodles that are sold fresh and are usually labeled "wonton noodles." They are quite thin and delicate, not thick and chewy like ramen noodles.

————

Bring a large pot of water to a boil for the noodles.

Make the chili vinegar by putting the pepper in a nonreactive bowl and covering with the vinegar.

Make the gravy by placing a wok or medium pot on medium heat. Add the oil and the garlic. Once the garlic is bubbling, stir until the pieces start to turn golden.

Add the stock, fermented soybean paste, soy sauce, seasoning sauce, sugar, and pepper; bring to a full boil over high heat. While you wait, dissolve the tapioca starch in the water and set aside. Once the gravy boils, add the shrimp and the Chinese broccoli, and cook for just 30 seconds.

Stir the tapioca starch slurry and pour about three-quarters of it into the sauce while stirring. Wait until the gravy returns to a boil to see how thick it is, and if it needs more thickening, add the remaining slurry. (The starch reaches full thickening power near boiling temperature, so you don't want to judge the thickness prematurely.)

(Continued)

SERVES 4
COOKING TIME: 20 minutes

1 jalapeño or other hot pepper, thinly sliced

2 to 3 tablespoons (30 to 45 ml) white vinegar

2 tablespoons (30 ml) neutral oil

6 cloves (30 g) garlic, chopped

3 cups (750 ml) unsalted Thai-style chicken or pork stock, store-bought or homemade (p. 265)

3 tablespoons (45 ml) fermented soybean paste

1½ tablespoons (22 ml) soy sauce

1 tablespoon (15 ml) Thai seasoning sauce

1½ tablespoons (22 ml) granulated sugar

½ teaspoon (2 ml) ground white pepper

¼ cup (30 g) tapioca starch or cornstarch

¼ cup (60 ml) water

12 ounces (340 g) shrimp, size 26/30 or larger, peeled and deveined

7 ounces (200 g) Chinese broccoli (*gai lan*), stems thinly sliced, leaves coarsely chopped (see note)

12 ounces (340 g) fresh wonton noodles

Note: Choose younger, smaller gai lan if possible, as they are more tender and less likely to be bitter.

Remove the wok from the heat, then taste and adjust the seasoning as needed.

Pull the noodles apart to loosen them. Add them to the boiling water and stir briefly, then cook for 1 to 2 minutes (the timing will vary for different noodles), until they are fully cooked.

Drain the noodles or scoop them out with a mesh skimmer. If not serving right away, toss the noodles with some oil to keep them from sticking together. Otherwise, divide them among the serving bowls and pour the gravy over the noodles.

Serve immediately with the chili vinegar. You can drizzle the noodles with a bit of the vinegar to add some tartness, and you can eat the pickled chilies as well.

The Mystery of Thinning Gravy

When you eat *raad na*, you'll discover that toward the end of the meal, the gravy becomes runny. By the time you're done, the gravy sometimes looks like there was no starch in it at all, but if you just leave it, it stays thick for days. Maybe you've noticed this similar thinning happening with clam chowder, potato soup, or other starch-thickened soups. It's common knowledge among Thai people that this is what happens to *raad na,* but few stop and wonder why it happens. After investigating, I found out that as you eat, the spoon carries digestive enzymes from your mouth back into the gravy, and these enzymes break down starches. The important takeaway: don't double-dip the communal bowl of gravy!

Street-Style Noodle Soup with Pork Meatballs

Guay Tiew Look Chin Moo | ก๋วยเตี๋ยวลูกชิ้นหมู

This is perhaps the most basic, classic noodle soup in Thailand. No matter where you are in the country, you won't be far from a vendor selling noodle soups with *look chin*, which are Asian-style meatballs. They're the perfect protein for weeknight meals because they're precooked and ready to go. Noodle soups can require a bit of organization, so using no-effort proteins makes it a lot easier. *Look chin moo*, or pork meatballs, are the most common type in Thailand, but you can substitute other types of meatballs in this recipe. If you have any leftover meats, like steak or cooked chicken, lingering in the fridge, thinly slice and add them to the soup—*guay tiew* is the perfect home for random odds and ends. For more tips on noodle soups, see Mastering Thai Noodle Soups (p. 178).

——

Soak the noodles in room temperature water until they are completely pliable, about 20 to 30 minutes. If you're short on time, use warm water and they will take less time to soften.

Bring a large pot of water to a full boil for blanching the noodles and vegetables.

Meanwhile, make the broth by adding the stock to a medium pot on high heat. Add the soy sauce, fish sauce, sugar, and pepper; bring to a simmer.

Add the meatballs to the broth and simmer for 1 minute to heat through. Cover and keep the broth hot on the lowest heat possible while you wait for the noodle water to boil.

(Continued)

SERVES 4

COOKING TIME: 30 minutes

NOODLE SOUP

8 ounces (227 g) dried rice noodles, size small (see note)

8 ounces (227 g) Asian-style pork meatballs (see note)

2 cups (120 g) bean sprouts

2 cups (10 g) spinach or another leafy green

About 1½ tablespoons (22 ml) fried garlic and garlic oil, store-bought or homemade (p. 262)

1 green onion and/or 5 to 6 sprigs cilantro, chopped

Roasted chili flakes, store-bought or homemade (p. 263) (optional)

BROTH

4½ cups (1.1 L) unsalted Thai-style pork or chicken stock, store-bought or homemade (p. 265)

2 tablespoons (30 ml) soy sauce

1 tablespoon (15 ml) fish sauce

1½ teaspoons (7 ml) granulated sugar

Freshly ground white pepper, to taste

Notes: Choose rice noodles from Thailand, and the size small should be about ⅟₁₆ inch (2 mm) wide when dried. I estimate about 2 ounces (60 g) of dried noodles per person, but if you've got big eaters, use 3 ounces (85 g) per person.

Asian supermarkets sell a large variety of meatballs in both the refrigerator and freezer sections. Pork is my favorite, but any kind will work.

Place one portion each of the noodles, bean sprouts, and spinach in a noodle strainer or a metal sieve that will fit into the pot. Dunk the strainer into the boiling water and wiggle it around for 5 to 8 seconds. Lift it out, shake off as much water as possible, and then plop the noodles and veggies into a serving bowl. Repeat with the remaining portions.

Divide the meatballs among the serving bowls and ladle the hot broth overtop until it just covers the noodles, about 1 cup (250 ml) per bowl.

Top each bowl with about 1 teaspoon (5 ml) fried garlic, a drizzle of garlic oil, and chopped green onions and/or cilantro to taste. Serve with chili flakes if you like it spicy.

Homemade Meatballs

Unlike Western-style meatballs, which are quite easy to make, Asian-style meatballs require a bit of time and special technique. So, while they may not be something you want to make on a weeknight, it's a fun project for the weekend or whenever you have some time, and you can freeze them for later. It's something that's best learned via video so that you can see the texture you are looking for and, most importantly, see the squeezing technique used to form the round, smooth meatballs. If you want to make them, check out my YouTube video:

Homemade Asian-Style Pork Meatballs

Braised Chicken Noodle Soup

Guay Tiew Gai Toon | ก๋วยเตี๋ยวไก่ตุ๋น

This dish is inspired by our popular duck noodle soup, in which duck legs are slowly stewed in a dark, rich broth bursting with spices. It's the perfect noodle soup for the fall or winter, when you might want something a little richer than clear broth soups. I like to use chicken instead of duck, which cuts down the braising time from 2 hours to only 45 minutes, and even less if you use a pressure cooker. If you don't want to mess with noodles, this soup is equally satisfying over rice with some veggies. For more tips on noodle soups, see page 178.

———

Soak the noodles in room temperature water until they are completely pliable, about 20 to 30 minutes. If you're short on time, use warm water and they will take less time to soften.

Optional step: If you're feeling ambitious, toast the whole dry spices by adding the cinnamon stick, star anise, coriander seeds and Sichuan peppercorns to a dry sauté pan over medium-high heat. Stir constantly until the coriander seeds darken slightly. Pour them onto a plate to cool.

If you have cheesecloth, wrap the galangal and all the whole dry spices inside it and tie it closed. You can add this bundle directly to the soup; it will make it easier to remove the spices afterward.

For the stovetop method: Place 4¾ cups (1.2 L) water in a large pot and add all the Braised Chicken Soup ingredients. Bring to a simmer over high heat, then turn the heat down to medium-low. Loosely cover the pot and cook for 40 to 45 minutes, until the chicken is fork-tender.

For the Instant Pot method: Place 4 cups (1 L) water and all the Braised Chicken Soup ingredients in the Instant Pot and cook on high pressure for 5 minutes. Allow it to naturally release for 10 minutes before releasing the remaining pressure.

(Continued)

SERVES 4

COOKING TIME: 40 minutes in Instant Pot, 1 hour on the stovetop

8 ounces (225 g) dried rice noodles, size small (see note p. 183)

4 to 6 leaves green-leaf lettuce (see note)

2 cups (120 g) bean sprouts

About 1½ tablespoons (22 ml) fried garlic and garlic oil, store-bought or homemade (p. 262)

1 green onion and/or 5 to 6 sprigs cilantro, chopped

Roasted chili flakes, store-bought or homemade (p. 263) (optional)

BRAISED CHICKEN SOUP

4 large chicken thighs (1½ pounds/680 g) bone-in, skin-on

½ small onion, chopped

8 inches (20 cm) cinnamon stick

2 pieces star anise

1 teaspoon (5 ml) coriander seeds

½ teaspoon (2 ml) Sichuan peppercorns (optional)

8 thin slices galangal (optional)

2 tablespoons (24 g) finely chopped palm sugar, packed

½ teaspoon (2 ml) ground white pepper

2 tablespoons (30 ml) soy sauce

2 tablespoons (30 ml) oyster sauce

1 tablespoon (15 ml) white or rice vinegar

½ to 1 tablespoon (7 to 15 ml) black or dark soy sauce

Note: *Yes, we put green-leaf lettuce in noodle soups! If this weirds you out, substitute any other leafy green.*

Bring a large pot of water to a boil for blanching the noodles and bean sprouts. Tear the lettuce leaves into bite-sized pieces and divide them among the serving bowls.

Once the chicken is done, remove the spice bag or use a mesh skimmer to skim off the floating spices. You can also skim off any excess fat from the surface, if you wish. Taste and adjust the seasoning with salt or soy sauce as needed. Cover and keep on the lowest heat, or the Keep Warm setting if using an Instant Pot, so it stays hot while you cook the noodles.

Place one portion each of the noodles and the bean sprouts in a noodle strainer or a metal sieve that will fit into the pot. Dunk the strainer into the boiling water and wiggle it around for 5 to 8 seconds. Lift it out, shake off as much water as possible, and plop the noodles and bean sprouts on top of the lettuce in a serving bowl. Repeat with the remaining portions.

Place a piece of chicken on top of the noodles and ladle the hot broth overtop until it just covers the noodles, about 1 cup (250 ml) per bowl.

Top each bowl with about 1 teaspoon (5 ml) fried garlic, a drizzle of garlic oil, and chopped green onions and/or cilantro to taste. Serve with chili flakes if you like it spicy.

Weeknight Chicken Khao Soi

Khao Soi Gai | ข้าวซอยไก่

SERVES 4

COOKING TIME: 50 minutes

1-inch piece (8 g) turmeric, or ½ teaspoon (2 ml) ground turmeric

¼ cup (60 ml) red curry paste, store-bought or homemade (p. 255)

1 tablespoon (15 ml) curry powder

1½ cups (375 ml) coconut milk, divided

3 cups (750 ml) water

2 black cardamom pods (see note)

4 to 8 chicken drumsticks (see note)

1½ tablespoons (18 g) finely chopped palm sugar, packed

1 to 2 tablespoons (15 to 30 ml) soy sauce

12 ounces (340 g) flat wonton noodles (see note)

FOR SERVING (OPTIONAL)

½ cup (75 g) chopped pickled mustard greens, rinsed (see note)

¼ cup (35 g) julienned shallots

4 lime wedges

Sautéed chili flakes (see note)

Do-ahead: The curry paste can be mixed with the spices (step 1) in bulk and then frozen.

The most famous dish of northern Thailand, *khao soi* is a noodle soup unlike any other. Egg noodles in an aromatic coconut curry broth are topped with crispy fried egg noodles. A fully loaded, from-scratch *khao soi* is a lot of work, but fortunately the parts that are tedious aren't crucial. So, when I'm short on time, I make only the most important parts—the noodles and the broth—and it's still very satisfying. The crispy noodles are impressive-looking, but I don't find them necessary taste-wise, so I'm not about to deep-fry something on a weeknight just for looks. The curry paste can also be simplified by modifying store-bought red curry paste.

———

Pound the turmeric into a fine paste with a mortar and pestle, then add the red curry paste and curry powder and pound to mix. If using ground turmeric, you can just mix them without pounding.

Add roughly ¼ cup (60 ml) coconut milk to a large pot and bring to a boil over medium heat. Add the turmeric-curry paste and stir for 2 to 3 minutes, until the paste is very thick. If the paste is sticking, deglaze with a bit of coconut milk. Add the remaining coconut milk and water, and bring to a boil over high heat.

While you wait for the broth to boil, smash the cardamom pods with a mortar and pestle until cracked, then wrap them in a piece of cheesecloth and add to the pot. (If you don't have cheesecloth, you can add them directly to the pot, but make sure they're not cracked so wide that the seeds inside will come out into the soup.)

Once the broth is boiling, add the chicken drumsticks, sugar, and 1 tablespoon (15 ml) soy sauce. Turn the heat down to medium-low and let simmer until the chicken is fork-tender, about 30 to 40 minutes. Once done, taste and add more soy sauce and sugar as needed.

While the curry is simmering, bring a large pot of water to a boil, for cooking the noodles.

Loosen the noodles and shake off any excess flour. If you like, you can cut them with scissors once or twice to shorten them and make them easier to separate and eat. Add them to the boiling water and cook for 1 to 2 minutes, until cooked through. Scoop them out with a wire skimmer or drain in a colander, and divide them evenly among the serving bowls. If not serving right away, toss them with some neutral oil to prevent them from sticking together.

Place the chicken in the serving bowls, then ladle the broth overtop just until it almost submerges the noodles, about 1 cup (250 ml) per serving. This is a rich broth, so you won't need too much of it. Serve with the accompaniments on the side.

To eat, top the noodles with the pickled mustard greens, shallots, and a squeeze of lime, if desired. Add the sautéed chili flakes for more heat.

Notes: *Black cardamom can be found at Asian or Indian grocery stores. If you can't find it, use 6 green cardamom pods instead.*

I usually serve 1 drumstick per person, but you can serve 2 to big eaters.

Wonton noodles are a type of fresh egg noodles sold in refrigerated section of Asian grocery stores.

Pickled mustard greens come in clear plastic bags at Asian grocery stores. Another tart pickle can also be used.

To make sautéed chili flakes, combine chili flakes with just enough neutral oil to make a paste, then sauté over low heat for a few minutes, until dark and smoky.

Tossed Rice Vermicelli with Skinless Wontons

Sen Mee Hang | เส้นหมี่แห้ง

If you're at a noodle soup vendor in Thailand but it's too hot a day for a soup, you can order the dry version. Instead of broth, the noodles are tossed in seasonings, but all the other components remain the same. For home cooking, this is an easy option because you don't have to deal with the broth! Wontons are a popular topping, but for a quick meal I make them "skinless," because who has time to wrap wontons on a Tuesday? But if you've got time, you can definitely wrap them. Top the dish with store-bought Chinese BBQ pork to complete the street look, though it's also perfectly satisfying without. PS. Don't let the length of the ingredient list deter you; it's all basic stuff and you probably have most of it already!

———

Soak the noodles in room temperature water until they are soft and fully pliable, 3 to 5 minutes for Wai Wai brand, and 10 to 15 minutes for Erawan brand. If using Wai Wai, after the noodles are soaked, feel the noodles for any big clumps and pull them off; small clumps are okay. Drain and set aside.

Bring a large pot of water to a boil for blanching the yu choy, the wontons, and the noodles.

Combine all the ingredients for the noodle seasoning except the black soy sauce in a large mixing bowl. The noodles will eventually end up here, so use a bowl large enough to hold everything.

Make the skinless wontons by pounding the cilantro stems, garlic, and peppercorns into a fine paste with a mortar and pestle. In a mixing bowl, combine the ground pork, cornstarch, sugar, soy sauce, oyster sauce, and pounded garlic mixture. Use gloved or clean hands to mix everything together well.

Blanch the yu choy in the boiling water for 30 seconds, or longer if you prefer them tender, then scoop them out with a mesh skimmer and set aside. Bring the water back to a full boil.

(Continued)

SERVES 4
COOKING TIME: 30 minutes

NOODLES & TOPPINGS

8 ounces (225 g) dry Thai rice vermicelli (see sidebar, p. 194)

4 ounces (115 g) yu choy or bok choy, cut in 2-inch (2.5 cm) pieces

Chinese BBQ pork, store-bought, thinly sliced (optional, see note, p. 194)

Fried garlic (p. 262)

Chopped cilantro, for garnish

Roasted chili flakes, store-bought or homemade (p. 263) (optional)

NOODLE SEASONING

3 tablespoons (45 ml) garlic oil (p. 262)

4 teaspoons (20 ml) granulated sugar

4 teaspoons (20 ml) white vinegar

1 tablespoon (15 ml) fish sauce

2 teaspoons (10 ml) soy sauce

2 teaspoons (10 ml) Thai seasoning sauce

Ground white pepper, to taste

½ to 1 teaspoon (2 to 5 ml) black soy sauce (optional)

SKINLESS WONTONS

6 cilantro stems, chopped

2 cloves (10 g) garlic

¼ teaspoon (1 ml) white peppercorns

12 ounces (340 g) ground pork

1 tablespoon (15 ml) cornstarch

1 teaspoon (5 ml) granulated sugar

1 tablespoon (15 ml) soy sauce

1 tablespoon (15 ml) oyster sauce

Use a dessert spoon to scoop a bite-sized chunk of pork mixture, and use another spoon to flick it directly into the boiling water. You can be quick here; they don't need to look neat. Once the last piece goes in, bring the water back to a simmer and let the pork pieces cook for 1 more minute. Scoop out with a slotted spoon or wire skimmer and set aside in a bowl. Bring the water back to a full boil.

Add the noodles to the boiling water and cook for 3 seconds if using Wai Wai brand or 15 seconds if using Erawan brand. Scoop the noodles out with a wire skimmer, shake off excess water, and check that they are cooked through. If they're not, return to the pot and stir them around for another 5 seconds or so. Once they're cooked, immediately transfer the noodles to the bowl with the seasoning and toss them thoroughly, making sure the sauce is evenly and fully absorbed.

Drizzle about ½ teaspoon (2 ml) black soy sauce over the noodles, and toss them well, adding more as needed until you have the desired color.

Divide the noodles among the serving bowls and top with the skinless wontons, yu choy, Chinese BBQ pork, fried garlic, and chopped cilantro. Sprinkle chili flakes overtop for extra heat. Serve immediately.

The Right and the Best Rice Vermicelli

There are a few products on the market labeled "rice vermicelli," but they are not all the same. Vietnamese versions come in thick, straight sticks that are not right for this dish. Look for a product of Thailand— and they should be thread-thin. Erawan and Wai Wai are the two most common brands, and I highly recommend you get Erawan if you can find it. Wai Wai noodles are a little too thin for this dish, though I do prefer them for stir fries. You can also substitute fresh egg noodles (wonton noodles) like the ones used in Egg Noodles with Shrimp Gravy (p. 181), or the small-size rice noodles used in Street-Style Noodle Soup with Pork Meatballs (p. 183).

Minimalist Pad Thai

Pad Thai | ผัดไท

Traditional *pad thai* is quick to make but tedious to prep for. There are a lot of ingredients, some of which aren't pantry staples even for Thai people. But that's because *pad thai* is not a dish meant for home cooking—it's something most people buy. But I wondered, what is the "minimum viable *pad thai*"? How much can I simplify it and still have it taste great and proudly be called *pad thai*? This is it right here. Faster, simpler, but still tastier than takeout. What I have removed are the dried shrimp, pressed tofu, and sweet preserved radish, and I've also provided a quick-soak method for the noodles. Everything that's left I consider important, but the peanuts can go if you can't eat them. You can find the recipe for my original *pad thai* on my website and in my first book, *Hot Thai Kitchen*.

FOR THE SAUCE

Melt the sugar in a small pot over medium-high heat. Once melted, let it cook for a bit longer, until the color becomes a deeper caramel but not quite dark brown. Once this color is achieved, immediately add the water; it will splatter aggressively and the sugar will harden. Turn the heat down to medium and swirl it around until most of the sugar is dissolved.

Turn off the heat and stir in the tamarind paste and fish sauce. Don't worry about a few stubborn chunks of sugar; they'll have dissolved by the time you need the sauce.

FOR THE PAD THAI

Using scissors, cut the soaked noodles roughly in half so it's easier to mix them with the veggies. Place all your prepped ingredients by the stove, ready to go.

Place a wok or large nonstick skillet on high heat and pour in just enough oil to coat the bottom. Once the oil is very hot, lay the shrimp down in one layer and let them sear without moving them until at least halfway cooked, about 2 minutes. Flip and cook on the other side until they are done. Turn off the heat and transfer the shrimp to a bowl, leaving all the oil and any juices behind.

(Continued)

SERVES 2

COOKING TIME: 15 minutes

SAUCE

3 tablespoons + 1 teaspoon (40 g) finely chopped palm sugar, packed

3 tablespoons (45 ml) water

4 tablespoons (60 ml) tamarind paste, store-bought or homemade (p. 266)

2 tablespoons (30 ml) fish sauce

PAD THAI

4 ounces (115 g) dried rice noodles, medium size, rehydrated (see note, p. 196)

3 to 4 tablespoons (45 to 60 ml) neutral oil

8 to 10 medium to large shrimp, about 21/25 count, peeled, deveined and patted dry

5 cloves (25 g) garlic, chopped

⅓ cup (40 g) thinly sliced shallots

2 large eggs

2½ cups (150 g) bean sprouts

8–10 stalks garlic chives, cut in 2-inch (5 cm) pieces (see note, p. 196)

¼ cup (35 g) unsalted roasted peanuts, coarsely chopped, divided

½ lime, cut in wedges

Roasted chili flakes, store-bought or homemade (p. 263) (optional)

Do-ahead: *Make the sauce in advance; it can be kept in the fridge indefinitely. Soak the noodles in advance, drain, and refrigerate for up to 3 days.*

Add a bit more oil to the pan if needed so that you have about 3 tablespoons (45 ml). Having enough oil is important to make sure that the noodles don't clump together.

Add the garlic and shallots, and turn the heat to medium. Stir until the shallots are translucent, about 2 minutes.

Turn the heat up to the hottest it can go, and add the noodles and sauce. Toss together until most of the sauce has been absorbed. At this point it will look like there aren't nearly enough noodles, but don't panic, the dish will bulk up with the veggies and proteins.

Push the noodles to one side of the pan to create space for the eggs, then break the eggs into the pan. Scramble slightly just to break the yolks, then move the noodles on top of the eggs and let the eggs continue to cook for another 30 to 45 seconds, until they are mostly cooked. Flip the noodles and then toss to break up the eggs.

Give the noodles a quick taste to check their doneness. If they're too chewy, add a splash of water and keep tossing for 1 minute or so to allow the water to absorb.

Add the shrimp back to the pan, along with any juices, and toss to mix. Turn off the heat and add the bean sprouts, garlic chives, and half of the peanuts. Use tongs to mix just until everything is evenly distributed. Plate immediately—you want the bean sprouts to be as fresh as possible, so don't let them linger in the hot pan unnecessarily.

Top with the remaining peanuts and serve with wedges of lime. Add some roasted chili flakes for heat, if desired.

Avoiding Soggy Noodles

Most recipes in my book serve four, but for *pad thai* I recommend you stir-fry the noodles in batches of two servings. Crowding the pan, especially with a low-BTU home stove, can result in soggy noodles because steam gets trapped under all the food and your noodles end up simmering in liquid longer than they should. If you've got a powerful stove and a large wok, you may be able to get away with a larger batch, so use your judgment here. You can also try reducing the amount of water in the sauce, or omitting it altogether, if you feel like you might be crowding the pan.

Quick Hainanese Chicken Rice

Kao Mun Gai | ข้าวมันไก่

Kao mun gai is my answer to both "What would be your last meal on Earth?" and "If you could only eat one dish for the rest of your life, what would it be?" I have sentimental attachment to it because my grandmother is from Hainan, and this is her signature dish that she makes for me every time I see her. Making *kao mun gai* the traditional way is a small project—you poach a whole chicken and then make the rice with the resulting broth. This method simplifies it into a weeknight-friendly meal without compromising the flavor. The rice becomes even more flavorful because it absorbs the chicken juices as they cook together. The only thing I actually don't like about it is that it takes away the labor of love that is part of the traditional process, but this weeknight-friendly recipe does make me appreciate my grandma's version even more.

———

Rinse the rice a few times, until the water runs clear, then drain well in a sieve.

Trim excess fat off the chicken thighs and reserve. If the chicken breast is large, cut it on a diagonal, splitting it along the thick half of the breast, to make two equal pieces. Sprinkle ½ teaspoon (2 ml) salt over the chicken pieces and rub it in.

In a wok, combine the oil and chicken fat trimmings, and turn the heat to medium-low. Sauté the chicken fat until the chicken bits are browned and the fat is rendered, about 4 minutes. You need about 2 tablespoons (30 ml) rendered fat, so if there is too much, remove some. If there isn't enough, add a little more oil to supplement. Remove the chicken bits, leaving the fat behind.

Add the garlic and ginger to the pan and turn the heat up to medium. Stir for about 2 minutes, until the garlic starts to turn golden.

Add the rice and the remaining salt, then turn the heat up to high. Toss for about 2 minutes, until the rice is hot throughout and dry.

Transfer the rice to a rice cooker or heavy-bottomed pot. Stir in the stock and place the chicken pieces in one layer on top of the rice.

(Continued)

SERVES 4
COOKING TIME: 45 minutes
SPECIAL TOOLS: A heavy-bottomed pot or rice cooker big enough so that the chicken pieces can be laid in one layer.

1½ cups (375 ml) uncooked jasmine rice

3 pieces (1 pound/450 g) bone-in, skin-on chicken thighs (see note, p. 200)

1 large (8 ounce/225 g) chicken breast, boneless, skin optional

1 teaspoon (5 ml) table salt, divided

1 teaspoon (5 ml) neutral oil

4 cloves (20 g) garlic, chopped

2 tablespoons (15 g) chopped ginger

1⅔ cups (40 ml) unsalted chicken stock (see note, p. 200)

English cucumber slices, for serving

DIPPING SAUCE

2 cloves (10 g) garlic

1 to 2 Thai chilies, or to taste

1½ tablespoons (10 g) chopped ginger

3 tablespoons (45 ml) fermented soybean paste

1 tablespoon (15 ml) granulated sugar

2 teaspoons (10 ml) soy sauce

1 to 2 teaspoons (5 to 10 ml) black soy sauce

1 teaspoon (5 ml) white vinegar

3 to 4 sprigs cilantro, chopped (optional)

Notes: You can mix and match dark and white meat depending on what people prefer, but you will need some chicken fat for the rice, so have at least two thighs, or buy whole bone-in, skin-on breasts, which should have some fat at the edges you can trim off.

For an authentic flavor, I highly recommend using homemade Asian-style stock (p. 265). Also, if you have extra stock, it's traditional to serve a small bowl of simply seasoned chicken broth on the side to help wash down the rice, since this is a dry dish.

If using a rice cooker, just click the "Cook" button and let it do its thing.

If using a pot, with the heat still on high, watch until you see the first sign of bubbling, then turn the heat down to low, cover with a tight-fitting lid, and cook for 20 to 25 minutes, until both the chicken and rice are done.

While you wait for the chicken rice to cook, make the dipping sauce. Using a mortar and pestle, pound the garlic, chilies, and ginger into a rough paste. Add all the remaining dipping sauce ingredients except the cilantro, and stir until the sugar is dissolved. Stir in the chopped cilantro just before serving.

Once the chicken is cooked, remove it from the rice cooker or pot and let it rest for at least 5 minutes before slicing. The rice right under the chicken might look a little mushy; this is normal and fine. Fluff the rice with a spatula, gently folding the bottom up to the top, and the mushy layer will mix in and disappear.

You can serve the chicken in whole pieces and have people cut it themselves, or you can slice the meat into thin pieces and place them on top of the rice in the traditional way. Serve with the dipping sauce, fresh cucumber slices, and, if you wish, a bowl of chicken broth.

Preventing Rice from Sticking to the Pot

You might wonder why I don't sauté the rice right in the pot that I'm using to cook it and make one less dirty dish. You could do that, but in my experience, this causes more rice to get stuck on the bottom. I'm not entirely sure why, but without fail, this has been the case. My theory is that an invisible amount of loose starch from the freshly washed rice gets cooked onto the bottom of the pot and makes it more grippy. But when you add rice that has already been sautéed, the excess starch is left behind. This doesn't apply to a nonstick pot, obviously, so if you're using one of those, feel free to do everything in the same pot.

Quick-Salted Fish Fried Rice

Kao Pad Kana Pla Kem | ข้าวผัดคะน้าปลาเค็ม

To me, salted fish fried rice is the poster child of Thai rustic solo meals—something you get at the food court during a lunch break. It's so basic, yet the salty, chewy fish makes this fried rice extremely satisfying and incredibly hard to stop eating. In Thailand, we typically buy salted king mackerel for this, but it's easy to make using any firm fish. I prefer making it myself because I make it less salty so I can use more fish. I love using salmon, as it makes the final dish so colorful. Dicing the fish before salting means you need only 20 minutes—so no planning required.

——————

Mix the salmon with the salt and let it sit for 20 minutes, or longer longer if you want extra-salty fish. Rinse off the excess salt with cold water and pat the fish dry.

Place a wok over medium-high heat and add the oil. Once hot, add the salmon pieces and fry without moving them until the underside is browned. Toss the salmon so most of the pieces flip, then flip those pieces that didn't. Let the second side sear until well browned.

Once the two sides are browned, keep them cooking, stirring frequently for another 1 to 2 minutes, until you get really firm, well-browned pieces—yes, you want these a bit overcooked. As you cook, break the pieces with your spatula to get more rustic-looking bits. Turn off the heat and remove the salmon from the pan, leaving all the oil behind. If you're cooking the fried rice in two batches (see sidebar on p. 203), poor out half of the oil and reserve it for your second batch.

Add more oil to the wok if the pan looks dry, and turn the heat to medium. Add the garlic and sauté until it starts to turn golden.

Add the eggs, break the yolks, let them set about halfway, then quickly scramble them. Add the Chinese broccoli and toss briefly just to get everything mixed together.

(Continued)

SERVES 4

COOKING TIME: 10 minutes, plus 20 minutes salting

7 ounces (200 g) salmon, diced in ½-inch (1.2 cm) pieces

1 teaspoon (5 ml) table salt

3 to 4 tablespoons (45 to 60 ml) neutral oil

6 cloves (30 g) garlic, chopped

4 large eggs

5 to 6 stalks (100 g) Chinese broccoli (*gai lan*), stems thinly sliced, leaves coarsely chopped

4½ cups (700 g) cooked jasmine rice, (see sidebar on p. 203)

4 teaspoons (20 ml) fish sauce

1 tablespoon (15 ml) granulated sugar

1 teaspoon (5 ml) ground white pepper

10 sprigs cilantro, chopped (optional)

Lime wedges, for serving

Turn the heat up to high, then add the rice, fish sauce, sugar, and pepper. Toss to mix well, breaking up any lumps of rice with your spatula.

Toss in the salmon, then let the rice sit without stirring for 10 to 15 seconds so that it can toast and develop some browning and flavor. Toss again to mix, and repeat this toasting step a few more times. Turn off the heat, then taste and adjust the seasoning.

Plate the rice, top with the cilantro, and serve with wedges of lime. Be sure to squeeze the lime over the rice and mix it up before eating.

A Few Tips for the Perfect Fried Rice

Old, cold rice for fried rice is great, but you don't need it. If cooking fresh rice, wash the rice at least three times, until the water runs clear, then use a little bit less water to cook it than you normally would (I do a one-to-one ratio for jasmine rice). If you have time, spread the rice out onto a plate to let it dry out before cooking. I also recommend weighing the cooked rice for accuracy, but if measuring by cup, press the rice in just enough so there aren't any big gaps, but do not pack it tightly. Finally, if you don't have a large wok, I recommend cooking in two batches to maximize rice toasting, though you can cook all the protein at once.

Chinese Sausage Fried Rice

Kao Pad Goonchiang | ข้าวผัดกุนเชียง

This is a childhood favorite of many Asian kids, including us in Thailand. Chinese sausages are sweet, salty, umami cured sausages that can be made with chicken, pork, and/or liver, but the classic is pork. A little goes a long way, since these sausages are intensely flavored, which makes them great for a budget meal. The sausages last a long time in the fridge, so they're handy to keep for a quick dinner. One note: even though they may look like pepperoni sticks, they cannot be eaten raw, so don't be snacking on them while you prep!

———

Spread the sausage slices in a dry wok in a single layer. Turn the heat to medium and let them cook without stirring until they start to brown on the underside and a little bit of fat is rendered. Once browned, stir for 30 seconds or so, until cooked through. Do not cook them for too long or you will render out too much fat and cause the sausage to become too salty. Turn off the heat and remove the sausage from the pan, leaving any rendered fat behind.

Add oil to coat the bottom of the pan and turn the heat to medium. Add the onions and carrots and sauté for about 2 minutes, until the onions are translucent.

Add the garlic and cook for another 30 seconds, until the garlic starts to turn golden, then add the Chinese broccoli and toss just until wilted.

Push the veggies to one side to create space for the eggs, and move the wok so the veggies are sitting a bit off the element. If the pan is dry, add a bit more oil, then add the eggs, break the yolks, and let them set about halfway. Scramble the eggs briefly, then add the rice on top of the eggs, and return the sausages to the pan. Toss everything briefly to mix.

Drizzle the soy sauce and fish sauce overtop, then sprinkle with the sugar and pepper. Toss until all the rice is evenly coated with the sauce.

Let the rice sit without stirring for 10 to 15 seconds to allow it to toast slightly, then toss and let it toast again. Do this three times or until the rice is dry and some of the grains have browned.

Remove from the heat and plate. Top with chopped cilantro or green onions, and serve with fresh cucumber slices and lime wedges. I like to squeeze the lime over the rice to cut the richness. Enjoy!

SERVES 4

COOKING TIME: 5 minutes

5 ounces (150 g) Chinese sausage, cut in ¼-inch (6 mm) thick slices (see note)

2 tablespoons (30 ml) neutral oil

⅔ cup (90 g) small-diced yellow onion

⅔ cup (90 g) small-diced carrot

6 cloves (30 g) garlic, chopped

1.8 ounces (50 g) Chinese broccoli (*gai lan*), stems cut in thin rounds, leaves in ½-inch (1.2 cm) thick ribbons

4 large eggs

4 cups (600 g) cooked jasmine rice (see sidebar on p. 203)

2 tablespoons (30 ml) soy sauce

4 teaspoons (20 ml) fish sauce

2 teaspoons (10 ml) granulated sugar

½ teaspoon (2 ml) ground white pepper, or to taste

Chopped cilantro or green onions, for garnish (optional)

FOR SERVING

English cucumber slices

Lime wedges

Note: *In my experience, good Chinese sausages tend to have a simpler ingredient list with few or no additives. Some brands are saltier than others, so if you find one that's too salty, try a different one next time.*

Leftover Anything Fried Rice

Kao Pad Kong Leua | ข้าวผัดของเหลือ

SERVES 2

COOKING TIME: 5 minutes

2 tablespoons (30 ml) neutral oil

6 cloves (30 g) garlic, chopped

2 large eggs

2½ cups (375 g) cooked jasmine rice (see sidebar on p. 203)

1 tablespoon (15 ml) soy sauce, preferably Thai (use a bit less if your leftovers are salty)

2 teaspoons (10 ml) fish sauce

1 teaspoon (5 ml) granulated sugar

¼ teaspoon (1 ml) ground white pepper

4.6 ounces (130 g) leftover protein, shredded or chopped

1 green onion and/or 4 to 6 sprigs cilantro, chopped

FOR SERVING

English cucumber slices

Lime wedges

Prik nam pla (Fish Sauce & Chilies Condiment, p. 269)

Fried rice is for Thai people what pizza is for North Americans: a standard base that you can then top with just about anything, making it the ideal dish for using up leftover bits of meat and veg. But unlike pizza, fried rice is easy and fast to make! A basic fried rice recipe such as this one is a good tool to have in your back pocket, and it will work with any protein, even strongly flavored ones. We don't usually add veggies to our basic fried rice, but to serve it Thai style, you've got to have fresh cucumber slices, a lime wedge, and some *prik nam pla* on the side!

———

Place a wok on medium heat and add the oil and garlic. Once the garlic bubbles, stir for 1 to 2 minutes, until the smallest pieces start to turn golden.

Add the eggs, scramble slightly, then let them set about halfway before stirring to break up the pieces.

Turn the heat up to high, then add the rice, soy sauce, fish sauce, sugar, and pepper; toss to distribute the sauce evenly.

Add the protein and toss to mix, then let the rice sit without stirring for 10 to 15 seconds so that it can toast and develop some browning and flavor. Toss to mix and repeat this toasting step a few more times. Turn off the heat, then taste and adjust the seasoning.

Toss in the green onions and/or cilantro to taste, then plate and garnish with more fresh herbs, if desired. Serve with cucumber slices, lime wedges, and some *prik nam pla*, if you wish.

> **Use Those Drippings**
> I first used this recipe with leftover supermarket rotisserie chicken, and if you've ever had rotisserie chicken, you'll know that at the bottom of the container lie delicious chicken juices. And the same might be true with whatever leftover meats you have—drippings or juices sitting at the bottom of the plate. This is liquid gold that should absolutely go into your fried rice. However, be mindful of how salty the liquid is, and cut down on the soy sauce or fish sauce accordingly. Also, don't add more than 2 to 3 tablespoons (30 to 45 ml) liquid for this recipe, so as to not make it too wet.

SIMPLE SWEETS

Kong Waan | ของหวาน

Desserts in Thailand

Thai desserts are not well known outside Thailand, but we are definitely sweets people. Go to any weekend market in Thailand and you'll see endless types of dessert for sale. However, our sweets are more commonly eaten as snacks, rather than as an after-meal indulgence.

Like Western desserts, many Thai sweets are quite time-consuming to make and require special skills, which is probably why most restaurants offer such a small selection. But there are many desserts that could not be easier to make, and I have included them here.

What Are Thai Desserts Like?

If you're not familiar with Southeast Asian sweets, they will look very different from what you're used to. Instead of wheat flour, we use rice flour, glutinous rice flour or tapioca starch, among other things. Instead of dairy, we use coconut milk for fat, liquid, and creaminess. Instead of brown and granulated sugar, we use palm and granulated. Instead of chocolate and berries, we add beans, squashes, and bananas.

Oven use is rare for traditional Thai sweets, so most of our desserts are steamed or stirred on the stove. We have a lot of puddings and dessert soups, and a lot of items that are dense and chewy, much like mochi and boba. Many of our desserts are whole ingredients, like fruits, squashes, rice, and beans, that are simply cooked in syrup, though not quite candied so that we can really enjoy the taste of the ingredient.

Steamed Kabocha Squash Coconut Custard

Faktong Sangkaya | ฟักทองสังขยา

If you love a good creamy squash, and you love custard, this is the perfect dessert for you. In Thailand, there are two versions of this dessert. The original version is made by pouring the custard into a whole hollowed-out squash, which is then steamed and sliced into wedges. I've shared this recipe on my YouTube channel, but some people have trouble with it because the varying sizes of the squash and the imprecise nature of steaming make it difficult to determine how long it needs to cook. So I want to share the easier, "reversed" version, where the squash pieces are steamed in the custard. And since we don't have to worry about cutting it into pieces that can hold their own, I'm also making the custard a little softer and richer, the way I prefer it.

———

Preheat the steamer over low heat, keeping the water at a very gentle simmer.

Place the sugar in a small pot, then add the coconut milk, salt, and pandan leaf. Turn the heat to low and cook, stirring occasionally, until the sugar is mostly dissolved. Push on the pandan leaf as you cook to help bruise it and release more aroma. After the sugar starts to soften, use a spatula to press down on any big chunks to help it dissolve more quickly; you do not want this mixture to boil and reduce, you just want to dissolve the sugar while maintaining the liquid volume. Once the sugar has dissolved, remove the pot from the heat and let the mixture cool while you prep the squash.

To prep the squash, cut it in half vertically with a big chef's knife. Using a spoon, scrape out all the seeds, then peel the squash with a vegetable peeler; if you're having trouble getting to some of the skin in the grooves, leave it for now. Cut the squash into ¼-inch (6 mm) thick wedges, then use a knife to trim off any remaining skin. Slice each wedge crosswise into ¼-inch (6 mm) thick pieces, erring on the side of too thin rather than too thick. Place the squash in the dish you're using to steam, or divide it evenly among the ramekins.

Steam the squash over simmering water for 7 to 8 minutes, until a fork easily pierces through but it's not mushy.

(Continued)

SERVES 6

COOKING TIME: 45 minutes for ramekins, 70 minutes for a big dish, plus cooling time

SPECIAL TOOLS: Six 4-ounce (120 ml) ramekins or a 3-cup (750 ml) heatproof dish for steaming (see note)

4.5 ounces (130 g) finely chopped palm sugar, packed

1¼ cups (310 ml) coconut milk (see note)

¼ + ⅛ teaspoon (1.5 ml) table salt

½ pandan leaf, tied into a knot (optional; see sidebar on p. 213)

9 ounces (250 g) kabocha squash (see note)

3 large eggs + 3 egg yolks

Do-ahead: *It's best to make this 1 day in advance to allow the flavors to mingle. It will last for up to 1 week in the fridge.*

Notes: *You can make individual servings in ramekins or use one big heatproof dish; a small casserole or a glass food storage container will work.*

If you want a richer and creamier custard, don't shake or stir the coconut milk before using; that way, you can use the fattier part of the coconut milk, which rises to the top as the milk sits.

The weight called for is for the squash already prepped as per the instructions.

While the squash steams, make the custard by whisking together the eggs and yolks in a mixing bowl, using a circular motion and without lifting the whisk, so you don't whip too much air into it. Remove the pandan leaf from the coconut milk mixture and discard, then gradually pour the mixture into the eggs as you whisk. Strain the custard through a fine-mesh sieve into a spouted container, such as a liquid measuring cup. Toward the end, if you see some lumps of egg whites caught in the sieve, try to push them through, but don't obsess over stubborn bits.

Once the squash is done steaming, remove the dish or ramekins from the steamer, turn the heat down to the lowest setting, and wait until the water is steaming but not simmering—a few bubbles here and there is fine, but there shouldn't be constant bubbling. It helps to use the smallest burner on your stove.

Give the strained custard a quick stir and pour it over the squash, leaving at least ¼ inch (6 mm) headroom to allow for a bit of puffing. Steam the custard for 15 minutes if using ramekins, and 40 to 50 minutes if using a large dish. This timing is a rough estimate, because steaming temperatures are not precise and will vary from stove to stove. Keep an eye on the heat to make sure the water doesn't boil or even simmer, as heat too high will cause the custard to puff up and the texture will not be smooth, though if it does happen, don't panic, it will still be fine to eat.

To check doneness, press down gently on the center of the custard; it should feel firm. If it is not cooked yet, some liquid will flow to the top when pressed. Or you can use an instant-read thermometer to check that the custard has reached 175°F (80°C).

Let the custard cool to room temperature or chill before serving. If possible, let it sit for a few hours or up to overnight to allow the flavors to mingle. If keeping overnight, wrap it well and refrigerate.

Pandan Knots

When we simmer pandan leaves in liquid, we tie them into a simple knot. Not only does this shorten the long, unwieldy leaves into a manageable size that fits neatly in the pot, but it bruises the leaves and helps release the flavor. If working with a very long leaf, you will want to fold it in half, or even thirds, before tying the knot. You can make multiple knots if needed.

Banana Coconut Sundae

Itim Raad Sauce Gluay Hom | ไอติมราดซอสกล้วยหอม

SERVES 4
COOKING TIME: 5 minutes

2 tablespoons (30 ml) unsalted butter

3 tablespoons (35 g) finely chopped palm sugar, packed

½ cup (125 ml) coconut milk

⅛ teaspoon (0.5 ml) table salt

2 tablespoons (30 ml) coconut-flavored rum (optional)

2 slightly underripe bananas, cut in ⅓-inch (8 mm) thick slices on a sharp diagonal

Vanilla or coconut ice cream

Roasted peanuts, coarsely chopped

Using Sweet Plantains or Thai Bananas

The challenge with using regular bananas is that there is only a small window of perfect ripeness. Too green and it's starchy, too ripe and it'll turn to mush very quickly in the pan. Of course, if you can get ahold of the short, chubby Thai *namwa* bananas, those would be perfect, but there is another terrific option that is more forgiving: sweet plantain. Choose ripe plantains with mostly black skin. They do require a longer cooking time, so you'll want to first sear the slices in the butter on both sides until browned, then remove them from the pan and make the sauce. Return the plantains to the pan once the sauce is done. If using *namwa* bananas, choose ones that are yellow, or yellow with a little bit of green, and sear them first, as with the plantains.

I love this recipe so much I put it on the menu of the Thai restaurant where I used to be a chef, and everyone who tried it loved it. It's a mashup of bananas Foster, which I learned to make in culinary school, and one of my favorite Thai street snacks, *gluay ping*, which is grilled bananas with a to-die-for coconut palm sugar caramel sauce. I love the idea of a dessert that's made à la minute, so your guests can watch it being made, and you don't have to do any work in advance! The chopped peanuts are an ode to Thai ice cream carts, which have various toppings you can choose from, but the peanuts are always added, like the cherry on a sundae.

———

Melt the butter in a 12-inch (30 cm) skillet over medium heat, then add the palm sugar and cook, stirring occasionally, until it melts and caramelizes into a deeper brown, caramel color.

Once the sugar has darkened to the desired color, immediately add the coconut milk; the sugar will seize up and bubble aggressively. When the bubbling subsides, add the salt and rum. Stir over medium heat until the sugar is completely dissolved and the sauce has thickened slightly.

Place the bananas in the pan in one layer. Cook just until heated through, about 30 seconds, flipping the pieces halfway through or basting the tops with the sauce.

Remove the pan from the heat and let cool for a few minutes, until warm but no longer hot. If you do decide to make this dessert in advance, heat it up just until it's warm before serving.

To serve, place a few pieces of banana around some ice cream in a small bowl and drizzle the sauce overtop. Sprinkle with chopped roasted peanuts.

Pineapple & Coconut on Ice

Subparod Nam Gati | สับปะรดน้ำกะทิ

SERVES 4

COOKING TIME: 10 minutes, plus optional chilling time

1 cup (250 ml) water

⅔ cup (160 ml) coconut milk

6 tablespoons (90 ml) granulated sugar

Small pinch of salt

1 pandan leaf, tied into a knot (optional; see sidebar, p. 213)

12 ounces (340 g) fresh pineapple, cut in ½-inch (1.2 cm) thick bite-sized pieces

½ cup (10 g) canned young coconut meat (see note)

Crushed or cubed ice, for serving

Note: You can omit the young coconut, or substitute other canned Thai fruits, such as lychee or rambutan.

One of the simplest ways Thai people make desserts is to simmer fruits, beans, or squash in syrup or sweetened coconut milk. I've always loved these types of desserts because nature has essentially made half of it for us, and we're just adding a bit of sweetness to enhance what's already there. This combination of pineapple and coconut is not done in Thailand, though, and I really don't know why not, because it's a match made in heaven. (Piña colada, anyone?) Light, refreshing, and marvelously low effort, it's the perfect way to end a big, filling meal on a hot summer night.

——

Combine the water, coconut milk, sugar, salt, and pandan leaf in a small pot and bring to a boil over high heat.

Add the pineapple and return the mixture to a boil, then turn the heat down to medium and simmer for about 3 minutes, until the pineapple looks darker in color and is heated through.

Add the young coconut meat, cook for 1 more minute, then turn off the heat. Taste and add more sugar as needed. Remove and discard the pandan leaf, then cool completely, and if you have time, chill in the fridge before serving. If you will not be able to chill it before serving, I recommend making the broth a little sweeter and creamier, as more of the ice will melt and therefore dilute the syrup.

To serve, ladle into small bowls, add lots of ice and stir well before eating.

Mango Coconut Tapioca Pudding

Pudding Sakoo Mamuang Sohd | พุดดิ้งสาคูมะม่วงสด

I wanted to create a mango-coconut dessert that's faster to make than mango and sticky rice. One day, after seeing the tapioca-mango dessert cups that are always sold at my local Chinese supermarket, I got this idea. Tiny tapioca pearls are folded into a silky coconut cream and topped with fresh, juicy mango. It's the same flavor combination as mango and sticky rice, yet a vastly different eating experience. Tapioca pearls lose their soft chewy texture after many hours in the fridge, so this isn't something you want to make too far ahead, but they're so quick that you can prep the coconut cream in advance and cook the pearls while people are digesting dinner!

———

Bring at least 6 cups (1.5 L) water to a full boil over high heat to cook the tapioca pearls. Make the coconut cream by placing the coconut milk and pandan leaf in a small pot and bringing the milk to a boil over medium heat. Add the sugar and salt; stir until dissolved.

Dissolve the rice flour in the water, then pour it into the coconut milk while you stir with a rubber spatula. Keep stirring constantly until the coconut milk returns to a boil and the mixture has thickened. Remove the coconut cream from the heat, discard the pandan leaf, and let cool.

Sprinkle the tapioca pearls into the boiling water and stir until the water returns to a boil. Then stop stirring and let them boil for 12 to 13 minutes. Meanwhile, prepare a small bowl of cold water to check doneness.

Check the doneness of the pearls by putting a small amount into the cold water. The pearls are done when any white centers remaining in the pearls look no larger than a tiny dot.

Drain the pearls through a metal fine-mesh sieve and run cold water through them until completely cool. Shake off excess water and transfer to a mixing bowl. If you're not ready to serve, you can leave them at room temperature, covered, for up to 4 hours. For the best texture, it's better to not refrigerate them.

(Continued)

SERVES 4 TO 6
COOKING TIME: 30 minutes

1 cup (250 ml) coconut milk

1 pandan leaf, tied into a knot (optional; see sidebar, p. 213 and see note below)

5 to 7 tablespoons (62 to 75 g) finely chopped palm or granulated sugar (see note)

¼ teaspoon (1 ml) table salt

2 tablespoons (15 g) rice flour

2 tablespoons (30 ml) water

½ cup (85 g) small tapioca pearls (see note)

½ cup (10 g) julienned young coconut meat, fresh or canned

2 to 3 sweet ripe mangoes, cut in ½-inch (1.2 cm) cubes

Notes: If not using pandan leaf, use palm sugar instead of granulated sugar for added flavor.

If the mango is very sweet, use less sugar, and vice versa. Also, if you're serving right after assembly, use less sugar, as the sugar will not have had time to absorb into the pearls and the dish will taste sweeter than if it had.

Make sure you use the tiny tapioca pearls that are no larger than 1/16 inch (2 mm) in diameter; they're available in white or a mix of pink, green, and white.

Do-ahead: *You can make the coconut cream in advance and either keep it at room temperature for up to 8 hours or refrigerate it for up to 3 days. Tapioca pearls can be cooked up to 4 hours in advance and left at room temperature.*

To assemble, stir the coconut cream (it can be warm, room temperature, or cold) and the young coconut meat into the pearls, mixing well. You can taste the pudding with a piece of mango and add more sugar and/or salt as needed, depending on the sweetness and tartness of the mangoes.

Spoon into a small serving bowl and top with a generous helping of mango pieces. Serve within 30 minutes of mixing. The tapioca pearls will continue to absorb moisture from the cream as they sit, so the longer they sit, the less soft and creamy the texture will be. If you have any leftovers, you can store them in the fridge, but the texture will not be as good the next day.

The Number One Rule for Working with Tapioca

"My tapioca pearls turned into mush in the water!" This has been the cry of far too many people, and I know exactly what has happened when they tell me this. They add the tapioca to room temperature water and bring it to a boil, like you would do with rice. This is understandable, since tapioca pearls kind of remind you of rice, right? So I need to stress the number one rule when working with tapioca pearls: do not add them to anything other than fully boiling liquid. This makes sense once you understand what tapioca pearls actually are: simply tapioca starch that has been clumped together into tiny balls, similar to the way old cornstarch can get clumpy in the bag. So, if you put them in not-hot-enough water, they will just dissolve. But when they go into boiling water, the outside instantly gels up, creating a shell that holds the inside together while it cooks through.

Black Beans & Sticky Rice

Kao Niew Tua Dum | ข้าวเหนียวถั่วดำ

It's rice and beans, but for dessert! Thai people love beans for dessert, and *only* in dessert. That's right, we don't eat beans in savory foods, so you can imagine it took me a while to appreciate Mexican food! But if bean desserts are new to you, you owe it to yourself to try one, and this simple dish is a great place to start. The flavor and texture combination of chewy sticky rice, creamy black beans, and silky coconut milk is fantastically comforting. Traditionally, the beans are cooked from dried and the rice is macerated in coconut syrup (see sidebar, p. 223), but I have come up with a shortcut method that uses plain sticky rice and canned black beans, and it works so well, you couldn't even tell this was a "cheat."

——

Cook the sticky rice using any of the methods described on page 238 (I prefer the soak-and-steam method, for a chewier texture).

While the rice is cooking, make the beans. Place the coconut milk, water, sugar, salt, and pandan leaf in a pot. Bring to a simmer over medium heat, using a wooden spoon to occasionally break the sugar into smaller pieces, to help it dissolve.

Once the sugar has dissolved, add the black beans and simmer gently for about 3 minutes to allow them to heat through and absorb some of the sweetness from the broth. Remove the pot from the heat. Remove and discard the pandan leaf.

To assemble, reheat the beans (if they cooled) until they start to steam but are not boiling. If the rice has cooled down, also reheat it until hot—the microwave is fine for this task. Distribute the rice among the serving bowls, then use a slotted spoon to distribute the beans over the rice. Ladle the broth over the beans, starting with ½ cup (125 ml) per bowl, then you can top each bowl off with any remaining broth. Let the rice sit in the broth for 10 to 15 minutes before serving, to allow the rice to absorb the sweetness from the broth.

see photo on page 223

SERVES 6

COOKING TIME: 35 minutes, plus optional 3 hours of rice soaking

¾ cup (150 g) Thai white glutinous rice

1¾ cups (435 ml) coconut milk

1¼ cups (310 ml) water

4.4 ounces (120 g) palm sugar (see note)

½ teaspoon (2 ml) table salt

1 pandan leaf, tied into a knot (optional; see sidebar, p. 213)

1 (14 ounce/398 ml) can black beans, rinsed and drained

Do-ahead: *The beans and the rice can be made up to a few days in advance and kept separately in the fridge.*

Note: *If the sugar comes in pucks, you do not have to chop it.*

Reducing Redundancy

Technically, the sticky rice for Black Beans & Sticky Rice should be macerated in a coconut syrup, a process that takes about 40 minutes, to create a sweet, plump rice that we use in various desserts, including mango and sticky rice. When you buy this dessert in Thailand, the beans and the rice are sold separately, and you would only put them together when serving so that the rice wouldn't over-swell. I saw the opportunity to simplify by using plain sticky rice and allowing it to sit in the coconut broth for 10 to 15 minutes before serving, to mimic the macerating step. I had to make extra broth to allow for this, but it turned out so well, I don't foresee myself doing it the long way ever again!

Coconut Jelly Duo

Woon Gati Maprao On | วุ้นกะทิมะพร้าวอ่อน

Agar jelly desserts, or *woon*, were my first viral recipes on YouTube—to my complete surprise, because for a Thai person, they are the most basic of sweets, like Jell-O to North Americans. When I was a kid, my mom would often come home with an assortment of *woon* from the market for me—colorful, sweet, refreshing, and a different mix of flavors every time, so it was always an exciting discovery. They are *the* treat that represents the joy of food for me as a child. Although there are hundreds of *woon* flavors these days, this coconut flavor is the most classic, the original.

———

Think about which layer needs to be poured into the mold(s) first, as you will need to make that mixture first. This will depend on which color you want to be the top *and* on whether you're unmolding upside down for serving.

FOR THE COCONUT MILK LAYER

Combine the coconut milk, coconut water, and agar agar powder in a small pot; stir to mix. Add the pandan leaf and bring to a boil over high heat, stirring constantly, as the powder will settle to the bottom at first. Once the mixture comes to a full boil, boil for about 15 seconds, then turn off the heat. Do not walk away, as it can boil over.

Check that the agar agar powder has completely dissolved by scooping some liquid up into a metal spoon, then pouring it back into the pot—there should be no tiny grains stuck to the spoon, and the liquid should look completely clear, with no specks floating around.

Remove and discard the pandan leaf, add the sugar and salt, and stir to dissolve. If this is the first layer, fill the mold(s) about halfway. Scoop any bubbles from the surface with a spoon and leave to set at room temperature while you make the next layer. If this is the second layer, make sure the surface of the first layer has set enough (it doesn't have to be completely set) before *gently* pouring this second layer overtop. Also make sure the liquid is very hot, to ensure that the two layers stick together.

FOR THE COCONUT WATER LAYER

In a small pot, stir together the coconut water and agar agar powder. Add the pandan leaf and bring to a boil over medium-high heat, stirring constantly, as the powder will settle to the bottom at first. Once the mixture comes to a full boil, boil for about 15 seconds, then turn off the heat. Do not walk away, as it can boil over.

(Continued)

SERVES 6 TO 8

COOKING TIME: 20 minutes, plus at least 2 hours of chilling

SPECIAL TOOL: Jelly mold(s) of your choice (see note)

COCONUT MILK LAYER

1 cup (250 ml) coconut milk

1 cup (250 ml) coconut water (see note)

1½ teaspoons (7 ml) agar agar powder (see note)

½ pandan leaf, tied into a knot (optional; see sidebar, p. 213)

5 tablespoons (62 g) granulated sugar

Pinch of salt

COCONUT WATER LAYER

2 cups (500 ml) coconut water

1½ teaspoons (7 ml) agar agar powder

½ pandan leaf, tied into a knot (optional)

3 tablespoons (37 g) granulated sugar

½ cup (90 g) diced young coconut meat, canned (optional)

Notes: You can make this dessert in one big dish, then cut and serve, or use small individual molds. If you want to unmold the jelly whole for serving, I recommend using a flexible silicone mold for easy removal; otherwise, use small individual molds—the jelly can be easily nudged out.

Choose 100% coconut water, preferably a brand that tastes quite sweet but without any added sugar. If you can get it fresh out of a young coconut, even better.

Make sure you are buying pure agar agar powder with no sugar or anything else added. Also make sure it is powder, not flakes, which will measure differently. The powder is available at some Asian grocery stores and at health food stores, as well as online.

Do-ahead: *The jelly can be made up to a few days in advance, but do not unmold or cut it until close to serving time.*

Check that the agar agar powder has completely dissolved by scooping some liquid up into a metal spoon, then pouring it back into the pot—there should be no tiny grains stuck to the spoon, and the liquid should look completely clear, with no specks floating around.

Remove and discard the pandan leaf, then add the sugar and stir to dissolve. Add the coconut meat, then pour into your mold(s). If this is the first layer, fill the mold(s) up about halfway. Scoop any bubbles from the surface with a spoon and leave to set at room temperature while you make the next layer. If this is the second layer, make sure the surface of the first layer has set enough (it doesn't have to be completely set) before *gently* pouring this second layer overtop. Also make sure the liquid is very hot, to ensure that the two layers stick together.

CHILLING & SERVING

Let the assembled jelly cool until it solidifies, which happens once it reaches room temperature, and refrigerate for at least 2 hours. Cut or unmold the jelly within 30 minutes of serving, because once it's taken out of the mold, water will gradually seep out, which is not ideal, but a small amount of water loss won't affect the taste.

To unmold, if you're using a flexible mold, you should be able to plop it out with a little pushing or bending of the mold. If you're using a small hard mold, you can insert a skewer or a small flat utensil along the edge and nudge it out; all you need is a little air gap on the side and it will release. If you're using a big, solid mold (for instance, a casserole dish), I recommend cutting and serving from the mold like you would with brownies, as it's a bit tricky to get a big jelly out of a hard mold without it breaking.

> **Agar Agar vs. Gelatin**
> Agar agar is made from a type of seaweed and comes in various forms, but powder is the easiest to use. It can set liquid into a gel like gelatin can, but that's pretty much where the similarities end. Agar agar sets at room temperature, whereas gelatin needs to be chilled, making agar agar much faster to work with when creating multiple layers. Agar jelly can also be left out at room temperature without melting. Gelatin is bouncy, jiggly, and melts just from the warmth of your mouth, whereas agar jelly is firm and crumbles when you eat it, and yes, you actually have to chew it! The two also require different ratios of liquid to powder. In other words, you cannot substitute gelatin in this recipe without majorly modifying the methods. If you want to use gelatin because you cannot find agar agar, I would follow a layered gelatin recipe for instructions and ratios.

Thai Street-Style Sundae

Itim Kanom Pung | ไอติมขนมปัง

When I was a kid, there was an uncle who rode around our neighborhood on a scooter with an ice cream tank attached to it. When I heard his bell, it was a mad rush to catch him before he was gone. His light-yet-satisfying ice cream was, and still is, the best I've ever had, and if you brought your own bowl, he always gave you extra. It was such a highlight of my childhood. Part of what made the ice cream so delightful was the way it was served. You had two options: in a bowl or in a fluffy bun that was like a small hot dog bun. And then there were several toppings to choose from, which was the especially fun part. It's hard to find these old-school ice cream carts today, but it's not hard to recreate your own Thai sundae bar. For me, the sticky rice and the peanuts are an absolute must, and when I go for the bun option, my favorite part is letting the bun soak up the melted ice cream. I haven't given amounts for the ingredients, as you can put as much as you want of everything.

———

If using sticky rice, place a small amount in the bottom of a bowl or on the bun bottom, then top with the ice cream and your choice of toppings. Finish it with a light drizzle of condensed milk, if you like.

To eat the bun version, you can bite into it like you would a hot dog, but eat quickly, as it will be messy once it starts dripping! If you want to enjoy it more gracefully, use a knife and fork, but the key is to get some bread with every bite of ice cream.

(Continued)

Hot dog buns or other fluffy white buns (see note)

Coconut ice cream (see note), or another flavor (I like Thai tea, matcha, coffee, Earl Grey tea, or black sesame)

OPTIONAL TOPPINGS

Sweet Sticky Rice (highly recommended; recipe follows)

Roasted peanuts, coarsely chopped

Canned pineapple in syrup, drained and chopped

Canned attap palm seeds, rinsed (see sidebar)

Jarred nata de coco, drained (see sidebar)

Canned sweet jackfruit, drained and sliced against the grain

Cooked corn kernels

Candied Sweet Potatoes (recipe follows)

Sweetened condensed milk, for drizzling

Notes: *Small fluffy dinner rolls, slider rolls, or brioche buns work well. You can also use a thick-sliced sandwich bread and shape it like a taco shell. If using a hot dog bun, trimming the ends or cutting them in half makes a more reasonable size for an after-meal dessert.*

If you want to make your own authentic Thai coconut ice cream or no-churn Thai tea ice cream, see the recipes on my website, QR codes below.

 Coconut Ice Cream Recipe

 No-Churn Thai Tea Ice Cream

Attap Palm Seeds and Nata de Coco

These two jelly-like treats are popular in desserts in Southeast Asia, and are as delicious as they are interesting. Attap palm seeds are oval, translucent seeds with a satisfying chewy texture that cannot be described and must be experienced firsthand. They come in a syrup that is very thick due to the starch from the seeds, so I like to rinse it off before eating. Nata de coco are little cubes packed in syrup with a unique chewiness unlike anything else. They come in glass jars and are sometimes flavored, though I recommend getting the plain ones. The gel is formed naturally as a byproduct of the fermentation of coconut water. Cool, right?

Sweet Sticky Rice

MAKES ENOUGH FOR 8 SUNDAES
COOKING TIME: 25 minutes, plus 40 minutes of macerating and optional 3 hours of soaking

1 cup (200 g) white glutinous rice

⅔ cup (160 ml) coconut milk

⅓ cup (65 g) granulated sugar

½ teaspoon (2 ml) table salt

Steam the rice using any of the methods on page 238.

While the rice is cooking, make the coconut syrup by combining the coconut milk, sugar, and salt in a small pot over medium heat, stirring occasionally, just until the sugar has dissolved. If the coconut milk is done before the rice, keep it covered so it stays warm.

Transfer the cooked sticky rice to a bowl and immediately pour the syrup overtop, then stir to mix well. Cover the bowl and let the rice sit and absorb the liquid for at least 40 minutes, folding well halfway through to distribute the syrup. Keep covered at room temperature until ready to serve. The sticky rice will last up to 4 hours at room temperature. Leftovers can be refrigerated for up to 3 days, though the texture will become progressively less chewy. Reheat in the microwave, covered with a moist paper towel, until steaming hot and soft.

Candied Sweet Potatoes

MAKES ENOUGH FOR 8 SUNDAES
COOKING TIME: 15 minutes

5 ounces (150 g) yellow- or purple-flesh sweet potato, ¼-inch (6 mm) diced (see note)

¾ cup (150 g) granulated sugar

¾ cup (185 ml) water

Pinch of table salt

Place all the ingredients in a small pot and bring to a simmer over medium heat. Once simmering, turn the heat down to low and cook gently for about 10 minutes, until the potatoes are cooked through. Remove from the heat and drain. The potatoes will keep in the fridge for a few weeks.

Note: I don't recommend using orange yams, as they are too moist for this recipe and don't have a good texture when candied. You want one with a drier, starchier flesh.

RICE

Kao | ข้าว

The Heart of a Thai Meal

Rice is the foundation upon which a Thai meal is built. It is the canvas upon which each dish is painted. We eat rice for breakfast, lunch, dinner, and dessert. In a Thai home, the rice is cooked before the meal has even been decided on, because whatever dinner is going to be, there will be rice. Rice is not a side dish.

The importance of rice shows in our language. For us, when we want to say "Let's have a meal," we say, "Let's eat rice." And our term for the dishes on the table—the curries, the stir-fries, and all of that—is *gub kao*, which literally means "with rice." If there is no rice in the meal, then it's highly likely that there are rice noodles.

I discuss rice and sticky rice at length in this chapter because it is important to get them right in order for the meal to be a success. I also included a recipe for *kao tom*, or plain rice porridge, because there are many dishes in this book that make a wonderful *kao tom* pairing.

Don't Add Anything to Your Rice

When I posted a video on how to cook rice on YouTube, I had a few people ask, "Wait, you don't add any salt?" And my reaction was, "Wait, you *do*?"

In Asia, our rice is always served plain. No salt, no oil, no butter—just rice. This is because, as I said, rice is meant to be a canvas for other dishes. It's not a carb you eat *alongside* other things, like mashed potatoes, it is supposed to be eaten *in the same bite* as other things. (Note: There is such a thing as coconut rice, but that's traditionally served with only a few specific dishes, and is actually not all that common in Thailand.)

Also, if your experience with rice has been with generic "long grain white rice" or rice that comes in a box, I can understand why you might need to add salt and butter to it. But properly cooked, genuine Thai jasmine rice is delicious. It's soft, fragrant, and slightly sweet . . . it really doesn't need anything.

Perfect Jasmine Rice
Kao Suay | ข้าวสวย

For many of you, it may seem silly that I should dedicate a section to how to cook rice, especially if you grew up cooking and/or eating rice every single day, like I did. But for others, it's going to resolve all your frustrations over rice that never quite turns out perfectly, even when cooked in a rice cooker.

Use Thai Jasmine Rice

Most Thai meals are served with Thai jasmine rice, known as *hom mali* rice. If you want brown rice, go for brown jasmine rice. It's not about patriotism here; it really is the perfect rice for the kind of food that we eat.

Our dishes include a lot of sauces that need to be absorbed into the rice, and jasmine rice has the perfect combination of fluffiness, softness, and stickiness to allow for that. Short-grain rice is too dense to absorb the liquid. And while basmati rice goes well with thick Indian curries, the grains do not hold on to each other well enough and will just end up swimming in the thinner sauces of Thai curries and stir-fries. Not surprisingly, different cuisines have designed their food to pair perfectly with their kind of rice!

For some Thai meals, sticky rice is the rice of choice. More on that on page 238.

How Much Rice to Cook

For a Thai meal, where rice is the main carb, estimate 1 cup (250 ml) uncooked rice for two people. This will yield about 3 cups (750 ml) cooked rice, which is probably a little more than two people will eat (though if you've got big eaters, you might want to make even more), but it is an absolute catastrophe if rice runs out during a Thai meal, so making just enough is not good enough.

If you didn't grow up in an Asian household, you might think that 1½ cups (375 ml) cooked rice per person sounds like a lot. But remember that rice is the *foundation* of the meal. It is not a side dish. Every bite of food you take is supposed to have rice in it.

Storing and Reheating Rice

Don't worry about cooking too much rice, since it keeps well in the fridge or freezer. In my house, there is always rice. If it's not hot or ready to go into the rice cooker, it's in the fridge. Leftover cooked rice should always be refrigerated, as it can be a source of foodborne illness if left at room temperature for too long.

Jasmine rice will keep in the fridge for a few days with no issues, but if it has been several days, you might want to mix a little water into it when you reheat, to make up for lost moisture. You can also freeze it for up to a month before it starts to dry out. When you freeze rice, keep it separated in portions, in flat disks for easy reheating.

Microwaving is how I reheat it, but be sure to get it back up to steaming hot or it will not regain its softness fully. If you don't have a microwave, steaming is the best way.

Washing the Rice

WHY WASH RICE? You need to wash white rice before cooking, not because the rice is dirty but because there is a tiny amount of loose starch in the rice that's left from the process of removing the bran. If not washed away, it will behave like rice flour in your cooking water, resulting in a layer of rice goo at the bottom of the pot, and also the grains will stick to each other a bit more.

HOW TO WASH RICE: Add plenty of water to the rice and swish it around vigorously with your hands until the water is cloudy, then pour off the water and repeat. For plain rice, wash it two to three times, until the water is significantly clearer than the first rinse; a little cloudiness is okay. If making fried rice, however, you need to minimize stickiness between the grains, so give it a few extra washes, until the water runs clear.

DO YOU NEED TO WASH BROWN RICE? Brown and any other whole-grain rice doesn't have any loose starch needing to be removed because the bran is still intact. But I always give it one rinse, as there can sometimes be loose rice hulls or dust that will float to the top of the rinsing water and can be poured off.

How Much Water to Use for White Jasmine Rice

In general, for 1 cup (250 ml) white jasmine rice, you will need 1¼ cups (310 ml) water. You can use any kind of cup—it doesn't have to be a measuring cup—because what matters is the ratio of rice to water.

However, this is just a starting point. How long the rice was dried before packaging, the specific variety of rice, and your own preferences will affect how much water is really needed. For example, "new crop" rice, which is rice that has been dried for a shorter amount of time after harvesting, doesn't need as much water because it's not as dry. After trying this ratio once, you can then determine whether you need more or less water for the rice you currently have in your cupboard, and you may need to adjust again with a new brand of rice.

How Much Water to Use for Brown Jasmine Rice

If you don't like brown rice, maybe it's because you have not tried Thai brown jasmine rice! Brown jasmine rice is tender and fragrant, and doesn't taste like twigs the way some brown rice can.

In general, for 1 cup (250 ml) brown jasmine rice, you will need 1½ cups (375 ml) water. Again, it is about the ratio, so you can use any kind of cup to measure, even a coffee cup. If possible, allow the rice to soak in the water for at least 30 minutes before cooking, to yield more evenly cooked grains. You could even start soaking it in the morning, before you leave the house, and cook it when you get home. To be clear, the rice should be soaked in the measured amount of water, and cooked in that same water. You're just giving the rice time to absorb the water before cooking.

Cooking Jasmine Rice in the Rice Cooker

Just because you have a rice cooker doesn't mean all your rice problems are solved. You still need to do the most important thing: add the correct amount of water. Now, you might be wondering, if the rice cooker pot comes with those lines inside that tell you how much water to add, can't you just go by that? Well . . . sometimes.

Those lines are for specific kinds of rice, so for Japanese machines, for example, they are for short-grain rice, which takes water at a one-to-one ratio—quite different from jasmine rice. Most non-Japanese brands of rice cookers have lines for long-grain rice, which generally works for jasmine rice. But again, you may need to adjust.

Note too that these lines are made for the rice measuring cup that comes with the rice cooker, not a standard measuring cup. The rice cup is equivalent to ¾ cup (185 ml) of a standard measuring cup.

How to Cook Jasmine Rice on the Stovetop

Wash the rice as per the instructions on page 235, then drain and place in a heavy-bottomed pot with a tight-fitting lid.

Add the measured amount of water (see page 235 or above for ratio) to the rice, cover the pot, and bring to a simmer over medium heat.

Once simmering, turn the heat down to low and allow the rice to cook gently for about 20 minutes, until all the water has been absorbed.

After 20 minutes, check that the water has been absorbed by inserting a rubber or silicone spatula along the side of the pot and pushing it slightly to reveal the bottom of the pot. If the bottom of the pot is dry, you can turn off the heat, cover the pot, and let it sit for another 10 minutes to allow any residual moisture to fully absorb into the rice.

Fluff the rice and keep warm until serving. If the rice is too firm, you can add a splash of water, drizzling it evenly over the rice, and let it cook for another 5 to 10 minutes.

Perfect Sticky Rice
Kao Niew | ข้าวเหนียว

Sticky rice is the second most important grain in Thailand, next to jasmine rice, and it's eaten most commonly in the northern and northeastern regions of the country. In desserts, however, it is unquestionably the most important grain because of its chewy and dense texture, which holds up to sweetness really well.

When to Serve Sticky Rice

In savory applications, sticky rice is served in a couple of situations. The first is with a northern or northeastern (*Isaan*) meal, reflecting the two regions in Thailand where sticky rice is most consumed. The other is with grilled or fried meats, such as grilled pork skewers, barbecued chicken, or fried chicken. Eating fried chicken with jasmine rice just isn't as satisfying as eating it with sticky rice, for reasons I cannot explain. I find that any protein-heavy dish is perfect with sticky rice, even the Thai Tuna Salad (p. 52).

Choosing the Right Sticky Rice

Not all types of sticky rice are the same, so make sure you buy sticky rice from Thailand. The bag is labeled as either "glutinous rice" or "sweet rice," even though the rice itself is not sweet—it just signifies that the rice is commonly used for dessert. The grain should be thin and medium length, and opaque white. Short-grain glutinous rice is not what we use in Thailand.

Storing and Reheating Sticky Rice

If you have leftover sticky rice that you don't plan on eating in the next day or two, it's preferable to freeze it for up to 1 month. Sticky rice gradually loses its stickiness when refrigerated, and this becomes obvious after more than two days in the fridge. When you freeze sticky rice, keep it separated in portions, in flat disks for easy reheating.

Because sticky rice dries out easily, the less convenient but best way to reheat it is to steam it. Microwaving is fine, but you'll want to spray or sprinkle the sticky rice with a little bit of water and then cover it with a moist paper towel first. Microwave it until it is steaming hot all the way through; otherwise, it will not regain its softness and stickiness.

To Soak or Not to Soak the Rice

There are generally two methods for making sticky rice. The best and the traditional way is to first soak the rice for at least 3 hours, or 4 hours if your rice is older, until the grains are fully saturated with water. Then you steam the rice *out* of water, allowing the absorbed water to cook the grains from within. This is a foolproof method because there is no chance of adding too much or too little water, so the texture is perfect every time. The downside is that you need at least 3 to 4 hours, which of course we don't always have.

Because of this, people have tried to figure out how to get around the soaking. And while there are ways to do it, they are more finicky and aren't foolproof, since sticky rice is not forgiving when it comes to using the wrong amount of water. Add even a little bit too much, and it'll be too soft. Not enough, and it'll be too crunchy. Not to mention that the amount of water needed varies depending on the brand, the specific variety, and even the age of the rice, so the process will always require a bit of trial and error. This is why soaking is, again, ideal. Once you nail one of the no-soak methods, though, the result can be perfectly satisfactory, considering that now you can have sticky rice any time without any advance planning!

How to Cook Sticky Rice: 7 Methods

There are many different ways to make sticky rice, and one of these should work with the equipment and time you have. It might be easier to see these methods in action, so check out the video for all seven methods in the QR code below.

7 Ways to Cook Thai Sticky Rice

SOAK AND STEAM METHODS

The first four methods require soaking the rice first. Regardless of which you choose, start by washing your rice in room temperature water a few times, until the water runs mostly clear.

Soak the rice in plenty of room temperature water for a minimum of 3 hours, preferably 4, and up to 12 hours.

Drain the rice directly into your steaming implement, being gentle with it, as the soaked rice grains are quite brittle. Steam the rice until cooked through, using one of the following four methods.

1. TRADITIONAL BAMBOO CONE STEAMER: Add about 2 inches (5 cm) of water to the pot and bring to a boil, making sure the water will be at least 1 inch (2.5 cm) lower than the bottom of the cone. Meanwhile, soak the bottom half of the bamboo cone in water, to prevent the rice from sticking.

Once the water boils, place the rice in the cone and put a lid on top (any pot lid that fits will do). Set over the hot water and steam for a total of 20 to 30 minutes over high heat (a large batch will take closer to 30), flipping the rice halfway through. To flip the rice, simply grab the edges of the cone and take it off the water, toss it until the rice ball is flipped over, then put it back on the water to finish steaming. Roll the finished rice into a serving bowl then use a spatula to loosen up the rice ball. Keep covered with a folded kitchen towel until ready to serve.

2. STEAMER RACK: You can use a regular steamer rack that sits on top of a pot, like the bamboo ones you see at dim sum, lined with damp muslin or a double layer of damp cheesecloth. You want to make sure the cloth is damp, to prevent the rice from sticking to the cloth. Fill the pot with about 3 inches (8 cm) of water and bring to a boil.

Place the rice in the cloth-lined steamer and clear a hole in the middle (so you have a rice doughnut) to allow steam to escape. Leave some space for the steam at the edges as well. Fold the edges of the cloth up to cover the rice and steam for 20 to 25 minutes over high heat. Place the finished rice into a serving bowl then use a spatula to loosen up the rice. Keep covered with a folded kitchen towel until ready to serve.

3. METAL SIEVE: This is a bit of a hack, but it'll work if you have a metal sieve that is the same diameter as a pot. Add some water to the pot, making sure there will be at least 1 inch (2.5 cm) of space between the water and the bottom of the sieve. Bring the water to a boil.

Place the soaked rice in the sieve, but don't fill up the whole sieve or the rice will block the steam from coming up the sides and reaching the rice on top, making a hole in the middle also helps. Put the sieve on top of the pot and cover with a lid. Steam for 20 to 25 minutes over high heat. Place the finished rice into a serving bowl then use a spatula to loosen up the rice. Keep covered with a folded kitchen towel until ready to serve.

4. SOAK-STEEP-STEAM: *For extra-soft sticky rice that stays soft when cool.* Sticky rice made using the traditional soak-and-steam method is perfect when hot, but once cool it dries out and hardens quite quickly, and it needs to be remoistened and reheated to get soft again. So, if you're going to serve it at a potluck, or if you're taking it on a picnic where the rice will sit out for a while, there is a hack to make rice that will stay soft when cool.

After soaking, drain the rice and place it in a heatproof bowl. Pour hot off-the-boil water over the rice, just enough to cover it, and steep uncovered for 10 minutes. Drain the rice and then steam as usual.

This method forces the rice to absorb a little bit more water. The rice will cook up softer, and it won't be quite as chewy when it's hot, but after it cools down to room temperature it will stay soft and is perfectly fine to eat without reheating.

NO-SOAK METHODS

Still game to try making sticky rice without soaking? Below are a few methods I've used successfully. But first . . .

Wash the rice in room temperature water a few times until the water runs mostly clear.

Using a sieve, drain the rice extremely well, as any extra water can make the rice mushy. Shake the sieve until water is no longer dripping from the rice.

Measure the water at the ratio of one part rice to two-thirds part water. So, if you're using 1 cup (250 ml) rice, you'll need ⅔ cup (160 ml) water. This is a starting point only, so if you find that your rice comes out a little too firm or too soft with this ratio, which is normal because of the natural variability of rice, you can adjust the amount of water next time.

Now cook the rice using one of the following methods.

5. STEAM THE BOWL: Put the rice and water in a heatproof bowl and stir the rice to break up any clusters. Cover the bowl with a plate to prevent condensation from dripping into the rice, and steam the bowl over boiling water for 25 to 30 minutes. You will need more time if making a larger amount. If you can, let the rice sit in the bowl for as long as you have time for before steaming it; even a very brief soak will be better than nothing!

6. RICE COOKER: This method doesn't work with all rice cookers, but if you have one, it's worth a try to find out, because it'll mean making sticky rice is as easy as making any other rice.

For rice cookers with only one "Cook" button, it's hit and miss depending on how high the heat is. If it cooks the rice gently enough, it can work, but if the heat is too high, it'll overcook the outside and undercook the inside.

If you have a multifunction machine that has a "sweet rice" mode, use that—it's meant for sticky rice and it should do the job very well. My Zojirushi rice cooker has this function and does an excellent job, but it's best with a small amount of rice. Larger amounts yield some unevenness, though it is still acceptable. If your rice cooker doesn't have a sweet rice function but does have a brown rice function, it's worth trying that out, as it's supposed to cook rice more slowly.

Simply add the washed rice and the measured amount of water to the rice cooker, give it a stir to break up any clusters of rice, and let it do its thing. As with the steam-the-bowl method, if you can, let the rice sit in the water for as long as you have time for before cooking it; even a very brief soak will be better than nothing.

7. MICROWAVE: This method should be your last resort, as it's quite finicky and yields less than ideal rice. But in times of desperation—when you have BBQ chicken in your dorm room and only *kao niew* will do—it will work well enough.

Start out with a quick soak by placing the rice in a microwave-safe bowl and adding hot off-the-boil water so it comes up about ½ inch (1.2 cm) over the rice; let it sit for 15 minutes. Drain very well, then add the measured amount of cold water.

Cover the rice with a microwave-safe plate and microwave on full power for 3 minutes. Stir the rice to distribute any hot spots, then microwave it again for 2 minutes, then stir, being sure to fold the bottom up to the top. Microwave it one last time for 1 minute, then stir and let it sit, covered, for 5 minutes before serving.

Note: I tested this using a 900-watt microwave, and when I used a 1100-watt machine, I reduced the first round to 2 minutes. Your machine might require more or less time, but the idea is that you want to take it out and stir it a couple of times in between intervals of cooking. You can also experiment with a longer soaking time and using a little less water, or try using a longer cooking time at lower power. There are lots of variables you can play around with here!

Plain Rice Porridge
Kao Tom | ข้าวต้ม

While we eat jasmine rice with most meals, sometimes we eat something a little more comforting and soothing: rice porridge. Rice porridge, or *kao tom*, is an integral part of the Thai diet, yet it is so little known outside Thailand. Simply put, it's rice cooked with a lot of water so that it has the consistency of loose oatmeal. Because of the large amount of water, a bowl of *kao tom* actually contains very little rice, making it very light, which is why it is most commonly consumed when you don't want a heavy meal: at breakfast, late at night, or when you're sick.

I have a theory that the tradition of *kao tom* for breakfast started because it's the perfect way to repurpose old, dry rice left over from last night's dinner. And indeed, when I see rice in the fridge looking dry, it's my cue to make *kao tom*.

What to Eat with Kao Tom

You can eat anything with *kao tom* provided it's not too soupy or saucy, since the rice is already wet—so no curries. But salads, stir-fries, egg dishes, and fried fish are all commonly eaten with *kao tom*. Also, because of its plain flavor, we love to pair it with salty preserved ingredients such as salted duck eggs, salted fish, pickled mustard greens, or preserved daikon radish. Try serving it with Thai Tuna Salad (p. 52), Chinese Sausage Salad (p. 56), Ginger Soy Chicken (p. 107), or Kabocha Squash & Thai Basil Stir-Fry (p. 174).

How to Make Kao Tom

Although you can make *kao tom* from uncooked rice, it's much easier and faster to start with cooked rice. For a healthier *kao tom,* you can mix in some brown, red, or black rice, but keep at least 30% white rice to maintain a creamy texture.

For water, use a ratio of one part cooked rice to two parts water, and you can cook it either on the stovetop or in a rice cooker (see the instructions for both methods on p. 246).

An important note for serving: after it's done, *kao tom* will continue to thicken as it sits, as the rice continues to absorb more water. So, if you find it has gotten too thick when you're ready to serve, simply stir in some hot water to loosen it.

STOVETOP: Add the rice and the water to a pot and bring to a boil over high heat. Once boiling, turn the heat down to low to maintain a gentle simmer. Let it simmer for about 15 to 20 minutes, uncovered, stirring occasionally once it starts to thicken to make sure nothing is sticking. The rice is done when the grains are burst open and the porridge has a loose oatmeal consistency. You can adjust the thickness of the porridge to your taste by adding more water to loosen or by simmering it longer to thicken.

RICE COOKER: Add the water and the rice to a rice cooker and press the "Cook" button. Let it cook until the rice cooker stops, but check in on it occasionally after about 15 minutes or so to give it a stir and make sure there's still enough water in the pot. You may also decide that it's done before the rice cooker stops, depending on the consistency you want. Here I'm assuming you have a simple rice cooker with no porridge function; if you have a porridge mode, you can follow the manufacturer's instructions for that.

RECIPES TO MAKE IN BULK

Tum Wai Tid Krua | ทำไว้ติดครัว

To Make or To Buy

If you want to make Thai cooking a regular part of your weeknight repertoire, there are some things you will want to have ready to go. Many of these items can be bought, and there is nothing wrong with doing that, but these recipes are here if you want to DIY. These all either freeze or last in the fridge for a long time.

To help you decide whether to make these recipes or to buy, here's what I usually do.

I Make:

TAMARIND PASTE | Homemade has a richer flavor and stronger acidity.

FRIED GARLIC | The garlic flavor is much stronger when homemade, plus you get to keep the oil which is where half of the flavor is.

ROASTED CHILI FLAKES | I like to make it so I know that all the chilies used are thoroughly cleaned and that they're toasted to my liking.

FIVE-SPICE POWDER | I prefer the flavor of my homemade version to most store-bought ones. Also, I make a little at a time, so the spices remain fresh.

STOCKS | Western-style stocks have different flavors from Thai ones. They also tend to be salted and not very full-bodied (they don't gel up in the fridge) unless you buy bone broths, which are expensive.

THAI CHILI PASTE | I sometimes make this and use it as a spread or for a special occasion, but for everyday cooking I use a store-bought one.

I Buy:

RED, YELLOW AND GREEN CURRY PASTES | It's too much work for my busy life right now, and the good brands are perfectly delicious. I also buy red curry paste to use as a base for building up other curry pastes that are not readily available.

THAI CHILI PASTE | Store-bought ones are perfectly fine for everyday use.

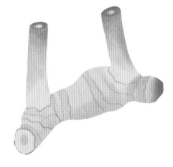

How to Make Curry Pastes: The Basics

Choosing Dried Chilies

Most Thai curry pastes use dried red chilies as the base, the source of flavor and color. The good news is that you don't have to use Thai chilies to make an authentic-tasting curry paste, as most dried chilies will give you similar flavors. The big variable here is heat.

Mild dried red chilies: You want the bulk of your chilies to be on the milder side so that you can add more color and flavor without the paste being overwhelmingly spicy. You can tell how spicy chilies are based on their size: the larger, the milder. In Thailand, spur chilies, or *prik chee fa*, are typically used, but guajillo and puya peppers also work beautifully; they can be found at stores that sell Latin American ingredients. I have also have had great results with gochugaru, Korean dried pepper flakes.

If you can only find smaller, spicier chilies, remove all the seeds and the white pith to reduce the heat.

Spicy dried red chilies: If you want some real heat, add small chilies. You can add as many as you want, so long as your mouth can handle it, or none at all. Dried Thai chilies, chiles de árbol, or the generic dried chilies at Chinese markets are among those that will work.

Wash Those Dried Chilies!

It might seem strange to wash a dried product, but it is important because some brands can be quite dusty, and you can even feel this dustiness with your hands. I wash the whole bag of chilies when I get them home so that I don't need to worry about it every time I use them.

Before you wash, inspect the chilies and discard any that are moldy. This isn't that common, but it's always good to check. Mold on dried chilies will look like grayish-green dust.

To wash them, fill a large bowl with plenty of cold water, then put the chilies in the water and quickly swish them around for just a few seconds; do not let them linger in the water or they'll absorb it.

Drain well and spread them out on a towel–lined baking sheet, and use a kitchen towel to dry the tops as much as you can. Let them dry at least overnight, preferably with a fan to help them dry faster. Once they are dried *completely*, pack them up for storage. If you've got lots of sunshine where you live, you can dry them out in the sun for the day (as long as there are no birds around that might come for a snack!). It's important that they are completely dried before packaging, so feel them for any soft, moist spots, to be sure.

Shrimp Paste

Most recipes for Thai curry pastes call for a small amount of fermented shrimp paste, or *gapi*, which provides some umami funk and also saltiness. You can omit this if you cannot find it; the fish sauce you will use to season the curry will provide a similar effect. But in some cases, such as with our sour curries, shrimp paste is a key flavor, so you should not omit it. There is no good flavor substitute for shrimp paste; if you've tried it, you'll know that nothing else tastes like it! Having said that, Japanese miso or Korean doenjang can be used instead to provide umami and saltiness.

Tools for Making Curry Paste

The tools you use will be the biggest determinant of how curry paste making will go for you. The main challenge is that we want the paste to be very fine so that it will infuse seamlessly into the sauce and yield a smooth texture. If your paste is coarse, there will be a lot of flavor locked up in the chunky pieces, and the texture of the curry sauce will not be as luscious and silky as it should be. Here are all the ways to make curry pastes:

MORTAR & PESTLE: If you want to experience the traditional way of making curry paste and you have lots of time on your hands, this is the way to do it. A mortar and pestle is also great for making small amounts of paste because, unlike with machines, there is no minimum volume required for it to be effective. In fact, it can only process a small amount of ingredients at a time—unless it's a giant set. You want to use a large, heavy-duty stone mortar and pestle for making curry pastes, so no wood, marble, or anything cute here. I recommend an 8-inch (20 cm) size (external diameter) for the job, or at the very least a 6-inch (15 cm).

COFFEE GRINDER + MORTAR & PESTLE: Using a coffee grinder will save you a huge amount of time. The grinder is used for dried chilies, which take a long time to break down, and any other dried spices called for in the recipe. You can grind the rest of the ingredients by hand, and add the ground dried chilies once you have a fine paste.

COFFEE GRINDER + IMMERSION BLENDER: This is currently my favorite combination of tools, as it yields a fine paste in the least time. The coffee grinder takes care of the dry spices, and the immersion blender takes care of the moist ingredients. Process the dry and moist separately, then combine them with a few final blitzes of the immersion blender. You will need to make at least one full recipe of curry paste; with any less than that, there will not be enough volume to blend.

BLENDER: This is not my favorite method, as you need a lot of volume before it blends effectively, and getting the paste out of the blender jug is a pain. The main thing here is that you will need to add liquid to the paste in order for it to grind effectively; water is fine, but you'll spend longer trying to cook all the moisture off when you go to sauté the paste, so try to add as little as possible. If you're making a coconut-based curry, you can add the first portion of coconut milk called for in the recipe to help it blend, and then use the remaining coconut milk for the rest of the recipe. Coconut milk will reduce the shelf life of the paste significantly, though, so I would freeze any extra, rather than storing it in the fridge.

FOOD PROCESSOR: I don't recommend using a food processor, as it can't really get the paste as fine as it should be. For items that don't need to be super fine, such as Thai chili paste, it works all right, though you do need a relatively large amount of ingredients to make it grind effectively.

NOTE: In the recipes, I've provided methods for using a coffee grinder for the dried chilies because I think it's the most important time-saver. If you don't have one, you will need to cut the chilies into ½-inch chunks and soak them in water for at least 30 minutes to soften. Then grind the rehydrated chilies with salt and any dry spices into a fine paste in a mortar and pestle before adding other herbs.

Curry Paste Storage

Curry paste will last in the fridge for up to 1 week, but I recommend freezing it to preserve the freshness if you're not using it within a day or two. I like to freeze it in flat disks, separated into portions for easy use.

Red Curry Paste

Prik Gaeng Kua/Prik Gaeng Ped | พริกแกงคั่ว พริกแกงเผ็ด

There are two types of red curry pastes in Thailand, and both are pretty similar, though some purists may excommunicate me for saying that. *Gaeng kua* is the most basic paste and uses no dry spices, whereas *gaeng ped* includes coriander seeds and cumin seeds—at least, this is the line I draw, but people don't always agree on what the differences actually are. I prefer to keep *gaeng kua* in stock, since it is the most basic paste and can be easily turned into other pastes, such as *panang* (p. 89), *massaman* (p. 79), or southern curry paste (p. 81). Because of this versatility, consider making a big batch of it and freezing it in small portions.

———

Using a coffee grinder, grind the dried chilies, peppercorns, and salt— and the coriander seeds and cumin seeds, if using—into a fine powder.

If using a heavy-duty mortar and pestle, add the lemongrass, galangal, cilantro roots, and makrut lime zest; pound into a fine paste. Add the garlic and shallots, and pound into a fine paste. Add the ground chili mixture and pound until well combined. Add the shrimp paste and pound to mix.

If using an immersion blender, place the lemongrass, galangal, cilantro roots, and makrut lime zest in a narrow container, such as a glass measuring cup. Top it off with the garlic, shallots, and shrimp paste (it is easier to blend with the moister ingredients on top). Use the immersion blender to blend everything until fine. You will need to lift and reposition the blender several times, stopping to scrape the bottom and bringing it to the top halfway through. Once the mixture is fine, add the ground chili mixture and blend to mix.

Use right away, store in the fridge for up to 3 days, or divide into two portions and freeze for up to a few months.

MAKES ABOUT ⅔ CUP (160 ML), FOR TWO BATCHES OF 4-SERVING CURRY

¾ ounce (20 g) mild dried red chilies, cut in ½-inch (1.2 cm) chunks (see p. 251)

½ ounce (10 g) spicy dried red chilies, or to taste, cut in ½-inch (1.2 cm) chunks (see note)

½ teaspoon (2 ml) white peppercorns

1 teaspoon (5 ml) table salt

1 stalk lemongrass, bottom half only, thinly sliced

2 tablespoons (15 g) finely chopped galangal

4 cilantro roots, or 10 to 12 cilantro stems, chopped

2 teaspoons (10 ml) chopped makrut lime zest (optional, see note)

6 cloves (30 g) garlic, chopped

½ cup (70 g) chopped shallots

2 teaspoons (10 ml) fermented shrimp paste (optional)

IF MAKING PRIK GAENG PED

2 teaspoons (10 ml) coriander seeds, toasted

1 teaspoon (5 ml) cumin seeds, toasted

Notes: *You can add as many of the small chilies as you like, depending on how spicy you want the paste to be. The seeds can be left in for more heat, or removed for less. For more on choices of chilies, see How to Make Curry Pastes: The Basics (p. 251).*

If you don't have makrut lime zest, you can add 2 to 3 makrut lime leaves, torn into chunks, when making the curry. Or substitute regular lime zest in the curry paste.

Green Curry Paste

Prik Gaeng Kaew Waan | พริกแกงเขียวหวาน

4 teaspoons (20 ml) coriander seeds, toasted

2 teaspoons (10 ml) cumin seeds, toasted

½ teaspoon (2 ml) white peppercorns

1 ounce (30 g) Thai green chilies or serrano peppers

1 ounce (30 g) mild green chilies (see note)

1 teaspoon (5 ml) table salt

25 Thai basil leaves, finely julienned (optional, see headnote)

1 stalk lemongrass, bottom half only, thinly sliced

3 tablespoons (22 g) chopped galangal

2 teaspoons (10 ml) makrut lime zest, finely chopped (or lime zest)

4 cilantro roots, or 10 to 12 cilantro stems, finely chopped

½ cup (70 g) chopped shallots

6 cloves (30 g) garlic, chopped

2 teaspoons (10 ml) fermented shrimp paste (optional)

Note: Using both spicy and mild chilies allows us to pack in more flavor without too much heat. Korean markets usually have mild green peppers available, and de-seeded jalapeños will also work.

Green curry is basically red curry made with fresh green chilies instead of dried red ones. But that one difference alone creates an entirely different flavor profile. The challenge with green curry paste is that green Thai chilies can be very spicy, and adding enough for good color and flavor may render it inedible for some. Removing the seeds and pith will help with that immensely, and I also like to add Thai basil leaves for a more vibrant green color without the heat, though any other neutral-flavored leafy greens will work here too. Or omit the leaves from the paste and, when making the curry, if you think it needs a boost, blend some greens with a bit of the liquid and add it in.

———

Grind the coriander seeds, cumin seeds, and peppercorns into a fine powder using a coffee grinder or mortar and pestle.

Remove the seeds and pith from some or all of the chilies to reduce the spiciness, then finely chop them. Err on the side of it being too mild, as you can always add more chilies back in when you make the curry.

If using a heavy-duty mortar and pestle, pound the chilies with the salt into a fine paste; if the mixture feels too wet at any point, add the ground spices to absorb the liquid. Add the basil leaves and pound until fine. Add the lemongrass, galangal, makrut lime zest, and cilantro roots, and pound into a fine paste. Add the shallots and garlic, and pound into a fine paste. Add the shrimp paste and pound to mix.

If using an immersion blender, place all the ingredients in a narrow container, such as a glass measuring cup, putting the shallots and garlic on top (it is easier to blend with the moister ingredients on top). Use the immersion blender to blend everything until fine. You will need to lift and reposition the blender several times, stopping to scrape the bottom and bringing it to the top halfway through.

Use right away, store in the fridge for up to 3 days, or divide into two portions and freeze for up to a few months.

Yellow Curry Paste

Prik Gaeng Garee | พริกแกงกะหรี่

The yellow in yellow curry comes from the fresh turmeric and the small amount of ground turmeric in the curry powder. You can use any kind of curry powder that you like here; the generic one commonly available at a non-Asian grocery store is fine. My rule of thumb when it comes to choosing curry powder is that if it smells good to you, it'll work. I do, however, prefer using fresh turmeric instead of ground, as I find the flavor smoother, and it is too easy to overdo it with the powder. Turmeric adds a unique flavor unlike any other spice, but too much, whether fresh or ground, will give an unpleasant medicinal taste. So treat it as one of those you-can-always-add-more-later-if-needed ingredients!

Using a coffee grinder, grind the dried chilies, coriander seeds, cumin seeds, peppercorns, and salt into a fine powder.

If using a heavy-duty mortar and pestle, add the lemongrass, ginger, galangal, and fresh turmeric, and pound into a fine paste. Add the garlic and shallots, and pound into a fine paste. Add the ground chili mixture and pound until well combined. Add the curry powder, ground turmeric, and shrimp paste; pound to mix.

If using an immersion blender, place the lemongrass, ginger, galangal, and turmeric in a narrow container, such as a glass measuring cup. Then top it off with the garlic, shallots, and shrimp paste (it is easier to blend with the moister ingredients on top). Use the immersion blender to blend everything until fine. You will need to lift and reposition the blender several times, stopping to scrape the bottom and bringing it to the top halfway through. Once the mixture is fine, add the ground chili mixture, curry powder, and ground turmeric, and blend to mix.

Use right away, store in the fridge for up to 3 days, or divide into two portions and freeze for up to a few months.

MAKES ABOUT ⅔ CUP (160 ML), FOR TWO BATCHES OF 4-SERVING CURRY

0.7 ounce (20 g) mild dried red chilies, cut in ½-inch (1.2 cm) chunks (see p. 251)

1 tablespoon (15 ml) coriander seeds, toasted

1½ teaspoons (7 ml) cumin seeds, toasted

½ teaspoon (2 ml) white peppercorns

1 teaspoon (5 ml) table salt

1 stalk lemongrass, bottom half only, finely sliced

2 tablespoons (15 g) chopped ginger

2 tablespoons (15 g) chopped galangal

1 tablespoon (8 g) chopped turmeric, or ½ teaspoon (2 ml) ground turmeric

6 cloves (30 g) garlic, chopped

½ cup (70 g) chopped shallots

1 tablespoon (15 ml) curry powder

2 teaspoons (10 ml) fermented shrimp paste (optional)

Thai Chili Paste

Nam Prik Pao | น้ำพริกเผา

MAKES ABOUT 2 CUPS (500 ML)
COOKING TIME: 50 minutes

1.7 ounces (50 g) mild dried red chilies (see note)

3.5 ounces (100 g) garlic, about 2 heads, unpeeled

7 ounces (200 g) shallots, peeled, cut in 1-inch (2.5 cm) chunks

¼ cup (30 g) dried shrimp, coarsely chopped if large

⅓ cup + 1 tablespoon (80 g) finely chopped palm sugar, packed

¼ cup (60 ml) tamarind paste, store-bought or homemade (p. 266)

3 tablespoons + 1 teaspoon (50 ml) fish sauce

1 teaspoon (5 ml) fermented shrimp paste (optional)

¾ cup (185 ml) neutral oil + more if needed

Note: Guajillo or puya peppers work well. If you can only find smaller spicy chilies, remove the seeds and pith from some or all of them.

If you were going to make only one paste from scratch, it should be this one. I don't think homemade curry pastes are necessarily better than store-bought, but homemade *nam prik pao* is always superior: You can use good-quality palm sugar and fish sauce as seasonings. You can use less sugar to make it more versatile, and use a healthy, neutral-flavored oil, such as avocado oil. Once made, it keeps for months in the fridge and can be used to add robustness and umami to soups, salads, stir-fries, or even fried rice and noodles. We also enjoy it as a spread on toast and sandwiches, and use it on a burger or as a base for a canapé. Traditionally, the paste is hand-pounded in a large mortar and pestle, but a food processor saves a lot of time and effort and works perfectly with this large volume of ingredients.

Preheat the broiler to high and set the rack 6 to 8 inches (15 to 20 cm) away from the element.

Place the dried chilies on a foil-lined baking sheet and broil them until charred in some spots, watching them *all the time*, as this takes less than 1 minute and they can burn in a few seconds. If you want a smokier flavor, flip the chilies and char the other side, which will take even less time than for the first. Remove the chilies from the oven, keeping the broiler on, and transfer them to a plate.

Separate the garlic into cloves but leave the skin on, and place them on one side of the baking sheet. Place the shallots on the other side of the baking sheet, cut side down. Move the rack to the top level, then broil the garlic and shallots until charred spots have formed on the shallots, about 5 minutes. The garlic peel will not look like it has browned much, but the cloves themselves will be.

Flip both the garlic and shallots and broil the other side until more charred spots form, about 3 minutes. Remove from the oven and allow to cool slightly before peeling the garlic. The garlic skin should come off easily.

Cut or break the chilies down into smaller pieces so they will fit in a coffee grinder. Grind them into a powder; you'll need to do this in batches. Place the ground chilies in a bowl.

Without cleaning the grinder, add the dried shrimp and grind into fine, fluffy flakes.

(Continued)

Place the garlic and shallots in a food processor, then add all the other ingredients except the oil and process into a paste. Try to get it as fine as possible, but it does not need to be smooth. You can add some of the oil to help it grind more easily. Scrape the sides of the food processor down once or twice during the process.

Pour the oil into a wok or large skillet, then add the chili paste. Don't use a small pot or it will take much longer to cook off the liquid. Turn the heat to medium or medium-low and, using a rubber or silicone spatula, stir the paste constantly as it cooks, scraping the bottom and sides of the pan frequently, until the paste turns dark and thick, about 20 minutes. If it's burning at the edges, lower the heat. When it's ready, the oil should be separated from the paste, and it should have the consistency of a spread. If you want a looser, oilier paste, add more oil to reach the consistency you like.

Taste the chili paste and adjust the seasoning with more fish sauce, sugar, or tamarind as needed. If it tastes generally weak, cook the paste longer to concentrate the flavors.

Store in a tightly sealed jar in the fridge for at least 6 months. It can also be frozen indefinitely.

Universal Stir-Fry Sauce

Sauce Pad | ซอสผัด

I learned about this technique from working in various Thai restaurants, where a premade mix of sauces is used in just about every stir-fry. The sauce is used as a base, then each dish gets its own modification with other ingredients, so you still end up with dishes with various flavors. Sometimes, for simpler dishes, the sauce is added by itself, and it's still totally tasty. Make a jar of this to keep in the fridge, and you will save yourself so much time later on!

––––––––

Whisk all the ingredients together and keep in a well-sealed jar in the fridge indefinitely. Shake or stir the sauce before using. When using, use about 1 tablespoon (15 ml) per serving of stir-fry.

MAKES ½ CUP (125 ML), ENOUGH FOR 8 SERVINGS
COOKING TIME: 5 minutes

¼ cup (60 ml) oyster sauce

2 tablespoons (30 ml) soy sauce

1 tablespoon (15 ml) fish sauce

1 tablespoon (15 ml) Thai seasoning sauce

What About the Sugar?

When you use this sauce in a stir-fry, I recommend adding a little bit of sugar as well, to balance the saltiness, but I don't add sugar to this recipe because different dishes need different amounts of sugar, and sugar doesn't dissolve well in this thick sauce. You can, however, dissolve 2 teaspoons (10 ml) of sugar in a little bit of hot water and add to the sauce, or add 1 tablespoon (15 ml) sweet soy sauce, as a baseline sweetness, then taste and add more as needed when you cook.

Fried Garlic & Garlic Oil

Gratiem Jiew | กระเทียมเจียว

MAKES ABOUT ⅓ CUP (80 ML) OF
FRIED GARLIC, AND ¼ CUP (60 ML) OF
GARLIC OIL
COOKING TIME: 10 minutes

1 head garlic (see note)

⅓ cup (80 ml) neutral oil

Note: *You can scale this recipe up as much as you want; just be sure to use enough oil to cover the garlic.*

I never have a Thai noodle soup without topping it with a drizzle of garlic oil and a sprinkling of fried garlic. And if you go to Thailand, all the noodle soups will come with it. At home, it means extra prep, but it takes a noodle soup from good to great, and it's worth making extra to have on hand for when the soup urge strikes. If you want the fried garlic to remain crispy, make it fresh. But for topping noodle soups, where the garlic will become soggy anyway, you can make this in advance and keep it in the fridge for months. If you want to take it to the next level, do it the old-school way, by rendering some pork fat and using that to fry the garlic!

——————

Chop the garlic so the pieces are no bigger than ⅛ inch (3 mm), but don't mince it finely.

Add the oil to a small pot or round-bottomed wok, then put a piece of garlic into the oil as your test piece. Turn the heat to medium. Once the garlic is bubbling, add the remaining garlic. If the oil doesn't quite submerge the garlic, add a little bit more to keep the garlic barely covered.

Turn the heat down to medium-low and stir constantly, keeping the bubbling gentle, until the garlic is golden and the bubbling has mostly subsided, 5 to 8 minutes. The more you make, the longer it will take. Don't let the garlic darken too much or it will be bitter; you want it golden, not brown. It will also continue to darken slightly after frying.

Drain the garlic through a metal sieve, catching the oil in a bowl underneath, and it's ready to use. Keep the garlic and oil separately in airtight containers; in the fridge they will last for at least a few months. The oil may harden in the fridge, depending on what kind you use, so be sure to bring it out to room temperature at least 30 minutes before using.

> **No Bubbling = Crispy**
> If you want your fried garlic crispy, a reliable indicator of crispiness is the lack of bubbling in the oil. When food is still moist, the moisture evaporates into vapor and pushes its way out of the food—that's what the bubbles are. So when there is very little moisture left, i.e. food is crispy, there is also very little bubbling left. You don't need to have zero bubbles, but the bubbles should definitely look "tired" before you pull the garlic from the oil.

Five-Spice Powder

Pohng Palo | ผงพะโล้

I know there are six spices on this list, but hey, some store-bought powders have only four, so I'm being generous here! As with most spice mixes, the combination of spices is not set in stone, but the four you absolutely need to have are cinnamon, star anise, clove, and coriander. Fennel seeds and Sichuan peppercorns I consider optional. Don't make too much at a time, as ground spices lose their aroma quickly.

In a dry skillet, toast the whole spices, including the cinnamon stick, if using, over medium-high heat until the coriander seeds darken slightly and there is smoke coming up from the pan. Pour immediately onto a plate to cool. This toasting step is optional, but it will be beneficial, especially in soups, where the spices will not be exposed to high heat.

Place the spices in a coffee grinder, add the ground cinnamon, if using, and grind until fine. Store in an airtight container for up to 6 months in a cool, dry, and dark place.

MAKES ABOUT ¼ CUP (60 ML)
COOKING TIME: 5 minutes

2 teaspoons (10 ml) coriander seeds (see note)

1 piece star anise

20 whole cloves

1 teaspoon (5 ml) Sichuan peppercorns (optional)

1 teaspoon (5 ml) fennel seeds (optional)

1 tablespoon (15 ml) ground cinnamon, or 6 inches (15 cm) cinnamon stick

Note: Always buy whole coriander seeds and grind them yourself. Store-bought ground coriander has very little aroma compared with whole seeds. If you can't find them at your usual stores, try stores that carry a lot of Indian ingredients.

Roasted Chili Flakes

Prik Pohn | พริกป่น

Prik pohn is a staple condiment in every Thai household. It's added to many dishes and also used as a table-side condiment for adding heat to any dish that needs it, without the extra flavors or oils that hot sauce or other spicy condiments would add. When you buy noodle dishes in Thailand, for example, they always comes with *prik pohn* for you to customize the spice level. And, if you use enough of it, it'll also add a slight smokiness, which comes from the roasting. You can use any type of dried chilies that are spicy, whether Thai, chiles de árbol, or the generic dried chilies sold at many Chinese markets.

In a dry wok or skillet, toast the chilies over medium heat, stirring constantly, until they develop some charred spots and smell smoky. If you're not making a huge amount, this will happen in just a few minutes, so keep an eye on them. Transfer the chilies to a plate to cool.

Grind the chilies into small flakes using a coffee grinder or mortar and pestle. If using a grinder, allow the chili dust to settle before slowly opening the lid. Store in the fridge or freezer, as over time dried chilies can get mold that won't be visible.

COOKING TIME: 10 minutes

Any amount of spicy dried red chilies, washed (see Wash Those Dried Chilies! p. 251)

Thai-Style Chicken or Pork Stock

Nam Stock | น้ำสต๊อก

Using store-bought stock in Thai cooking is okay . . . sometimes. For soups where the flavor of the stock is key, you will be much better off making your own, because store-bought stocks are made with Western aromatics and have the wrong flavors. In Thailand, pork stock is our basic stock that's used the most often, but chicken stock will work just fine.

———

Wash the bones in cold water and place them in a big stockpot. Add the water and bring to a simmer over high heat. Once simmering, turn the heat down to low.

After simmering for about 15 minutes, skim off any scum that has floated to the top, then add all the vegetables and aromatics. If making chicken stock, simmer for at least another 30 minutes (for a total of 45 minutes). If making pork stock, simmer for at least another 1 hour and 15 minutes (for a total of 1½ hours). The longer you simmer, the more flavorful it will be. Top it up with water as needed to keep the bones submerged.

Strain the stock. It is now ready to use. The stock will keep for 1 week in the fridge and indefinitely in the freezer. If using freezer bags, do not overfill or the bags may burst in the freezer. When thawing the stock in freezer bags, always put the bag in a bowl in case there's a small tear in the bag, especially if it's been rubbing against other things in the freezer.

MAKES ABOUT 12 CUPS (3 L)
COOKING TIME: at least 55 minutes for chicken stock, 1 hour 40 minutes for pork stock

Amounts do not need to be precise

2 pounds (1 kg) chicken or pork bones (see note)

14 cups (3.5 L) water

5 cloves (25 g) garlic, smashed

1 onion, large-diced

¼ teaspoon (1 ml) white peppercorns, crushed

4-inch (10 cm) piece daikon, peeled, large-diced (optional, see note)

2 to 3 cilantro roots, or about 8 stems (optional)

2 stalks lemongrass, top half only, cut in chunks (optional)

Notes: You can buy pork bones in the meat section of most Asian grocery stores; pork neck or back bones are perfect for making stock.

When peeling daikon, peel off a few layers until the color turns from a bright, opaque white to a darker, translucent white. The outer layer of the daikon is a bit bitter.

Waste Not!

Depending on what kind of bones you're using, there can be a lot of meat left on the bones. I always use pork neck bones because they're particularly meaty, and in addition to a great stock I also end up with enough meat for another meal for two! So once you've made the stock, pick all the meat off the bones and throw it into soups, stews, stir-fries, fried rice . . . anything! The meat will very tender but rather bland, so I always toss it with a bit of soy sauce first before adding it to dishes.

Homemade Tamarind Paste

Nam Makaam Piak | น้ำมะขามเปียก

MAKES ABOUT 2 CUPS (500 ML)

COOKING TIME: 20 minutes plus 20 minutes soaking

½ pound (225 g) seedless tamarind pulp (see note)

2 cups (500 ml) hot water

Note: *Buy tamarind pulp that comes in a rectangular block, and it should be a product of Thailand. Do not use tamarind pulp from whole pods, as those are sweet tamarind meant for eating, not cooking.*

How to Make Tamarind Paste

I grew up making tamarind paste at home fresh whenever we needed some. When I came to Canada, I was over-the-moon excited at the convenient premade jars you can buy. But I was quickly disappointed, as that paste can be quite diluted and barely sour, and I needed to use so much of it to get good flavor. So I'm going back to basics here. Homemade tamarind paste is packed with acidity and flavor, not to mention that it's easy and costs you much less than store-bought. You can keep the paste in mason jars—it will keep for many months in the fridge—or freeze it into ice cubes and it'll last indefinitely. The process of making tamarind paste is probably easiest to understand by watching a video, so check it out by scanning the QR code on the left.

———

Use your hands to pull apart the tamarind block into small chunks and place them in a large, heatproof mixing bowl.

Pour the hot water over the tamarind and let it sit until it's cool enough for you to handle, at least 20 minutes. You can let it sit for as long as you need at this point—the longer it sits, the easier the next step will be.

Use your hand, preferably gloved if you don't want tamarind stuck in your nails, to squeeze and scrunch the pulp to loosen it from the fibers. You should end up with something that has the consistency of a smoothie.

Once you can feel that most of the pulp has been released from the fibers, strain the tamarind mixture into a pot through a sieve, but avoid a fine-mesh sieve, as the paste will be thick (Asian noodle strainers work great for this). Push as much of the liquid through as possible, and scrape the bottom of the sieve occasionally.

Gradually pour about ½ cup (125 ml) room temperature water over the remaining fibers in the sieve while using your hand to mix it all around. This will rinse off any last little bit of tamarind still stuck in the fibers.

You can use the tamarind paste right away for cooking, but for storage, cook it over medium-high heat until it boils, stirring constantly, *(Continued)*

because it is quite thick and can bubble and jump at you if you don't stir. Allow it to bubble for 4 to 5 minutes to ensure that it is thoroughly heated through before turning off the heat.

Transfer the hot tamarind paste to clean 1-cup (250 ml) mason jars. I like using the smaller ones so each jar will not be open for as long. Close the lids while the paste is still hot and let cool at room temperature before moving to the fridge for storage. You can also freeze the paste in ice cube trays and then store the cubes in freezer bags.

Fish Sauce & Chilies Condiment

Prik Nam Pla | พริกน้ำปลา

Some call it *prik nam pla*, others call it *nam pla prik*, but either way, this is the most beloved condiment in Thailand. If I ask for it at a Thai restaurant and the server doesn't know what I'm talking about, I'm taking a lot of points off that place. *Prik* means "chilies" and *nam pla* means "fish sauce," and at the basic level that's all you need, but often a squeeze of lime is added for a touch of acidity. It's our all-purpose condiment that can be added to anything that needs extra seasoning. Salty, acidic, and a little spicy (or a lot if you eat the chilies), it just boosts all the flavors and brings to life any dish that seems a little dull. It's our salt and pepper, our general fix-all.

You don't really need a recipe for this because you can just make as much as you need, and the ratios are entirely up to you, depending on how spicy or tart you want to make it. I make *prik nam pla* only when I need it, so that the lime juice flavor stays fresh, but it will keep indefinitely in the fridge.

———

Place the fish sauce in a bowl, then add as many chopped chilies as you like, depending on how spicy you want it. Add a squeeze of lime. I never measure for this recipe, but a rough ratio is about three parts fish sauce to one part lime juice, though you can add more if you want it tarter. Add chopped garlic and shallots, if desired.

If you add shallots and garlic, let it sit for 15 minutes before using, to allow the flavors to infuse.

Fish sauce

Thai chilies, chopped (see note)

Lime juice

Chopped garlic (optional)

Chopped shallots (optional)

Note: *If you do not want to eat the chili pieces, leave them quite chunky so it's easy to avoid them. Otherwise, chop them finely.*

Acknowledgments

Kob Kun Ka (Thank you).

Thank you to Hot Thai Kitchen fans around the world, who fuel all of my work, and a special thanks to my Patreon supporters, whose generosity cannot be overstated.

Craig, thank you for holding the fort while I took extra time; your sacrifices helped make this book possible. Adam, thank you for your never-ending dedication to our fans and our work. T.J., your beautiful pottery made my food shine once again. Janis and Lawren, it was a blast; thank you for helping me make these dishes come to life. Robert and Zoe, thank you for your belief in me once again.

To my family, Mom, Dad, P'Art, and P'Erd, thank you for always making me feel supported and loved.

To Grandma, I owe it to you for teaching me that love can be shown through food.

Index